No One is a Mystery

How to Use the Planets

to

Understand Anybody

Randall Curtis
Amrita Publications
Kentfield, California
1998

No One is a Mystery. Copyright © 1998 by Randall Curtis. All rights reserved. No part of this book may be used or reproduced in any manner whatsoever without written permission from Amrita Publications except in the case of brief quotations embodied in critical articles and reviews.

First Edition
Printed in the United States of America

Publisher's Cataloging in Publication
(Provided by Quality Books, Inc.)

Curtis, Randall, 1929-
   No One is a Mystery: how to use the planets to understand anybody/Randall Curtis. -- 1st ed.
   p.cm.
   ISBN 0-9644459-5-6

   1. Astrology and psychology. 2. Interpersonal relations--Miscellanea. 1. Title.
   BF11729.P8C87 1998   133.5
                                    QBI98-688

Amrita Publications
P.O. Box 367
Kentfield, CA 94914
E-Mail: amrita@skysage.com
www.skysage.com

   Typesetting and Technical Support by Elizabeth Curtis
   Cover Painting by Gail Weissman
   Cover Design by Elizabeth Curtis
   Copyediting by Netty Kahan

Special Thanks and Appreciation

I am indebted eternally to my beloved wife, Elizabeth, for her countless hours of typesetting, layout, design and technical support. Without her passion and sacrifice for getting everything right, it would be several more years before this book could go to press. My heartfelt appreciation to Gail Weissman for creating the beautiful painting for the cover of this book. Many words of praise to Netty Kahan for her expert editing and uncompromising attention to the details. She deserves a special applause. Finally, a million hugs to all my clients who shared the stories of their lives and inspired the writing of this book.

Also by Randall Curtis

The Heart of a Man is a Woman

To my beloved Elizabeth who has always been there

Contents

NORA'S STORY

THE SECRET CHEMISTRY OF RELATIONSHIPS

    Introduction   72
    Your Journey Through Planetary Psychology   74

THE LESSONS

Lesson 1   LET'S MEET THE PLANETS   75
    Discover the hidden energies of the planets and how you are affected by them.

Lesson 2   THE SECRET CHEMISTRY OF RELATIONSHIPS   86
    Discover how the planetary patterns of a person affect another

Lesson 3   SIGNS OF THE TIMES   97
    Descriptions of the Twelve Human Attitudes
    Summary of the Signs   108

Lesson 4   WHEN THE PLANETS COME VISITING   110
    How the visiting planet's continue to affect your birth planets

Lesson 5   HOW TO CREATE PLANETARY PROFILES   117
    Lelia Thore's Planetary Profile   117
    The Basic Attitudes of Lelia's Personal Planets   119
    How the Impersonal Planets Impact your Personal Planets   119
    Creating a Summary with Analysis Forms   127

Lesson 6   HOW TO EXPLORE THE HIDDEN CHEMISTRY
           IN A RELATIONSHIP   132

           Analyzing the relationship between two planetary profiles
           How to Avoid Fatal Attractions   134

THE CHEMISTRY

Part 1   DESCRIPTIONS OF THE PERSONAL PLANETS IN
         THE SIGNS

         The SUN (Ego/Survival Instinct)   138
         The Differences Between the MOON and VENUS   148
         The MOON (Feelings/Habits)   149
         MERCURY (Thinking/Communication)   156
         The Differences Between VENUS and MARS   165
         VENUS (Values/Feminine)   165
         MARS (Passion/Masculine)   175

Part 2   THE EFFECTS OF THE IMPERSONAL PLANETS

         JUPITER (Expansion/Optimism)   186
         SATURN (Contraction/Restriction)   191
         URANUS (Radical Change/Independence)   198
         NEPTUNE (Imagination/Escape)   204
         PLUTO (Transformation/Extreme Pressure)   212

APPENDIX

         Master Table   A-2
         The Element Chart   A-4
         The Sign Table   A-6
         The Personal and Impersonal Planets   A-7
         The Relationship Table   A-8
         Analysis Forms   A-10
         Important Steps for Obtaining Chart Information   A-12

1

I found the old iron gate that Rachel told me about. Like she said, there was no address—only the word "Christos," carved in wood, hanging on the fence. I walked through the gate and found a long, stone pathway that wound through rich, green pines and ancient redwoods. The pungent pines and perfumed flowers soothed my senses and the cold, dark memories of the city faded into the soft sunlight that was coming down through the trees.

After a hundred yards or so, I came upon the porch to a canary-colored, two-story house with white trim. An old black-and-white cat leaped upon a log and stared at me. I felt love for it right away and a warm feeling filled my body. I reached up to ring the rusty cowbell hanging from the door but stopped when I saw a tall man coming from a small white cottage beyond the house. He waved as he moved gracefully among the trees. He looked like the picture of one of those Indian sages my mother used to keep in her meditation room. His long, white hair waved in the breeze as he glided towards me.

"Hi, I'm Nora Lakewood," I said, reaching out to shake his hand. "Are you Mr. Christos?"

"Call me Robert."

"Hope I'm not too early."

"Oh, no, not at all. I seldom follow a schedule, anyway." He opened the door and motioned me into the house. We turned a corner into the kitchen.

"Rachel really thinks a lot of you," he said.

"She's always been so good to me, ever since I was a little bumpkin." He smiled and nodded.

Rainbows danced across a polished oak table, giving the kitchen a magical feeling, but I couldn't tell where the colors were coming from. The deep purple princess plants hovering over a deck railing seemed to smile at me as I sat down. Even though I could see the San Francisco Bay through the window, I was relieved that the bridge was far away from me now. I shivered even thinking about it.

"Would you like something to drink?" he asked.

"I could use a glass of water."

I glanced around the room looking for the source of the rainbows, searching for something strange, but there was nothing unusual—except the air was so full of silence I could almost hear it. I breathed in a faint wisp of incense. It smelled like Yellow Rose.

"Your flowers are beautiful," I said, looking out the window.

He handed me the glass of water.

"My wife, Lelia, planted them. She's the guardian of the plant kingdom—calls them her friends. We also have goldfinches, gray squirrels, squadrons of hummingbirds . . ."

"Nice."

It was refreshing to hear a man say something touching about his wife.

"I hope you can tell *me* something nice," I blurted out in my usual fashion. "Rachel said I should come to see you, so here I am. I've always been curious about this stuff, but music and theater's been my thing." My throat went dry and I downed most of the water. "I guess I'm afraid you'll tell me I'm going to die or something." I felt stupid for saying that, but my tongue always races ahead of my head. On the other hand, the question didn't seem that dumb to me. After nearly two years of heart-wrenching pain, I had been about ready to go off the bridge.

I watched the rainbows bounce off his thick, snowy hair. His angular nose and well-defined chin gave him a clear, but austere presence. Then his face softened. "You don't need to worry about anything I might tell you," he said sitting down. "Even if there was some trouble, we'd find a way to work through it. Anyway, there's nothing to fear, Nora. Ask Rachel. She's spent a lot of years watching her planets. Besides, if you know what they're doing, you can handle things a lot better."

My eyes focused on a tattered book on the table, *Bhrigu Nandi Nadi: A Classical Work Based on NADI Technique of Prediction*. I guessed it was Sanskrit. "Can you tell what's happening to me? I can't seem to trust myself anymore. It feels like I'm holding on to sand. I guess Rachel told you what happened?"

"We talked on the phone."

"If it wasn't for her, I probably wouldn't be here. I can't believe that I almost . . . Well . . . my mother died and I didn't want to live anymore."

"I'm so sorry about your mother. She certainly was a beautiful woman."

"You knew her?"

"Yes," he said staring into space. He did not want to tell Nora that years ago he had almost lost himself in her mother's unusual charms and painful, teasing aloofness. He had dared to chase her only in his fantasies, never saying a word. Before his fascination would have ripened into an unfulfilled longing, Lelia burst into his life and stole his heart. With her, it was more than a tantalizing attraction—her honest blue eyes and open sweetness made his heart leap. One day he woke up and knew she *was* his heart. "You have the same sparkling, auburn hair as your mother," he said, breaking his reverie.

"But where did you meet her?"

"I heard her play the piano once at the Conservatory. I loved her Chopin. I saw her several times at the Vedanta Temple in the City, and at Rachel's Place. It's amazing how much you look like her—even the blue green eyes."

"Mother said my eyes are Aquarian. She was an Aquarian, too, you know." A deep sadness rushed through me and I went stone quiet.

"I know how much it hurts to lose someone," he said. "I lost my sweetheart when I was about your age."

"What happened?"

He stared into space again.

"We were out at the beach climbing the rocks. The waves were spraying mist everywhere and the surf was thundering in my ears. Sarah was right behind me. Then I didn't hear her anymore. I turned around and she was gone—gone without a sound. We never found her. The waves just swallowed her up. Can you imagine what that's like? No chance to say good-bye? Never again would I be able to tell her all the things I loved about her. I wandered the streets for days and nights. Every day for more than a week I went back to the beach, looking for some trace of her, but it was useless. It took me forever to realize that she just wasn't going to be around anymore. When the reality finally sank in, I felt I would never love anyone that much again. It was just too heartbreaking."

"What did you do after that?" I asked, tears filling my eyes.

"It was a strange time when nothing meant anything to me anymore. I keep searching for a reason to keep living. Then I met this powerful spiritual teacher from India, Raman—a great Vedic astrologer.

One day he took me over to the cemetery—I can still hear him talking: 'Look around you, Robert,' he said. 'Everybody ends up here, but they go on. Your Sarah—maybe already reincarnated—starting another round in some other place. Don't just exist in memories and suffering,' he said. 'Engage in living. See those wild Rhododendrons on that hillside? They bloom; they die. Live like those mysterious flowers. Learn how to live in the eternal presence and hold communion with the one who breathes you. Every day must be released. It is not easy, but it is a practice you must be willing to commit to if you are going to find any peace at all in this terrible place.'

"I learned so many things from him. He was a master at reading my planets. He took one look at them and told me who I was, where I was going, and what I was meant to do with the rest of my life."

"Could you do the same thing for me?"

"We'll see," he said, sliding a sheet of paper toward me. "Here's a chart of your planets. It may look like a bunch of symbols, but there's a whole universe of information hidden in those little characters. They are the patterns of your planets that were forming at the time you were born—they reveal your unique chemistry, who you really are."

I looked closer at the chart. "What can you tell me?"

"As you probably know by now, I take the date, time, and place of your birth and calculate all the positions of your planets. As you will soon learn, this moment holds the secret to your life."

He got up from the table, poured something into a blue-and-yellow cup, and sat back down. Then he pushed a button on the tape-recorder. "We'll put this on tape so you'll be able to review it. Some people type it up or listen to it in their car when they are driving around. Do whatever you like."

He took a long sip of whatever he was drinking.

"To understand all of this you will have to accept some things on faith until I can prove them to you—or until you can prove them to yourself."

"Fine with me," I shrugged. "Anything's better than this."

"I can see by the way your planets are positioned that it is not part of your nature to be depressed. What I mean is you weren't born depressed. Some people are born to struggle with depression, but the depression you're going through now is only temporary. I know it doesn't seem like it because it's been around for a couple of years."

"How did you know that?"

"We're all born with different psychic energy patterns which are shown by the relationship of the planets to each other. Some of these patterns are more difficult for us to cope with than others. But your planets show that you were not born with a depressed emotional pattern—anger, yes, but not depression. That's caused by something else."

"What's that?"

"Let me explain. As we analyze the psychic energy patterns of your planets at the time you were born, you will come to understand who you are. This planetary chemistry reveals your inner world—what goes on inside your psyche. This is why we can find out if you were born depressed by simply looking at your Moon."

"Why my Moon?"

"Because the position of the Moon at birth reveals how you are connected to your source of nurturing."

"What can you tell me about my Moon?"

"It's in Libra. After thousands of years of observation, ancient astrologers discovered that when the planet Saturn is located at the same point along the sky circle as the Moon at the time of a person's birth, the individual is born depressed. Historically, this indicates a very dark childhood. We don't really know why it works this way, but when the Moon joins Saturn at the time of birth it darkens the spirit—makes the person feel unsustained emotionally. But fortunately you were not born with Saturn next to your Moon."

He pointed to the right side of my chart. "Your Saturn's over here in Sagittarius—a long ways from your Moon. So, you were not destined to struggle with depression all of your life. However, since the old scrooge Saturn continues to move around your chart after birth, he started visiting your Moon about two years ago."

"Two years ago? That's when I came back from New York; the time my mother found out she had cancer."

"Doesn't surprise me, because the Moon also shows the emotions and the mother—or our source of nurturing—in our chart. At the time Saturn started visiting your Moon, your mother found out she had cancer. This visit of Saturn to your Moon marked the beginning of your depression because it shows a sad experience having to do with your mother—the loss of the one who nurtured you. But now Saturn is nearly through visiting your Moon, so the darkness will soon be lifting."

"That's really hard to believe," I said shaking my head. "I've been down so long I've forgotten what it feels like to laugh. I sure hope you're right."

"Let's see if we can find you some daylight, Nora. Let me see when this depression is actually coming to an end—when you will feel secure again."

"Please. The pain is eating me up."

He rubbed his forehead with his long fingers.

"The end to your depression is not that far away. Hang in there a little longer—until about the second week of October—and your work will start to get easier. Saturn will be gone from your Moon and Venus will be holding hands with Jupiter. These two planets will bring you a lot of support. This may sound very strange to you, but if you will trust me for a while, you will soon find out that I'm telling you the truth. You will soon discover that the planets are the secret metaphors of your life."

"I'm open, really. I just never understood it this way before. It's really cool how you explain it—wish it were sooner, though. I'll just have to work through it, I guess."

"Well, I wish I could move old visiting Saturn off your Moon right now, but obviously I can't. We are all born to experience these things. A person who was born with Saturn on their Moon deserves a lot of sympathy—they have to struggle with depression and the loss of nurturing all their life. You can be thankful that your depression is only temporary. It will end in October."

"This is unbelievable. You can really see that?"

"It's really not that mysterious, once you understand that the planets are psychic parts of yourself. They're mirrors of your inner space. The tragedy is that the average person is not aware of them and it is very hard to wake people up. If this form of planetary psychology is not part of their culture, they reject it automatically. For most people in the West, the planets are mere physical objects floating in space for the amusement of scientists and astronomers. Look how astronomers are so fascinated by the rocks on Mars, but never think of exploring the psychic Mars that lives within them. Most people don't realize that they have a psychic connection to the planets."

"You make it sound so simple."

"This is odd," he said after sipping from his blue-and-yellow cup. "There are mixed messages in your planets. Some of the energies are stressful, others are helpful. Your career seems to be in some kind of delay pattern right now because the visiting planet, Jupiter, is going backwards there. This could explain the delay. Work is there for you, but it doesn't seem to be much help in your actual career area right now—at least not until October. Does this make any sense?"

"So far, you're right on."

"You should have a lot of success in the arts," he said placing his long index finger on the page. "Your Venus is right up here at the top of your chart in Pisces."

"Really?"

"Yes, she's been there since you were born, compelling you to pursue your music and acting. But right now, she's not able to bring you much benefit—at least not until those changes take place in October. What kind of work do you do?"

"I play keyboard. I was a rock musician in an off-Broadway black comedy called 'Rene's Renegades.' Ever heard of it?"

"No, I haven't, but I'm not out in the world much these days."

"It had a long run but it finally came to an end—too much jealousy and infighting. One of the guys even broke my best friend's jaw—it was never the same after that. Besides, I was burned out. That was about the time my mother got sick, so I came back to San Francisco. Lately, I've been doing word-processing. I've also been a legal secretary and worked as a waitress when I was going to school in New York."

"What kind of school?"

"They train actors. You know, for TV."

"Well, maybe you could temp as a legal secretary until something opens up for you. The pay's good."

"Maybe you're right."

"If you'd like, I'll call Gloria at Maxwell Associates. She does a lot of temp placement for law firms, and she comes to me for readings. I'm sure you'd like her. She's a Pisces and loves to help people. I'll call her later and see if she can find something for you."

"That's so sweet of you." Why was he being so nice? It was hard to believe. But I wasn't going to get into my critical side, as I usually do with a man. I was thankful for all the help I could get. "What kind of drink is that?" I asked, trying to be more friendly.

"Ginger and lemon grass with a touch of Fijian honey," he replied, taking another sip. "Would you like to try some?"

"No, thanks," I said making a face I didn't mean to make. "I'll just stick to water. Do you see anything there about my boyfriend, Richard?"

"What's his birthday?" he asked, picking up a big red book off the table.

I reached in my purse, pulled out a piece of paper, and read what I wrote: "He was born on June 10, 1966."

"His Sun's in Gemini, but we have to look at more than that." His long finger slid down the page past the tiny symbols and numbers. They reminded me of a bus schedule. He jotted down several notes around my chart and said, "Ah, hah. He's a lot like you."

"Like me?" I felt my face getting hot. "In what way?"

"He loves his freedom and can't stand commitment."

That sure hit hard. It was so right on that I held back my impulsive tongue hoping he would say more. . .but he didn't. Finally I said, "Richard was a pilot who turned actor after working as a technical director for a flying film. He's never stayed long in one place. I was really turned on by him but I didn't want to get too close. Fear of losing my freedom I guess. He used to say 'You only like me because you can't control me.'"

"What's going on between you now?" Robert asked.

"He's pissed off at me for standing him up. He wanted to go to this wild party and I didn't want any part of it. It was just a simple no on my part, but he blew the whole thing out of proportion. Now he wants me to pay back all the money he's claiming I borrowed from him. It's just out of spite."

"Can't you work it out with him? It seems he's very generous toward you."

"Really? How can you tell that?"

"His Jupiter is right next to your Venus. I'm sorry, I didn't mean to say that, but it's a habit I have gotten into over these years—going on about the planets as if you know what I was talking about. Just know that he likes giving you things. It's hard for him to be mean to you—he would have to work at it."

"How can you see all this in that piece of paper?" I asked.

"It's a mystery," he said, stretching his long arms into the air. He took a deep breath, exhaled, and rubbed his nose. "It would take too long to explain it here. But is this true about Richard? Is he generous towards you?"

"Yes, I have to admit it. He's given me a lot of money. At first I found it hard to accept. I told him it was just a loan. I did keep track of most of it though. Well—not down to the penny—but most of it. I never dreamed he would push me for it, especially when he said he liked giving it to me."

"See? He is generous toward you. Ask him if you can make payments on what you owe him. Besides, I'm not so sure he's all that concerned about getting his money back. Maybe he just wants you to eat crow."

"Eat crow?" That was a phrase I'd heard on TV but never knew what it meant.

"It's an old saying, but in your case it means to be humble. Your planets show that you're a very strong-willed woman. Do you like to be in charge?"

I got the feeling that he already knew the answer to that. "I guess so. Most guys seem to be afraid of me. They think I'm too aggressive."

"I think Richard just wants you to eat humble pie. You know, cry on his shoulder. It may surprise him if you do that. He might even feel sympathy for you."

I shook my head. "I'm not very good at crying on a guy's shoulder." My stomach felt like it was flopping around inside of me. "How can you see all these things from this one piece of paper?" I asked again.

He cleared his throat and turned the tape over in the machine. "As I said, this piece of paper holds secrets you wouldn't believe. But after all this time, I still don't know why it works—nobody does—but look how much we've discovered so far."

An idea floated into my mind and I leaped at the chance to change the subject. "Is there some way I could use the planets to understand my characters better?"

"You would probably have to work with the writer, but you could create a fictitious chart for your character. There's one very effective way that you can make them more believable."

"How's that?"

"By adding in contradiction."

"What do you mean?"

"Have you ever noticed that what makes a character seem real are the contradictions in their nature?"

"I'm not following you."

"Let's take you for instance. You're like an angel with a sword. You have a very soft heart, but part of you is tough as ironwood. Doesn't this seem to be a contradiction? How can you be soft and tough at the same time? The answer is simple. Your soft side is hidden. Anyone who really got to know you would see your caring side. Another kind of contradiction is the 'cake and eat it too' variety. I find this in people who have intense desires for relationship but can't commit to one partner."

Was he being subtle?

"One of my clients had her Sun in the detached sign of Aquarius and another planet in the possessive sign of Scorpio. I should explain that the signs are simply human attitudes. Planets energize these particular attitudes in our chart when we are born. The basic attitude of Aquarius is detachment and the basic attitude of Scorpio is attachment. These attitudes are in conflict because you can't be attached and detached toward someone at the same time. She didn't want her lover to even look at another woman but she wanted to have a lot of men friends herself. This pattern shows that the intense desire for attachment, shown by the sign of Scorpio, is in conflict with the Aquarian desire to remain free and unattached."

This sounded like me. I was about to defend myself but he kept talking.

"If the actress Sharon Stone has her Moon in Scorpio, she might have these contradictions. This is because her Venus, the planet of love and relationship, is in Aquarius, the blue-green sign of detachment. As you can see, these desires are in conflict because they are seeking different forms of fulfillment. Maybe one day, when you're well known, you'll have a chance to show her how this works.

"It also helps to know the dark side of a character—the unseen motivations of her life. If you would like to know how to enrich your characters in this way I can help you."

"That really sounds exciting," I said, "but I don't have much money right now. I couldn't pay you to teach me."

He grinned. "I'll just keep a record and you can pay me back when you become a rich and famous actress."

I was squirming again. "You sure? You may have to wait a long time. Music gigs are very scarce for me these days and, as you know, my acting career's not going too well either."

"Don't worry about it. When you become a wealthy actress you can send all your famous friends to consult with me."

"Okay," I said. Why was he so sure about me becoming famous? Did he really know something about me that I didn't? Would Venus and Jupiter really help me out in October?

He looked at his appointment book on the table. "Can you come here on Saturdays at ten o'clock for a while?"

"Yes, I think so."

"I have something that will help you," he said, pushing away from the table. "I'll be right back." He walked out of the kitchen and then returned with something in his hand. "Here, I want you to have this."

I read the cover, *The Secret Chemistry of the Planets*, by Robert Christos.*

"This simple little book will help you understand everything we've talked about today and everything we will cover in the future. Read the first three chapters before you come next Saturday and we'll go from there. It's an ongoing dialogue between a student and a teacher—Lelia and me, actually, before we got together."

"Thank you. This is really cool."

He reached over and withdrew the cassette from the tape recorder and handed it to me. "Here's your tape. Don't forget to listen to it a few times. We'll be going into deeper things as you begin to study the contradictions and hidden side of people. Those discoveries will add a lot of depth to your acting. You're going to become very successful, Nora. Of course we have to discover who we are along the way, and that's what you'll be learning too. In fact you're going to discover a wonderful secret—something that will change your life."

"What's that?"

"It wouldn't mean much if *I* told you, but it will mean a lot when *you* tell me."

"Sounds mysterious."

"That's because most people don't know about it. I tried to explain it to some students of Tibetan teachings the other night after their meditation but most of them only stared at me. They were all too logical."

"But isn't that the way we understand things? Through reasoning?"

"Most things, yes, but this is different. You can only understand *this* secret from a deep well of feeling—from the heart."

---

* Dear Reader: See Robert's book starting on page 71.

"But how do you know I'm going to get it?"

"I can see it in your chart. The bigger planets are moving you in a direction that will give you that understanding. You're going to make a discovery that will set you free."

"But why can't you tell me what it is?"

"Because it has to be your awakening, Nora."

I stared at him for a moment waiting for more insight but he only smiled at me. Finally, I got up from the table. "I really appreciate your teaching me all of this—even though I'm not sure I understand a lot of it."

"You will," he said, continuing to smile. "See you next Saturday?"

"For sure. Thanks, Robert. Bye."

The faint clanging of the cowbell merged with my feelings as I stepped onto the stone path that led back to my uncertain world. It was so amazing. Robert had answers I didn't even know existed. I inhaled the pines and flowers in one deep breath and then walked out the old iron gate toward my car. As I turned toward San Francisco, I wondered what secret I was going to discover that would change my life. I hoped I would soon find out.

2

My brain was still spinning when I got home. Robert had stretched it like a balloon and I knew it would never be the same. I was bugged by not knowing the secret he talked about. I thought maybe I could find it in his book. I took a ginger beer from the fridge, sat down, and started reading. I spent hours studying the chapters, but I couldn't find any clues to the secret. I did find a lot of things that were very fascinating—like how visiting planets show events coming up in our lives, how we can understand children from the first day they're born, and what causes fatal attractions.

Since I always ended up having such intense arguments with men, I wondered if they were really fatal attractions. I decided to ask Robert about that when I arrived at his place the following Saturday.

Just before I rang the cowbell, I paused for a moment to absorb the haunting flute music coming from inside. "That's a cool melody," I said to Robert as he opened the door. "What is it?"

"Something for Raman."

"Sounds like a great theme for a film." I sensed it was something personal so I changed the subject. "Your book was so fascinating. That part about depression really helped me understand what's happening to me."

"I'm glad," he said, laying down his bamboo flute. "Do you want something to drink?"

"I think I'll try some of your lemon grass." After a long silence I asked, "What happened to your rainbows?"

"Rainbows?"

"The last time I was here, there were rainbows jumping around the room. I don't see them anymore."

"Oh, those are from the glass wind chimes from out there on the deck. The colors come into the kitchen only at certain times of the day—when the wind is blowing and the sun hits them just right. Lelia is always creating nice things to look at."

"You really love her, don't you?"

"Very much. After Sarah I never thought I'd love anybody again, but a broken heart was the best thing that ever happened to me—made me more sensitive to other people's suffering."

I liked listening to him talk about his feelings. I felt closer.

He placed the tea in front of me, pushed the record button on his machine, sat down, and picked up my chart. "Well, today is the day we begin to explore your life in depth. Like why you came to earth, what you were born to do. We talked about some of that the last time—now we can go deeper. It could get a little intense, so let me know if you need a break. Did you read the first three chapters of the book?"

"Yes. The whole book, in fact."

"That's great. Do you remember anything about the signs?"

I took a sip of the tea, hoping it would burn off the Saturday morning fog floating around in my brain. "On page 97 of your book you said that the signs are attitudes people express through the energy of their planets. They show how we look at things. You also used colors to explain them."

"That's interesting that you remember the page number."

"My memory's photographic. It's helped me a lot in music and remembering scripts, but it hasn't helped me much in other parts of my life."

"That's remarkable, but Aquarians usually are very bright. Since your Sun and Mercury are in that sign, you have some off-beat ideas about freedom and a strong desire to follow your own path. Can you relate to that?"

"Sounds like me."

"But sometimes our desire for freedom can be deceiving, because we could simply be avoiding the very thing that would make us happy. For instance, when a person gets too close to you, do you look for a way out?"

I began to feel the heat of old reactions. "You could say that," I said. I knew that was a weak way of admitting that he was right, but I began to wonder where he was heading.

"The Sun in a woman's chart shows her inner male, her heart—the kind of man she loves and is attracted to. You would naturally be attracted to Richard, a Gemini, as well as Aquarians. These types are freedom lovers. They reflect your own heart nature."

"Are you saying that a woman's heart is masculine? I don't see how that could be. I've always thought of my heart as being feminine."

"I can understand why this sounds strange to you, because upon first hearing, it doesn't make any sense. But let me say it to you in a different way and then I will explain. *The heart of a woman is a man and the heart of a man is a woman.*

"There is no doubt that you are a woman—you are present here in your feminine form—but there is a greater mystery at work that we must come to understand. When you feel love for a man, where does that love come from?"

"From me."

"So the love must *already* be there inside of you before you even meet the man."

"I guess, in a way, but he brings it out of me."

"So what is it about a man that awakens the love that is already inside of you?"

"I don't know. It's a mystery to me."

"Since he does not pour love into you but awakens it instead, he must be reflecting your heart—revealing it to you. Since that *reflection* is masculine, your heart is also masculine. This male part of you, your heart, is shown by the Sun in your chart. As I said, the sign your Sun is in shows the kind of man you are attracted to. This man has the potential for awakening your heart.

"If a woman's Sun is afflicted by other planets at the time of her birth, she feels that her true power is unavailable to her. If a woman's heart, the Sun, is obstructed by fear, pain, and anger—as shown by the bigger planets—she tends to attract men who reflect her neuroses—not her strength. If she is unable to feel the tremendous love of her own heart, she will be unable to feel and honor her own self-worth. She tends to attract men who reflect her doubts because she is deeply afraid of intimacy. Since true intimacy requires that she become vulnerable, the threat of the potential loss of an intimate relationship may be too much for her to bear."

"That's heavy. Do I have an afflicted Sun?"

"In my book, I talked about planets being hostile or unfriendly towards each other. In your chart, Neptune is unfriendly toward your Sun, your inner male. When this pattern is found in a woman's chart, it usually shows that she has no support from her father. She has a great distrust of men because she fears that they will abandon her. Did you receive much emotional support from your father?"

"With my father it was kind of strange. He was never mean to me but he didn't talk much. Mother said I reacted so violently to him whenever he tried to discipline me that he finally just left me alone. I guess he gave up trying to have a relationship with me."

"You know, you're really a very strong woman, but your aggressive side is a defense against being vulnerable. It appears to be a way of warding off intimacy. Do you always have to be in control of a relationship?"

"You can see that?"

"If this is too much probing—sometimes I get carried away."

"No, I can handle it. There was this guy named Chris who was in my acting class—a real wimp. I walked all over him. He was a very sensitive type, a couch potato. In the beginning I tried to help him, but I only made him weaker. The more he leaned on me, the worse it got. Men don't understand me—they want me to be their mother, or a sweet little thing or something. Then they sulk when I get upset over their weakness. My relationships have always been destructive like that. I hate them. I don't know why, but I always end up. . .you know. . .being a bitch. Is there something wrong with me? Are these fatal attractions?"

"I will let you judge that for yourself as we continue to explore your planets, but for now let me tell you something interesting about men. If a man is not strong—has an afflicted Moon or Venus—a woman tends to go for his jugular."

"His jugular?"

"His throat."

"Oh," I laughed. "I guess I have peeled the skin off of a few men. You know, looked for their weaknesses and then played on them. But I don't know why I do that?"

"Many women tend to develop a hatred for a man's weakness. If she's looking for strength and he can't give it to her, the situation will only get worse. The man has to go through a radical emotional experience before things will change."

"What kind of experience is that?"

"If he refuses to give his heart away, it has to be taken from him. Love has to come bursting out of him and force him to feel his insides. When he is neither supported nor consoled emotionally by the woman who has his heart, he becomes open and vulnerable to feeling his own pain and the emptiness of his soul. Although he may be unaware of this, he is forced to connect to himself as the source of his nurturing—he has no other place to turn, nothing to lean on. If he loves completely, he will find his own heart, which has been blocked off by his resistance to feeling, and this vulnerability will lead him to discover his own strength. But, of course, many men will avoid this self-confrontation; instead, most of them will turn to drink, drugs, sex or almost anything to numb their pain and help distract them from feeling what they're feeling. But if they have some wisdom or self-awareness, they will eventually see that they can't run away from themselves. They need to recognize the pain that's locked up in their body and be willing to engage it—even welcome and embrace it if that's what it takes to discover the power of their own heart. If they do this completely, they will discover that their heart is a woman, the source of their self-nurturing."

"I assume that this works the same with women?"

"Yes, it is very similar. A woman must find her inner male if she wants to be happy. The Sun reveals her heart and Mars shows her passion. If either one of these planets was frustrated by a larger, impersonal planet at the time she was born, she will find it very difficult to be truly intimate with a man."

"Don't I have some of that?"

"We talked about your Sun being afflicted by Neptune which is a larger, impersonal planet. That's why you would find it hard to trust men. But Pluto is also frustrating your Mars, which makes you want to control or dominate men. You would rather be the aggressor. Is this your defense against getting hurt?"

"I don't know. Could you look up Chris?"

"What's his birth date?" he asked.

"We celebrated it once at a cast party—March 6, 1966, but I don't have his time of birth."

"That's okay." He picked up his big red book and looked up the date. "Hmm, your Pluto is on his Moon in Virgo and your Saturn is squaring his Moon from Sagittarius."

"What does that mean?"

"There I go again. I keep using these planetary references that you aren't used to. But you did read about Saturn on the Moon in the first chapter of the book that I gave you. But here we are talking about your Pluto in an adverse or hostile relationship to Chris's Moon, which is a much more powerful and coercive influence. In this situation you were functioning as Pluto, the person with the power. You wanted to perform psychological surgery on Chris—you couldn't help it. It was a compulsion. It was like he had a boil, a wart, or some kind of disease you wanted to cut out of him."

"That's *so* true. He was always involved in some stupid little detail that used to bug the shit out of me. He would spend an hour in the bathroom getting every little hair straight, or take forever to butter and jam his toast. I used to go into a rage."

"He certainly must have been intimidated. Obviously, he was afraid of you—anyone would be if they had their Moon where your Pluto is located. It is simply a karmic relationship where the energies are naturally hostile toward each other. It's not your fault, nor was it Chris's. It is the combination that was bad—not the planets. Some planetary combinations make people natural enemies. Your soft side was seduced into helping Chris, but your angry and controlling side could not stand his weakness."

"What can I do about this? How can I keep from attracting these kinds of men?"

"Well, that's part of the secret you're going to discover. You're beginning to see that the planets hold the key to understanding all of your relationships. You need to learn how another person's planetary energies relate to your own *before* you establish a long-term relationship; this is the wisdom I think of as *planetary psychology*. That's why knowing your own chemistry is really the answer. We need to attract those people who reflect our heart instead of our neuroses. But how can we do that if we don't know our own heart? . . . If we are still neurotic ourselves?"

"But changing yourself is hard. It really hurts."

"I know, but that's the price we have to pay. We must feel our pain before we can become free of it. When our feelings are a mystery to us, they have a way of manipulating our lives; they beat us up despite all of our good intentions. But this is because we don't know who we are—we rarely get to the bottom of ourselves. Most of us wear a mask and pretend that's who we are. We don't see a real person in the mirror. But life is already cracking your mirror, Nora. Years ago I made the same trip. I guarantee that if you finish your journey, not only will you become a free woman but also a great actress."

He picked up my chart as if to double-check something. "Do you want me to continue?" he asked, still holding his eyes on the chart.

"Yes," I blurted out as if to tell him he didn't need to ask.

"Well, there is something else. Your father."

I shifted my chair as if to prepare myself for another onslaught of his penetrating mind. "Are we going back to him again? I thought we were finished with my father?"

"I just wanted to say that there was a very hostile energy between you."

"Well, like I said before, I would scream at him and pound on the table when he'd try to discipline me. My mother said she went to see a therapist about it because at that time they were getting along pretty well and she wanted to know what it was between me and my father. My mother said it seemed to be hate at first sight as far as I was concerned. The therapist suggested that my mother do all the discipline and that my father stay out of it. That was hard for him because, according to my mother, I was pretty reckless and he was afraid I would hurt myself. But I guess I've never wanted any part of him."

"When was your father born?"

I opened my notebook, turned to a list, and pointed to my father's birthdate.

Robert's face tensed up and then relaxed, and he remained silent for a moment. "The therapist was right," he said finally.

"There was no way you and your father could have gotten along. You would have had to be saints. That's too bad. He appears to have really cared for you, but the anger and resentment rose automatically between you two. You were born with a defiant spirit and his Mars, adverse to your Pluto in Virgo, only aroused that defiance. You didn't have to get to know your father in order to dislike him—it was instantaneous. It's like when we walk into a room. . .some people we avoid and others we are drawn to. It's a matter of planetary chemistry. I would have given your mother the same advice as the therapist did regarding your father. But it must have been very hard for him too."

"I never knew how he felt," I said. "I haven't seen him since I left for New York more than ten years ago. They divorced long before my mother died."

"With your Saturn on your Mars and Pluto forming a stressful line to these two planets at birth, it's very clear to me that you would have real trouble with men."

I felt I was swimming into deep water, but he kept baiting my curiosity. "What do you mean with Saturn on my Mars?"

"Well, as you probably remember from Lesson 1 in my book, Saturn functions as an old Scrooge by spoiling the good intentions of about every planet he touches. He obstructs, frustrates, and depresses people everywhere.

"Mars in a woman's chart shows her sexuality—her passion. The sign Mars was in when she was born shows the kind of man she desires sexually. But your Mars is hindered by Saturn and this makes it difficult for you to be truly intimate with a man. It appears that you may have a lot of body armor and don't want to be vulnerable sexually."

"Oh, god, that's true," I squinched. A hot bubble popped inside of me and a river of feeling flowed out. "I hate it, but that's the way it is. No man's ever going to get control of me—I won't allow it!" I shot up from my chair. "I don't want to talk about this anymore," I said, gathering my things.

"I understand, Nora. I have to go meet Lelia, anyway. We have covered a lot today. Do you still want to come back next Saturday?"

"Could I call you? I'm not sure. I may have to go somewhere with a friend." How clever of me. I was surprised how quickly I came up with that excuse. It was time for a breather; he had scraped a lot of raw nerves.

"Sure," he said. "Give me a call during the week and let me know what's happening." He got up from the table and turned off the tape recorder. "This one is full of really valuable material," he said handing me the tape. "But we don't need to continue in the same vein if you don't want to."

"Thank you," I said shaking his hand. "I'll call you." I gave him a weak smile and closed the door behind me. I didn't even remember walking through the pines and sniffing the flowers. All I wanted to do was to get away from Robert Christos.

3

I called Rachel on Monday morning and went up to her restaurant on Chestnut Street to talk to her about Robert. She was sitting at my favorite booth in the back where my mother and I used to sit. Blue and white flowers laced between rich, green vines hung from the giant logs that crossed the ceiling; it always felt like such a warm and cozy place to me. This was where I used to listen to Rachel and my mother tell stories about the Beatles, the Indian swamis, and Timothy Leary, the "acid guru." I was a mere twelve-year-old then and the Marina neighborhood seemed quieter in those days. Since the '89 earthquake, a lot of people have moved in, and now there are restaurants and coffee houses everywhere.

"How did your reading go with Robert?" Rachel asked, handing me my favorite latté.

I looked into her big brown eyes. Her moonlike face always reminded me of one of those cherubs in a religious painting. "The last session was real bad," I said. "Robert pissed me off. I feel like I've been burned to the bone."

"Really? What happened?"

"We talked a lot about my relationship to men, how I treat them, and my strategies around that. I've been 'going for the jugular,' he says, from the time I banged on the table at my father. A lot of things have been coming up for me—even stuff from the Sixth Grade. Remember that time I ran that boy's bike off the hill onto the freeway? It was twisted into a pretzel. What was his name? . . . Marvin Horn, that was it."

"I remember him. Your mother said he had it coming, trying to bully you and everybody else at school."

"I know I've done some mean things to guys—getting back at them for being such jerks, like Elmer."

"Who was Elmer?"

"Elmer Finch, the concert pianist. He was at the Conservatory when I was there. A real musical snob. He was always needling me about my technique and showing off his parallel thirds. He really pissed me off! One day I swiped his metronome and broke it into a zillion pieces. I even put some of the pieces on his piano bench hoping they would stick him in the ass. I know he knew I did it, but he couldn't prove it. He was so anal. When I think about it now, I know that was such a mean thing to do. A lot of stuff like that's been coming up for me."

"Don't be so hard on yourself, dear. That's all in the past now. Besides, you're forgetting the good things you've done for people. Remember that summer you took care of me when I had the accident? Boy, what timing that was! It was right after Fred left, the bastard. You shopped for all the groceries, filled my prescriptions, washed my clothes, cleaned the house, changed Odin's litter box, fixed my dinner, and even gave me back rubs."

I felt uncomfortable with her praise. "Where's Fred now?" I asked.

"I don't know and I don't care. He's probably 'spaced-out' at the Las Vegas books betting the horses. He was so obsessed with them that I told him to go marry one. So he did—I mean he left," she laughed. "After the accident I tried to get his help, but I couldn't find him. That's when you lit on my doorstep—an angel from down the street. That was you, Nora."

"Robert did say I have a soft side. But you're the real angel, Rachel. You're the one who got my butt off that bridge."

"Well, we won't get into that one, dear. At least you don't have cobwebs in your brain like me"

"How do you mean?"

"Robert said I was born with Neptune frustrating my Mercury, which makes me kind of distort things. And being a sensitive Pisces with Moon in Cancer doesn't help. I guess I make things up to fit my fantasies, which is *not* too good for business, you know. I don't mean I deceive people—I just fool myself sometimes by pretending everything is okay when it's not. Your mother used to shock me with the way she criticized me for wearing my rose-colored glasses, but she was usually right . . . it just made me uncomfortable at times. I guess that was her Aquarian way."

"I'm an Aquarian, too."

"That's right, you are. Well, don't Aquarians tell it like it is?"

"Yes we do, but it's not always that easy to look at our own stuff, no matter how honest we are. I mean, Robert sure gave me more heat than I could take, and I'm still blistering from it."

"But it sounds like you're getting on top of it, dear."

"Really? I don't feel like I'm on top of anything."

"What I mean is it sounds like you're processing stuff, that Robert's really helping you."

"He is? Could be I guess, but I'm really churned up inside."

"Oh, . . . there's Joe," she said, looking into the kitchen. "I gotta go, dear. My supplier's been bugging me to let him collect his money. Keep in touch, and let me know what happens with you and Robert. I love you," she said, kissing me on the cheek.

"I love you too," I said, hugging her.

"Talk to you later."

"Bye."

As soon as I returned to my apartment, I called Robert and told him that everything was okay for Saturday. He gave me Gloria's phone number at Maxwell Associates to call her for a possible job. I wrote her number down, put it in my purse, and went through the morning mail. "Bills, bills, bills," I grumbled. "Why don't they send *me* some money." Suddenly an envelope I saw sent a hot wave through me. I stared at the return address, savoring it. I even stroked the embossed letters with my fingers to feel how precious the words felt: "Delcroix Productions."

I had done a cold reading for David Delcroix more than a month ago and had given up on the part. Maybe he wanted me to do it after all. Silently praying, I slowly opened the envelope, unfolded the letter, and read it:

> *Dear <u>Ms. Lakewood</u>:*
>
> *We regret to inform you that your audition for <u>Lillian</u> in <u>Time for Silence</u> has been carefully considered by the casting director and we have decided we cannot use you at this time.*
>
> *Thank you for your participation.*
>
> *Sincerely yours,*
>
> *David Delcroix*

"Thank you for your participation," I mocked. "You're not welcome you jerk."

I jumped into my car and drove straight to Delcroix's office in downtown San Francisco. It was in a building right next to 101 California Street where a crazy guy shot all those people a few years back. As I pushed the elevator button for the 20th floor, I thought about that nut with the gun, and a part of me wanted to do something like that to Delcroix.

I knew his secretary wouldn't let me in so I waited until she was distracted, and then I charged into his office. "This is the third rejection I've gotten from you, you jerk." I shoved the crumpled notice in front of him. "How can you expect anybody to understand a character if they're reading cold all the time?"

"Who are you?" he demanded.

"That just shows you how stupid you are. I read for you three times and you don't even remember me."

He sneered. His beaky nose and mousy mouth made him look like a turtle as he leaned forward, glaring over the top of his glasses. "Doesn't that tell you something?" he shot back, as he pointed to his head with his right index finger and made a dumb face like I was an idiot. "Maybe you haven't gotten the message yet, sweetheart."

"You nerd," I blasted. I picked up a script off his desk and threw it at him. "You couldn't direct my ass across the street." I turned around and walked swiftly past the gawking heads in the hallway, barely noticing the red faces as I swept by.

"I lost it again," I thought later in the car. "I've just ruined my acting career. That wimp probably knows everybody in Hollywood. I'm still banging on that table at my father—at all men, I guess. I can't see how I'm ever going to stop getting pissed off at them; but I've got to find a way somehow. I can't keep shooting myself in the foot like this."

The next morning I walked up to Rachel's to indulge my ego before I hit the work jungle. Rachel said that eating her desserts was like making love—a real sensual experience. So I ordered her hazelnut mousse and swooned as my taste buds got lost in the cream. The pastry flakes disappeared into my tongue, what a delight. I took the piece of paper that had Gloria's number on it, walked over to the wall phone and punched it in. "

"Maxwell Associates, this is Gloria speaking. How may I help you?"

"Yes. This is Nora Lakewood. A friend of mine, Robert Christos, told me that you might have a temp job for me."

"Oh, hi Nora. Have you done litigation?"

"Yes, I have."

"Well, I have this job, but they don't need anyone until ten o'clock tomorrow morning. It's down on Market Street. Why don't you come in around nine and we can take care of the paperwork. Is that convenient for you?" she asked.

"Yes," I said. "I'll be there. Where are you located?"

"Three Eighty Pine, Suite 330. Do you know how to get here?"

"Yes. Thank you."

"You're welcome. See you tomorrow at nine."

I strolled back to my table. *This could be a nice day after all,* I thought. I picked up the *Times* and read the theater section. "Bad, bad, bad," I said out loud, shaking my head.

"What's that?" a male voice asked next to me.

I turned and felt dark, intense eyes drawing me in. For a second I didn't know where I was. "They're so bad," I said, catching myself. "These jerks in Hollywood are making so many dumb films; they write stupid scripts with no third act. It's really hard to find a good one these days—everything's about violating women or blowing somebody up."

"What kind of movies do you like?" he asked in a mellow tone. His wavy, pitch-black hair was well combed and his shirt looked freshly starched. He wore a crimson tie that was splashed with blue and yellow flowers. It was perfectly tied, but still he seemed looser than an ordinary business type. And he looked too neat to be an actor.

"Nice tie," I said.

"My mother sent it to me for my birthday."

"When's that?"

"The eleventh of November—I'm Scorpio."

I thought about what Robert says in his book about the *black sign attitude* of Scorpio: *They exude an intensely mysterious quality that makes them very seductive.* "What year?" I quizzed, to hide my staring.

"1965. Now I'm supposed to ask 'What's your sign?'" he laughed.

"Aquarian," I replied. "But, thank God, we're more than our Sun sign. There are nine other planets."

"Sounds like you're really into it," he said, moving his chair closer. He held out a suntanned hand. "I'm Andrew Kent."

"Nora Lakewood," I said, shaking his hand. He made me nervous but I didn't know why.

"Are you an astrologer?" he asked.

"Oh, no, I'm just a student. I'm studying it to learn about how to develop my characters for acting parts."

"I once had a friend who was really into it. He tried to make it work with the stock market by using the Gann system, but could never figure it out. He lost a bundle."

"I guess it won't work with some things." His eyes kept pulling me into them, and I forced myself to look away. My feelings were racing ahead of me. "What kind of work do you do?" I managed to ask.

"I'm a trader."

"What's that?"

"Commodities. I place orders to buy or sell contracts on gold, corn, wheat, coffee, or cattle and wait to see what happens. Then I sell or buy when the market is going in my favor. This is my office," he said showing me a cellular phone and a newspaper. "I can take my office any place in the world—France, Japan, Australia—even on the beach at Laguna."

"That's cool, but are you making any money at it? I mean I've heard that can be risky. Couldn't you get burned?"

"Most people do, but that's because they don't have any patience. They let their brokers make all their decisions and lose their shorts. Some of them don't even know how they lose their money. I read my own charts and do my own trading. Last year I made $320,000 on coffee."

"$320,000 on coffee?" I asked, dropping my head in disbelief.

"Yes, I figured coffee was going to go up a long time ago when I saw more and more people drinking lattés. So I loaded up on call options, watched the prices soar, and made a bundle."

"I guess you're just smarter than all those other people," I said a little sarcastically.

"It just takes patience and knowing when to move."

He's probably exaggerating just to impress me, I thought. I couldn't believe he made that much money.

"There are some other people who did the same thing as I did," he said, appearing to read my mind. Then he looked at his watch. "Well, I have to meet somebody. I would like to know more about your astrology. Do you have a card?"

"No, I don't."

"How about a phone number?"

"Why don't you give me your card?" I asked. "I can give you a call."

A dark fire filled his eyes and he looked annoyed. "I'm not in town much," he replied, looking at his watch again. "Well, I have to go." He got up from the table, paused for a moment, and then walked out the door. He waved a halfhearted good-bye as he walked down the street.

"I think I blew it," I whispered. A strange feeling danced through me as my heart swelled in ecstasy. Then an intense sadness swept the bliss away and circled my body. Every bone seemed to hurt as I sank into my seat. *I let him get away*, I thought. While I knew that a woman had to be careful with strangers these days, I still ached to call back that moment. His face, his eyes, and his voice sank deep inside of me—they wouldn't let go. Somehow he had awakened a wild energy that I couldn't control. I looked down the street, searching for him, but there was only dust and sunlight . . . He was gone.

4

The next morning I went downtown to see Gloria at Maxwell Associates. She was just like Robert said—a sweet Pisces lady who loved helping people. She got me a temp job at a fancy law firm on Market Street. The carpets were so thick, I felt like walking around with my shoes off. Despite the elegant surroundings, I hated being a lawyer's slave again but I was in no position to be picky. Anyway, it wasn't forever. Robert said things would be looking up for me in October.

When I saw Robert again, I begged him to tell me something about Andrew. "Do you think we would be compatible?" I asked.

He put Andrew's birth information into his computer. A few gray strands of hair slid across his deep blue eyes as he shook his head. "This is something," he mused. "You really love this man, don't you?"

"I don't know. It feels like he's got a hold of me and won't let me go."

"Your connection is really strong—it might go back to a past life."

I looked closer to see what he was seeing. "How do you do that?" I asked. "You don't even have my chart."

"I keep a lot of charts in my head, just like you keep scripts and music in yours. I close my eyes and they're right there."

"But what do you see?"

"For one thing, your Neptune's right next to his Sun. You could feel like you've known him for a thousand years. What this pattern does is stir up a love memory in you that may have been dormant for a long time. If you allow yourself to feel it, you'll sense that you already know him. Your reasoning may try to interfere, but if you allow yourself to acknowledge what you really feel, you will have your answer."

"But I don't understand how this can happen. I don't *really* know him."

"Actually you do know him, just as I've described. But it doesn't matter. It's the chemistry of your planets that tells me about your relationship. These feelings you have for him must be very strong. Isn't this true?"

"This is strange," I said. "First there's my mother and now this awful feeling. When will it all end?"

I got up from the table and stood at the window. A scrawny crow flew out of the mist and landed on a giant redwood branch. It looked cold and hungry. "What's really crazy is that I don't think I can survive without him. Isn't that dumb? To feel like this over somebody you don't even know? I just don't know what to do about it." *Was this me talking? A mousy little girl who didn't know how to take care of herself?*

"He's your teacher," Robert said.

"My teacher? How can you say that?"

"He has come into your life to open your heart."

"But how can you say that when you haven't even met him?"

"Oh, I've met him all right—he represents one of the planets moving in your chart. As you may recall, after we are born, the planets continue to move along their path through the signs. Some of the planets move into a position that stimulates our birth planets. These are called visiting planets. The visiting planet Pluto is presently changing your relationship to all men because it's passing right over your birth Mars, which was in Sagittarius at the time you were born. And as you know, Mars reflects the male energy in your life. This is a very emotional time for you. When Pluto visits a woman's Mars, as it is doing in your chart, she usually finds a very intense relationship. But for some women, it may be more lust than love. This is passion in its highest state and you could become obsessed with your desire for him. It is very difficult to refuse to engage in this affair, but I don't look at this as a bad thing. It is much deeper than mere lust or romance. Visiting Pluto represents Andrew and he has come into your life just as your heart process is beginning. That's how I know he's part of the changes you're going through. Mars is male, and the male within you is being awakened—he is now walking into your life. You are compelled by Pluto to embrace him despite your resistance."

"But I thought I was coming out of my bad time."

"This is not bad at all, Nora. Pluto, or Andrew, is part of the process that's going to help free you from a bad time."

"But I'm terrified," I said walking back to the table to grab a hunk of tissue. "If this is love I don't want any part of it—but you said it might just be about lust."

"In your case, it's more about love."

"I can't believe I'm such a wimp. I thought I was stronger than this. Does this happen to other people?"

"Sure, to some—when it does, almost everyone thinks they're losing their mind, but it's their defenses they're losing. Besides, you're no wimp, Nora. Wimps are people who are afraid to feel, to engage in life. You're just beginning to feel your true love for a man. Believe me, no one I know is ready to deal with the kind of love-intensity that's created by the visitation of Pluto. It's not something you can prepare for. At least, that's been my experience. True love has a way of making us care a lot more than we want to but there is no real strategy for stopping the feeling—although a lot of people try."

I felt like sliding under the table.

He reached over and placed his hand on my arm. A few of his eyebrow hairs stood out like lobster antennae, which gave him an impish look. But his eyes were the kindest I'd ever seen. "Just don't resist it, Nora," he said getting up from the table. "This man has your heart and you're not going to get it back. You can only love him." He stopped the tape and handed it to me.

I got up from the table and started moving toward the door. "I'll have to find him first. I don't even know where he lives."

"You will. I'm sure he hasn't forgotten someone as beautiful as you. He's probably looking for you just as much as you're looking for him."

"You're just too nice, Robert," I said opening the door. "Do you really think I'll find him?"

"The planets show that there's a man around you who will play a very important part in your life. I feel that Andrew's that man. Just look around—I'm sure you'll find him."

"Thanks," I said. "See you Saturday."

"Okay. Bye, Nora."

On Wednesday morning, I put on my spiffy blue-green outfit with my favorite white blouse and walked up to Rachel's Place in search of Andrew. The aroma of roasting coffee floated on the morning fog as I slipped through the old brass doors. I took a sweeping glance at the people sitting behind their newspapers and walked over to a man who seemed to be hiding behind his. I hoped it was Andrew—but no such luck. I ordered my favorite French Roast latte´ and splurged on Rachel's new peach Napoleon. It sent my taste buds dancing as I swirled my tongue through a sea of peachy cream. The caffeine jump-started my adrenal glands and I felt a new rush of courage. I was determined that if I would be lucky enough to see Andrew again, I wouldn't let him get away this time. It had only been a little over a week since I had seen him and I figured he'd have to show up sometime soon. I scanned the theater pages of the morning paper looking for a good movie to distract me from the pain that was still gnawing on me just beneath the surface. A little while later, I saw Rachel come in. We waved at each other and she went into the kitchen. I took a monologue from my bag and started working on the lines.

Nearly an hour later, one of the customers left the door open and a swift foggy breeze spread over me like a shock wave; the sharp air slapped me in the face like a cruel messenger. Andrew was not going to show. I got up from my seat, gathered my belongings, and paid my check. Then I went into the kitchen to see Rachel.

"Nora," she said, "you look beautiful this morning. What's the occasion?"

"I was looking for the man of my dreams."

"Tell me where you're going to look, dear, and maybe I'll join you."

"I thought he might be here."

"Here?" she asked, while turning on the gas under a kettle of soup.

"Yes. I met him here about a week ago, but I don't have his phone number. I thought he might show up this morning. Maybe you know him. His name's Andrew Kent."

"What's he look like?"

"He has a tan, black hair, intense eyes—a Scorpio—a fancy dresser with a cellular phone and a laptop."

"I think I *have* seen somebody like that but I don't know his name. Let's ask Sally. She knows just about everybody who comes in here."

I followed Rachel to a table in the back where Sally was folding napkins. "Sally?" Rachel asked. "Do you know an Andrew Kent who comes in here? He's a sexy Scorpio guy with black hair, suntanned, and wears fancy clothes."

"Andrew Kent," Sally mused. "Ummm. Oh—I do know an Andrew, but I don't remember his last name. Your description sounds like the same guy—he comes and goes a lot. I remember waiting on him a little while back."

"Do you know where he lives?" I asked.

"No—wait a minute," she said. She took some gum out of her mouth and stuck it on a saucer. "I may have something in my locker."

She went into the back room and came back out with something in her hand. "Here," she said. "I found this brochure he gave me a while ago. Looks like it's him—his address is stamped on the back. You can keep it, Nora. At first, I thought I would do some investing, but when I found out it was commodities, I chickened out."

"This is fantastic, Sally. I owe you. Now I better go find him."

"Yes," Rachel said. "You don't want him to get away this time."

"No way," I said. "Bye. See you soon."

I went straight to a phone station and called the number on the brochure. It was disconnected. I kicked the phone post and cursed the phone company. "What next?" I said in disgust. I walked down Pierce Street to check out the address. I was surprised that it was only a few blocks from where I lived. I scanned the mailboxes for Andrew's name but no luck. Just as I was about to leave, I looked back at the boxes in case I'd missed something. I noticed the word "Manager" under one of them and pushed the button. An old woman's voice came floating out of the speaker. "Yes?"

"Hello," I said moving closer. "My name's Nora Lakewood. I'm looking for Andrew Kent. Do you know where I can find him?"

"No, I don't. He moved out about a year ago and I don't have his forwarding address anymore. You a relative?"

"No, just a friend, but I really need to find him."

"Sorry dear, I can't help you."

"Okay. Thanks, anyway."

Just as I reached the sidewalk I heard the woman calling from the speaker. "Young lady, are you still there?"

I rushed back to the speaker. "Yes," I replied.

"I was just thinking. I remember him having a brother who worked as an attorney downtown someplace in the financial district, but I don't know where. Andrew called him his 'big brother Bruce.' He was always calling him his 'big brother Bruce.'"

"Oh, thank you so much," I cried. "That will help a lot."

"You're welcome, dear. Hope you find him."

"Thank you. Me too. Bye."

When I walked home and looked for Bruce Kent in the phone book, I slammed the book on the bed. There were more than a dozen Bruce Kents and I had no clue which was the one I was looking for. Then I turned to the yellow pages and looked under "Attorneys." There was only one Bruce Kent. I grabbed the phone and quickly punched in the number without knowing what I was going to say. I felt like I was falling off a cliff.

"Bruce Kent," a voice boomed in my ear.

"Mr. Kent, my name's Nora Lakewood. I'm a friend of Andrew Kent. Are you his brother?"

"Yes, " he replied in an expectant tone.

"I'm trying to locate him. Do you know where he might be?"

"No, I don't. I haven't heard from him in over a month. We have dinner once in a while, but he's on the road a lot. I never know where he's going to be. He was in New York City last month, but I don't know if he's still there. If you'll leave your number I'll tell him to get in touch with you when he calls. What's your name again?"

"Nora Lakewood," I said, giving him my number.

"Okay. I'll tell him you called."

"Thanks. I'd appreciate it."

The following Saturday, just when I had started to sit at the kitchen table to compare my planets with Andrew's, the phone rang.

"Is this Nora?" a man asked.

"Yes," I said.

"This is Andrew Kent. I got your message from Bruce. You're quite a detective. How'd you find me, anyway?"

"It was Sally at Rachel's Place. She had one of your brochures with your old address on it. Your former landlady told me about your brother, Bruce, so I called him. It's really amazing that you called," I said with my feelings bouncing around inside of me, "I was just looking at your chart this very moment."

"My chart? Are you playing the commodities now?"

"No, no," I laughed, "not that kind of chart. Your *astrology* chart. I was just looking up your planets."

"Checking up on me, huh?"

"You could say that. You're really big on travel and you have a great passion for detail."

"That's pretty good," he said. "How can you tell that?"

"According to my teacher, Robert, Jupiter is a planet that shows our urge to do something in a big way. Since your Jupiter's in the traveling sign of Sagittarius, travel is a big thing for you. It's part of your nature."

"That's true. I can't seem to stay in one place. Sometimes I feel like I have no home—my home is wherever I take my shoes off. How'd you know I was a nit picker?"

"Your Mars is in Virgo. That's a planet of passion and the sign of Virgo gives you the tendency to keep things organized. You must have a passion for little things."

"That seems logical. I do have this compulsion for keeping track of every little tick of the market."

"When you come out this way again, we should have dinner sometime and see how our planets relate to each other."

"There couldn't be a better time than now—I just happen to be arriving in San Francisco tomorrow afternoon. Are you free then? I could pick you up around seven and we could go over to Marin for a nice dinner. I know a great restaurant."

"Yes, that would be nice," I said trying not to sound too excited. "I live in Seashore Gardens. The old place was destroyed by the '89 earthquake. Do you know where that is?"

"Sure do. I used to walk by there all the time. Which house are you in?"

"The first one on the right, 351—the one with the bamboo wind chimes. Just double-park and ring the doorbell and I'll come out. That way you won't have to look for a parking place.

"Okay. By the way, don't forget to bring *your* chart. I'll have to check you out, too, you know."

"Okay," I laughed. "See you tomorrow at seven."

"I'll be there."

5

"What's the name of this place?" I asked Andrew after we were seated by a window overlooking the bay.

"Pietro's. Do you like it?"

"Yes," I replied, watching a small flock of snow geese gather on the grass near the edge of the water. "It's really peaceful here."

"Yes." He picked up a crimson-colored menu. "Would you like some wine?" he asked.

"That would be nice."

"Red or white? Dry or sweet?"

"I like chardonnay, it's not too sweet."

He motioned to the waitress. "Hi, Sheri," he said as she arrived at the table. "Could we have a bottle of the Far Niente chardonnay?"

"Sure thing," she said as she smiled softly, and then glided off toward the bar.

"You come here often?" I asked.

"Only when there's something special—like *you* for instance," he said winking.

"I'll bet," I said, hinting that I didn't believe him. "You probably flatter all the other women you bring here."

"Actually, to tell you the truth, I don't. I have only brought important clients here. Most of them have been older men and women, investors who want me to help fatten their portfolio."

Sheri brought the wine, showed the label to Andrew, and after uncorking it, she poured a little into his glass. He handed it to me. "Here, taste it—you be the judge."

I was almost overcome by the subtle flavor that washed over and around my tongue. "Ummm," I faked a swoon. "This I like."

Sheri smiled, poured the wine, pushed the bottle into a bucket of ice, and disappeared again.

"Oh, my god," Andrew said looking at the menu. "They have Columbia River salmon tonight. You gotta' have this. Don't look any further."

"How do they fix it?" I asked.

"They wrap this beautiful filet in banana leaves, sprinkle it with a touch of chives and scallions, and serve it with a fantastic sauce. The amazing thing is how moist the salmon stays by using the banana leaves."

"I'm sold—let's get it," I said, placing my menu back on the table.

"Actually, I think they stole the recipe from Yukol."

"Who's that?"

"A wonderful Thai chef who runs a little place over on Lombard. We'll have to go there sometime."

"I think I know where it is."

"I would also like to recommend the hot spinach salad. You know, I hate spinach, but the way they make it here has changed my mind."

"You sound like a real gourmet. I've never heard of a hot spinach salad before, but if you say its good, I'm willing to try it."

"It's good." He motioned to Sheri. She came over and took our order. When she left, Andrew said, "She's a dancer. Used to be on Broadway but said she got burned out. Didn't you say you were into acting?"

"Yes, but I'm not having much luck lately."

"Why's that?" he asked. His pitch-black hair shimmered against the bay rippling behind him.

A soft breeze came in through an open window and cooled my fiery skin. I looked into his eyes. They seemed almost hypnotic as I fell into them. "Too much karma between me and directors," I finally said, looking away.

"What do you mean?"

"Robert, my astrologer, says I'm going through this phase where everything is depressing. Things are just not working out for me."

"Don't you have an agent to help you?"

"No, I can't get one. They don't want to mess with you if you haven't done anything major. I've done leads in summer stock, neighborhood theaters, and an off Broadway musical. I've also played some bit parts in TV and was featured in a documentary film once—but they're looking for somebody with more experience."

Sheri dished out the hot spinach salad and I took a bite. "Oh, this is good," I said, happy to get the attention off of me. "I never knew spinach could taste like this."

"Me, neither," he said, sliding his fork into a leaf. "I can't imagine *you* being rejected. You're so photogenic—beautiful green eyes, auburn hair, a very sensual mouth. It certainly can't be your looks."

"I really get tired of hearing about *my* acting problem," I said laying down my fork. "Delcroix says I'm too disconnected and not in touch with my character. He says I'm trying to make the words carry the feeling instead of letting my feelings carry the words. But what does he expect? Most casting directors will let you do a monologue of a piece that's close to the part you're trying out for. The problem is that he wants the actors to read cold, not letting us see the script ahead of time. I need to improvise into my character—take some time to get to know her and create a history for her. Otherwise, it doesn't make any sense to me. I think he's just a control freak."

"What do other people say you should do?"

"An actor friend said that I should do some group improvisations and sharpen my auditioning skills. So, I started working with Marcia Kimmell at the Next Stage."

"Who's she?"

"A fantastic teacher of improvisation and theater games. She can change her character and mood in an instant. You should see her—her performances are amazing. I'm so fortunate to have her. She's teaching me to trust who I am more, coaching me on audition pieces, and helping me create some original work. Then there's Robert. He says something else." I picked up my fork and started eating again.

"The astrologer?"

"Yes. He says we have to know who we are before we can understand anybody else."

"What's he mean by that?"

"I'm not quite sure, but he keeps telling me that we can't know who we are until we have given our heart away to somebody."

"That would take a lot of courage. Have you ever done that?"

"No way," I said, hoping he didn't see that I was lying—hoping that he couldn't see that he already had my heart.

"I think that would be a real risky thing to do," he said. "You would lose control of your life and become somebody's plaything. Love has to work both ways—give and take. I don't think we have to give ourselves away to somebody before we can know who we are. That really sounds strange to me."

I back-paddled into a safe harbor behind my words. "You're probably right—it would be dangerous."

"This Robert sounds more like a love doctor. I thought astrology was about prediction and reading the stars, not psychology."

He sounded a little irritated, but I still felt glad that he'd said that. My emotions were moving way ahead of me and I was afraid I would say something foolish. I hid behind my words again. "It's really all about the planets," I said, "not the stars. He's great at seeing what a person's like on the inside. He says it all has to do with the position of the planets at the time we were born. The patterns they form show who we really are."

Just when I sensed we were heading for an argument, Sheri brought the salmon.

"I can't wait till you taste this," he said. "You're going to have a terrific surprise."

He was right about that. "It's the most tender salmon I've ever tasted, " I said. "Thank you for recommending it. You must eat out in restaurants a lot to know so much about food."

"I hate eating alone. I've probably spent a fortune in restaurants. They are my home, my place to relax. I feel mothered here."

"Don't you have a family?"

"No, not really. I do see my big brother Bruce once in a while. But I was never much into family even when I was a kid. I was always off with my friends someplace."

"How about your father and mother?"

"They're in England. They moved there after I graduated from high school, and I didn't want to leave the States. I moved in with a friend who was into the commodities market. He taught me how to play the futures." He took another drink of wine. "I do fly over to see my parents once in a while, but I guess I'm not very attached to them."

"Moon in Aquarius," I mused.

"What does that mean?"

"I apologize for that. I'm beginning to pick up Robert's habit—he's always talking to people about their planets as if it was an everyday conversation. The Moon was in Aquarius when you were born, so this means that your habits and feelings tend to be unpredictable. Aquarius is the sign of detachment."

"But aren't you an Aquarian?"

"Yes, my Sun's in Aquarius." I was surprised he had remembered that. I had mentioned it to him only briefly in our first encounter at Rachel's Place. "That means I can understand your detachment, because I've always been that way myself. When things get too sticky,

I always cut out. I've never had a long-lasting relationship with anyone."

He lifted the wine glass as if to take another drink, but put it back down. "Me neither. My relationships have never been very close, because I have always felt bound by a need to stay free. Sounds like we're a lot alike. Maybe it's just our way to avoid getting hurt."

"Probably. Who wants to get hurt? But, you know, I don't have any fears about you. It's very strange, I feel like I've known you for a long time— I can't explain it."

At this point Sheri cleared our plates. "Would you like to see the dessert menu? Coffee or after dinner drinks?" she asked.

"No dessert for me," I said. "I've had my calories for the day."

Andrew said, "No dessert for me either, but I'd like to share a glass of that Muscat with Nora. You know? The Bonny Doon Muscat?"

"You got it," Sheri said. "I'll be right back."

"What's a Muscat?"

"It's a dessert wine. It is so delicate you won't believe it. It's like perfume on your palate."

"Okay," I said. "You really do have an ongoing love affair with food, don't you?"

"I'm basically a hedonist," he smiled, "but an ongoing love affair with you would be even nicer."

My heart leaped, even though I tried not to show any pleasure. "You really think so?" I asked, baiting him.

"I know so," he said touching my hand. "It would be a wild thing to do."

A warm river rushed through my body. My hand turned over and grasped his instinctively. My face got hot.

"We're blushing," he said.

I smiled. "Yes, but you don't have a red face. There's too much tan."

"But it's hot. Feel it." He placed my hand against his face and I wanted to run it through his hair, but he kissed it. "Umm, nice perfume," he said. "Gardenia?"

"Lilac."

Sheri brought the small glass of Muscat and placed it between us. "Will there be anything else?" she asked.

"We'll take the check," Andrew said. He turned back to me, still holding my hand. He picked up the glass of Muscat and put it against my lips. "Take a sip of this."

"It is so subtle," I said. "You're so right. It does taste like some kind of perfume, but it's very light." I looked straight at him and let myself fall into his eyes. "You're a very sensuous man. You know that?"

He smiled, his dark eyes flashing. "Scorpio, you know."

"I've been wondering about that," I said.

"About what?"

"If a Scorpion and an Aquarian could get along. Robert says Scorpio people are very loyal if they love someone but Aquarians are usually very detached just because they want to be free."

"That's funny," he said. "I feel both ways. I mean I am usually a one-woman man, but then I don't want to be inhibited. I like to have options even though I might not do anything."

"A contradiction," I added.

"May be."

Sheri brought the check, thanked us, and walked away. We finished the Muscat and Andrew placed a crisp hundred-dollar bill on her tray. "Are you ready to go?" he asked.

"Yes," I said getting up from the table. I glanced at the tip tray. "Don't you want to wait for your change?"

"No," he said, "the rest is hers."

When we arrived at my place, Andrew walked me to the door. He took both of my hands and looked into me. "It was a great dinner," he said softly. "Too bad it has to end."

"It doesn't have to," I said moving closer.

He let go of my hands, slipped his arms around me, and placed his lips gently on mine. My body warmed, then turned to fire. "You're something special," he whispered. "I really could get attached to you."

I slid the key into the door, opened it, and turned on the living room light. "I'm already attached to you," I said. "It started with me the first time I saw you." I remember thinking I shouldn't have said that, but I couldn't hold myself back. I didn't want to scare him off, but I didn't feel like I had any control anymore. For the first time, I even felt light-hearted, free of the burden of self-protection. I felt my armor slip away.

I slipped off my shoes as he loosened his blue-speckled tie. He looked so delicious. He kissed me again. . .and I was gone. We glided into the bedroom and floated through the dark. Somehow we found my bed and slid onto it. I felt him take off my clothes piece by piece with a silent and graceful rhythm. His body moved like a slow motion silhouette against the distant light coming from the living room. An intense wave of ecstasy swept through me as his lips pressed gently against mine. Flashes of blue light burst forth in the center of my head and my heart swelled with an indescribable joy as he entered me. "Oh, you're so gorgeous," I whispered. The words felt like they came out of someone else or maybe from the real me for the first time.

"So are you," he whispered.

After our bodies were spent in the joy of intimacy, we lay there for an endless time. The silence seemed sacred as I breathed the bliss flowing through me. I remember feeling like someone new, as if I had found my heart for the first time. Then I drifted into sleep.

6

When I awakened the next morning, Andrew was standing over me dressed in his blue suit and same blue-speckled tie. "Good morning, sexy one," he said leaning down to kiss me.

I sat up in bed. "I love that tie," I said touching it.

"It's good luck."

"Does that mean we're lucky together?"

"Could be," he said, gently stroking my hair. "I have to be downtown for a meeting at eight. Want to meet someplace for lunch?"

"How about the Summit Grill? It's in Embarcadero Three. I could walk over from the firm and meet you there around 12:30."

"Sounds great." He kissed me again, and then walked over to the door and opened it. He turned around slowly, took a piece of mint candy from a bowl I had in the hallway, and said, "By the way, I just want to let you know I've been checked out by my doctor. I don't have any—well, you know, a disease or anything."

"Me, neither," I said smiling. "Thank god for that!"

He popped the mint into his mouth. "See you at lunch."

"Bye, handsome."

He waved good-bye and closed the door.

I sat there in my birthday suit reflecting upon how I ended up that way. For a brief moment, I wondered if I had made a big mistake—being so open and free with Andrew—but my body was smiling and my heart was singing. My inner critic was washed away by a lingering feeling of ecstasy.

My heart continued to swim in a river of bliss as I stared at Andrew across the table at lunch—but a part of me felt a little strange with such intense happiness. "Are you still getting rich on coffee?" I managed to asked him.

"No, but I'm about ready to make a move. My contacts tell me that Brazil is going to have a bumper crop this year. So, I expect the price is going down, and then I'll make another bundle with sell-orders."

"But how can you make money if the price goes down?"

"You do it with put-options—but I don't want to bore you with all that stuff. You really have to get your head into it to understand it."

"Thanks. I don't have much of a head for business. So what do you do for fun?" I asked, rubbing a shoeless foot against his leg.

"Oh, trading *is* great fun, but I do like running, watching football, and—making love," he said, winking. Then seeming embarrassed, he asked, "Do you ever watch the 49ers?"

"Sometimes."

"They're my favorite. Have you ever thought of using astrology on the players? Maybe you could figure out if they're going to have a bad day or not."

"Robert could do that but I'm not that good yet. Besides, I'm too busy developing my characters."

"Got it."

We held hands between bites of ocean scallop, and kissed after sharing a Tiramisu. I don't remember much after that except that I found myself on the street saying good-bye to him. We kissed again, and then he gazed briefly into my eyes. "I'll call you tonight," he said, turning toward the parking garage.

"Okay," I said. He waved good-bye as I watched him disappear into the parking tunnel. *Oh, how I love that man*, I thought, as I strolled back toward Market Street.

Andrew called around six that evening and asked me if I wanted to see the *Phantom of the Opera*. "One of my clients gave me tickets and I thought it would be perfect for another evening out," he said, "you want to go?"

"I'd love to," I said.

"We can have an early dinner at Pico's. It's near the theater. Can you be ready in a few minutes? I'm already in the area calling from my car phone."

"Just ring the bell. I'll be ready."

After the show, we went to the top of the Renaissance Hotel and sat in the bar overlooking the bay. It didn't take us long to finish a bottle of Dom Perignon, which loosened us up to the point of nibbling on each other's ears. Then he ordered another bottle.

"If we keep this up," I said, "we're going to have to find a designated driver to get us back home."

"Don't worry about that, lovely one. I have a suite on the 30th floor. All we have to do is get to the elevator, push a button or two, and we're home free."

I was still sober enough to ask a sensible question. "But how am I going to get to work tomorrow?"

"Call in sick."

I thought I would be upset by his suggestion, but instead I was amused. "Right," I said, raising my glass. "I'll call in sick." I ate some fresh crab hors d'oeuvre to slow down the champagne, but the champagne won out.

By the time the bartender said he was closing up, I think we managed to fake a decent "good-night" and headed for the elevator. I remember holding on to Andrew's arm, certain that he knew where he was going. Somehow we did find the right room—that's what he told me the next morning when he woke me up by doing push-ups.

"Where do you get all that energy?" I groaned, as I sat on the edge of the bed watching him.

"I don't know—sometimes I even surprise myself. But, right now, it's just a way to get the woozies out of my head from last night."

"I don't remember much after leaving the bar," I said. "Look at me, I still have my clothes on."

He got up from the floor and walked over to me. "Clothes on or off," he said, caressing my face, "you always look great to me."

I smiled and kissed him on the cheek. "Which way is the bathroom?" I asked.

"To your left. You'll find everything you need, even your own safety-sealed toothbrush. I'm going to have some breakfast sent up. How about some fresh raspberry juice, a latte´ and a hot croissant?"

"That sounds wonderful," I said, heading for the shower.

When I came out of the bathroom, I could smell fresh coffee. Andrew was hanging up the phone. "I had to sell some contracts before the market closed," he said.

"You amaze me. How do you keep up the pace?" I asked, picking up the phone after him.

"I always feel wired. I have to burn off energy."

After I called the office and told my boss I was sick and couldn't come in, Andrew motioned me to the table. "Here have a seat. These croissants are delicious—almost as good as Rachel's Place."

After breakfast he said, "I have to go to a seminar in Phoenix for a few days and I won't be back until Friday night." He slid on his shoes and stood up to tie his powder-blue tie. "Would you like to do some shopping?"

"For what?"

"Anything you want. It's on me. There's a great designer store over on Powell and "

"Oh, no, you've spent too much on me already. Besides I'd feel too guilty doing that. I'm happy just being with you."

"Money's no good if you can't spend it on the people you care about, but I think I understand how you feel. If you change your mind let me know." He reached in the closet and picked up his suitcase. "I'll give you a call from Phoenix. Maybe we could do something on Saturday when I get back. Will you be free then?"

"Call me Friday night when you get back and we can work out a time."

"Fantastic," he said, giving me a strong hug and kissing me gently on the lips. "I'll call you anyway before Friday. You can stay here until eleven if you would like."

"That's all right. I have to be going soon, anyway. I need to work on an audition piece before I see Marcia tonight."

"The theater lady?"

"Yes."

"I'll see you," he said, picking up his suitcase and heading for the door."

"Don't you need to *pack* your suitcase, first?" I asked.

"Oh, no. I always pack way ahead of time. It must be those picky Virgo planets you said I have. Gotta keep organized, you know. I'll be calling you."

"Okay. Bye."

"Bye, bye, beautiful."

I arranged for Andrew to pick me up after I got back from my lesson with Robert on Saturday morning. We took off for a picnic in Muir Woods to see the giant Redwoods that had been growing there for hundreds of years. As we lay quietly together on the forest floor between two huge logs, we inhaled the earthy scent of those ancient beings. We felt that they seemed greater than trees and had a presence we couldn't explain. I felt like hugging them—telling them how grateful I was that they were there. The giant logs that we lay between placed us apart from the rest of the world, and I wondered if others had made love there, too.

On Sunday, we climbed to the top of Mt. Tamalpais—actually we drove most of the way because I knew I wouldn't be able to keep up with Andrew. We sat down on a big rock at the top and held hands as we watched the seagulls glide over the bay. I wondered if my life with Andrew would always be that blissful.

A few weeks later I found out . . . We were driving back to San Francisco after having spent five fantastic days at Big Sur. I wanted to ask him something I had been thinking about for a long time. I started fidgeting with a match book I had taken as a souvenir, and I read the printed words, "Ventana – Big Sur – Country Inn Resort."

The memories flooded my mind. I savored the moment we had stood on a grassy hill watching the ocean swallow the sun. I recalled his warm arms taking the chill out of mine as the fog swept in from the shore. Memories of flames leaping from the fireplace, timeless dinners, and ecstatic lovemaking rushed through my heart. Then a swelling fear took over my body as the doubts darkened the bliss within me. Should I ask him now? . . . If I do, it may be the end of all that we've meant to each other . . . but I had to know. It wasn't like me to hold back a question so long. Then something inside shoved me forward.

"Andrew, do you love me?" I blurted out. My words seemed to scorch every inch of air in the car and an excruciating silence followed. Terror stung my heart.

He cleared his throat. "Sure, I'm crazy about you, Nora," he answered in an almost joking tone. Then seeming to realize that was not enough, he said "Yes, I do love you—in my own way."

"What way is that?" I asked.

"I don't know. I've never tried to analyze it—it's just what I feel."

"I feel you're holding back, that there's a part of you I can't reach. It feels separate from me, something you're not sharing."

"We're all separate from each other, Nora. Everybody needs their own space. Besides, I told you that I could only go so far. I always get an urge to run when this kind of conversation comes up. Remember? We didn't want this to get too sticky."

"*You* don't want it to get too sticky, but I told you it was different being with you." I turned in my seat to look straight at him. "It feels like you're withdrawing from me emotionally. You say nice words, but there's this coolness, a kind of indifferent attitude that shows up in the way you respond to me."

"Maybe you're talking about yourself, Nora. Aren't you the aloof Aquarian?"

"But your Moon's in Aquarius. You're the one who's detached emotionally."

"I think we're both detached emotionally."

"How can you say that? I guess you haven't noticed lately that I'm not detached from you. You're the only man I've ever really wanted to be this close to. I don't want to run away anymore."

He pulled over into a service station and stopped the car. "Look, Nora, I never promised you absolute, unconditional love. I feel you're closing in on me. I need breathing room." He took a restaurant mint from his shirt pocket, unwrapped it, and started eating it.

. . . And I started burning inside.

Then he got out of the car, went into the men's room, and came back out. "Look," he continued, "maybe I'm not able to love a woman completely. I've tried, but at some point they want a lot more than I'm able to give them. I don't know why, but it always seems to end up this way."

"But it doesn't have to end up this way," I said suddenly, realizing that I may have gone too far. I placed my hand on his leg. "We can work it out."

"Maybe," he said. He squeezed my hand and drove out of the service station. "I just need space."

I hated myself for holding on to him, but I was pleased that I had spoken my heart and said what I really felt. Still, I was terrified. I wondered how reliable a man could be with his Moon in Aquarius.

When we reached my place, he reached over and kissed me. "I'll give you a call," he said.

"Don't you want to come in for a while?" I asked. The look on his face twisted around in my heart like a knife. "I know," I said in a tone that exposed my pain, "you need your space." I slid out the door and slammed it shut.

"I have to go to Denver early in the morning," he said, stretching his head down to look at me through the open window. "I'll call you when I get back."

"Don't bother," I snapped. "Keep your space. Maybe you'll get lost in it." I spun away and walked toward the house, not looking back. I heard the sound of his car slip away into silence.

When I got inside, I dug out his chart and looked at his planets. I remember Robert saying that a man's Venus and Moon showed what his relationship with a woman would really be like. Andrew's Venus was next to his Uranus. I turned to Robert's book and opened it to a paragraph under the "Uranus supports Venus" section. It read: *They live on the edge of relationships because they believe in the freedom of love and the adventure of new encounters. They will find it difficult to remain loyal in relationship with others.* I burned for deeper answers, so I called Robert's number.

"Robert, this is Nora," I said. "I'm really sorry to bother you so late, but I'm really hurting. Could you help me?"

"What's the matter?" he asked softly.

"It's Andrew—he's pulling away from me. I can't seem to reach him. Could you tell me something about where he's coming from?"

"Just a minute. I'll pull his chart up on the computer. Let's see. Yes, his Moon's in Aquarius and his Venus is in Libra conjunct his Uranus. Generally, a man with his Moon in Aquarius is not very good at sustained intimacy or commitment. He always wants to be available in case another more fascinating relationship comes along. Also, with his Uranus next to his Venus, he tends to get bored very easily with relationships. All of these planetary energy patterns tend to cool the love between you that I first saw with your Neptune on his Sun. He looks at a woman as his friend and lover rather than as a heart intimate. He seems disconnected from his inner woman—his feelings—they could be a total mystery to him. Further, with his Sun and Mercury in Scorpio, he would want to maintain control and keep his distance. This may be the lack of emotional connection that you are sensing. I would say that he can't give you what you want. I don't think he's able to love you in the way that you'd like—maybe that's what he's trying to tell you. It's a fear of intimacy, fear of losing his freedom, or a feeling of being trapped."

"What can I do about it?"

"Nothing. You can only love him . . . but you may have to walk away at some point."

"I wish I could take my heart back. This is killing me."

"Once you give it, you can't take it back. It may sound strange, but those people who do give their heart away, find it. They are the ones who know what love really is."

"But how do you deal with it? The pain is almost unbearable."

"I know, I know—believe me, I've been there."

"How did you deal with it?"

"There was no way I could deal with it. Like you, I couldn't handle the pain either. Yet, I had no choice but to feel it. Sometimes it was so intense that I would just crawl up into a fetal position and cry. The woman I loved was someone I met during the summer of '67, the year all the hippies turned on in the Haight-Ashbury. I didn't feel much like a man in those days, but it was through her that I finally discovered who I was."

"What happened?"

"I had to face the fact that she didn't love me and then I asked myself what I could do about it. The answer was 'Nothing.' Then something hit me."

"What was that?"

"I realized that I could choose to let her go, that I didn't have to remain a victim and suffer the loss forever. Somehow I found the strength to bring it to an end, to say good-bye."

"But I don't know if I have that much courage. I don't think I can do that."

"Nobody says that you have to decide tonight, tomorrow, or even next week, if you don't want to, Nora."

"But feeling beat up like this, I don't know where he's coming from—it's a real torment. It feels like I have a knife stuck in my chest, and I can't get it out. It's cutting me up inside. I've never had such heartbreak."

"Just keep talking about it, feeling it, and crying it out. Don't try to shut down what's going on inside of you. Soon you'll be released from the pain, just as I was, and when you come out of it, you will be a very different person."

"This is really hard to take in, Robert. I sure hope I feel different from the way I feel now."

"It will take time, but it will happen. . .I promise you."

"Thank you so much. I really appreciate your being there for me. I guess I'll let you go—I don't want to keep you up all night."

"I'll be here if you need to talk."

"Thank you. Goodnight."

"Goodnight, Nora."

I crawled through work the next day. Somehow, I managed to file court documents, type up a temporary restraining order, and send out a summons and complaint for service on a deadbeat. The alleged crook was accused of ripping off an old man who was barely getting by with his shoe repair shop. "People are so mean to each other," I remember thinking. When I caught the "30 Express" back home to the Marina, a feeble old lady with gnarled fingers wobbled on to the bus, and I gave her my seat. I thought of the old shoe repairman and felt my eyes getting wet. I turned away from the other passengers to hide my face. Strange, why am I crying over people I don't even know?

When I got off the bus, instead of walking home, I went down to the bay's edge to watch the waves come in. I could see the Golden Gate Bridge through the patchy fog that was flowing across the giant, rusty red towers.

I thought about the lawyer who had leaped off the north tower last July—right where I once stood. What kind of pain was he feeling? I wondered if I could walk over to that place again and do what he did. In that instant, a sharp spray of salty water slapped me in the face as if to say, "A bad idea." The tide was coming in fast and the waves were getting higher. A chill ran through me as goose bumps popped up on my arms. . .but there was no Andrew to warm them. I turned away quickly and walked home.

I got a surprise when I reached my place. The old stray, black-and-white female cat that had been wandering in my yard the past couple of weeks was lying on my back doorstep. She reminded me of Robert's cat, but she was much older and really scarred. She looked up at me with sagging eyes. "Why have you come to me?" I asked. "Nobody loves you?" She didn't answer. "I know what that's like," I said. I brought her some milk, but she wouldn't touch it. Then I got her some water and left it on the doormat. Two hours later, when I looked out the window, she was still there. I opened the door, and she looked up at me as if trying to tell me something. It was beginning to get dark, and the cold Marina fog was coming in. I took her inside and placed her on a warm towel in the living room. I sat on the sofa watching her soft black-and-white stomach rise and fall in a quiet rhythm. She seemed asleep. I then went to bed.

The next morning the old cat was still in the same place. She did not eat or drink. I placed a heating pad under her to keep her warm and went to work.

When I came home that night, there were three messages on my answering machine—all from Andrew. It wasn't easy, but I erased them.

Just as I had started feeling sorry for myself, I looked over at the sofa and saw that the old cat was still lying on the heating pad where I had left her before going to work. There was something magnificent in the way she lay there—like an old warrior whose scarred body longed for rest. I sat down on the couch to review Robert's book. Then I felt a soft paw on my foot. I reached down, lifted her into my lap, and stroked her furry stomach. A few minutes later, I felt something change. I put my hand next to her nose—there was no breath, only a growing silence. Was she dead? . . . that fast? . . . Yes, gone. She had slipped away into an infinite silence. I pressed her gently against my breast as an invisible wire squeezed my heart. Then I closed my eyes and sank into the darkness. I cried and cried until I fell asleep.

When the morning sun warmed my face and woke me up, I shuddered at what I found. The old cat's body was as cold and hard as a log. I wondered if my body would be like that when the last breath would leave me. I slid her carefully into a large brown bag and carried her down the street to the vet. He called the Humane Society and they took her away.

It seemed like I kept wiping my eyes all day long over that sweet old cat. How quietly she went away, how easily she seemed to let go—if only I had her courage. When I got home that evening I felt I had to do something. Since I had no interest in food, I went directly to my desk and began to write.

Dear Andrew,

This letter is my confession to you. I didn't answer your calls because it's been too painful for me. It's okay that you don't love me, Andrew—you can't help feeling the way you feel. But being with you, knowing that you don't feel the way I do, is just too much of a heartbreak for me. But that's still okay—you don't need to feel any guilt about it. The problem is that I gave you my heart and I can't get it back. I'm learning to let go, though. I know that sounds strange coming from me, because I've always been able to let people go. Now I see that I just didn't care enough with other men. But it's different with you—now I know how much it hurts when we really care. I do release you, Andrew. You're free. For some strange reason, by loving you, I have found more of myself. Maybe that's your gift to me. Anyway, I'm grateful that you came into my life, no matter how painfully brief it has been.

I hope that someday you will find someone you can really love. Take care, wherever you are, and wherever you go. You will always live inside of me because you are the first man I've ever let into my heart. Good-bye, Andrew.

I do love you.

Nora

7

I was still numb after mailing Andrew's letter on my way to work the next day. I should have called in sick—it was one of those days when my bosses were a pain in the butt. I checked the Moon. It was in Virgo. I knew everybody would be picky, picky, picky. Judith Marble, an anal-retentive associate, made me do a letter over again eight times. She kept putting "final" on it when it was really a redraft. When I printed it out on top-grade bond each time, she would find another flaw or word she wanted to change, and I'd print it out all over again. I wondered if I would ever be done with the damn thing—not to mention the senseless slaughter of sacred trees. Old Harvey Sapper couldn't find his pleading file and blamed me for not keeping track of it. When he later found it under his desk among the dirty and discarded coffee cups, he peered at me sheepishly and gave me a restrained "sorry." Now I knew why I was looking for a more creative life outside Yuppieville.

My tension was broken by Sylvia, an overworked paralegal, who told me the latest lawyer joke while I was on my way to the copier. "Hey, Nora, you know what a lawyer uses for birth control?"

"No, what?" I asked.

"His personality."

"Fun-ny," I chuckled.

When I got back to my desk, I checked my home answering machine for messages. A director friend of mine, Lenny—actually Leonard Pace—had left a message for me to call Mildred Sword, a casting director for Golden Gate Films. I called her up and she asked me to bring my portfolio. Lenny wanted me to read for the lead. I was really scared, but I sure wasn't going to turn down a chance to do the female lead in a TV movie. I called Mildred and made an appointment for a Saturday reading. I asked her if I could have a script, and she promised to Fed Ex me one that afternoon.

When the script arrived, I read it three times and then concentrated on my character. The story was about one of those "poor little rich girls" whom nobody understood. But the problem was that the writer made her out to be a real bitch and the ending was very weak. I felt the writer had overdone the bitchy part. The character, Tanya, needed more depth. She was too shallow; the audience would have no sympathy for her. I tried to find some planetary patterns to understand her conflicts, but I could tell I needed help. When Saturday came around for my lesson, I asked Robert.

"What kind of pattern could I choose for Tanya that would explain her being so bitchy and demanding?" He gave me a cup of tea, lemon grass, like I drank before.

"Why not make Pluto frustrate her Mercury or Pluto frustrate her Moon?" he asked. "As you know, my book tells you what signs frustrate each other. Why not put her Pluto in Virgo and her Mercury in Sagittarius? The actress, Joan Crawford, had this pattern. Only in her case, Pluto was in the Sign of Gemini, which was hostile to her Mercury in the Sign of Pisces. Even though Mercury and Pluto are far apart in her chart, they are still very unfriendly. Pluto definitely frustrates Mercury with this pattern.

"Oh, I remember her in the movie *Mommie, Dearest*, I said sipping the lemon grass. "Crawford was played by Faye Dunaway."

"This pattern makes the mind very intolerant. Even though the person may be highly intelligent, an emotional reaction bursts forth from the unconscious and causes them to be unreasonable. They have a compulsion for having their own way at the expense of other people."

"Crawford seemed to be like that. But what can I do to make Tanya a more sympathetic character?"

"Consider that if we take the larger planet Jupiter (expansion) and put it next to the Moon (feelings), we get *expanded feelings*. Now, if we put her Moon and Jupiter in Pisces, we get *expanded caring feelings*. With this pattern, Tanya would be an extremely caring person."

"I'm beginning to see how it works now," I said. "Susan Pace, the woman who wrote the script, has already shown a transformation of Tanya's negative side by having her make a serious mistake that indirectly causes her friend's death. Tanya loses a lot of her arrogance after that. So now the Moon and Jupiter in the Sign of Pisces would be much stronger—her true caring side would have a chance to come out."

"Let's do another one just to make sure you understand it. Why not make Neptune also support her Moon? What would you say about that combination?"

"Well, Neptune is the planet of inspiration, and the Moon is feeling. From this, I get inspired feelings—a caring person."

"Great. Now you have some key patterns for understanding your character. All you need to do is use your imagination on how she expresses them. You understand her problems and the kind of planetary energies that show her responses to life. Obviously, this will be reflected in her dialogue with the other characters in the story."

"Right."

"Of course, if you were really ambitious, you could create imaginary patterns for all the other characters in the story based on how the author has portrayed them and you could even help the writer make the characters more interesting."

"That's really cool. Maybe I'll do that one of these days, but right now I'm happy just knowing who *my* character is."

"By the way, I forgot to ask. How are you doing with Andrew?"

"I wrote him a good-bye letter. It was so hard—but I knew I had to do it."

"What made you decide to end it?"

"It was so painful being with him and knowing he didn't care that much. You said I might have to walk away. Somehow I found the strength to do it after that old cat died."

"What cat was that?"

"I took in this black-and-white cat, and she died on me. I know she was in a lot of pain, but she never complained. She just surrendered and let go. I guess writing the letter was my way of letting go of Andrew. Maybe I felt like I was honoring the old cat in some way."

"I honor you, Nora. The old cat would be proud of you, I'm sure."

"I still miss her. I still miss Andrew. It hurts to know I won't be seeing them anymore. But for some reason, I feel stronger for doing what I did."

"I know exactly what you mean. Later, I realized that it was actually in giving my heart away that I found it. You seem to be heading in the same direction—opening up, taking risks, getting stronger."

"I do feel stronger, but I'm still hurting over the loss."

"It does hurt to be vulnerable, but it's the only way I know to find your heart. There's a great gift for those who have crossed that line."

"What's that?"

"Consider that most people don't have much passion for life, don't know what they want. But how can they know what they want if they don't know who they really are—what they really feel and value about themselves? When a person gains this true feeling of self-respect, they will have passion. There is a clarity that comes from being open at the heart, vulnerable, and not afraid to let our feelings be known. This is where you are now, Nora."

"You're too kind, Robert. I don't feel like I've done a very good job at it. I've been stumbling around a lot, acting like a fool."

He laughed. "You're in a far better place than you think," he said, getting up from his seat and becoming very animated. "Once in a rare moment comes the chance to lose our heart to someone—where we don't have a choice. If we allow that impulse to take us to the end and don't fight it, it will lead us to freedom. Rare is the person who will *choose* to give their heart away. Usually it has to be stolen from us, taken away by an intensity of love that overwhelms our mind and our usual strategies of self-protection and control.

"It is hard to realize that such a moment is a graceful gift, because it is usually too painful for us to look at. The mind tangles the heart with all its reasons for not loving, and fear hides love from all of us. It is simply the fear of surrendering our heart to what attracts us. Most of us refuse to make this surrender, we only pretend it. It rarely happens.

"I know we would be far better off if we truly lost our heart to another. We would emerge as a new person. But there are those who will not give up their pain. They will hold onto all the hurting memories and refuse to love again. They become scarred by their experiences of love—charred but not consumed, severely burned by the fire but not transformed by it. They usually fail to release their lover from their heart and therefore prevent their own transformation. We need to be burned up, not just burned. The transformation is incomplete if we hold on to the pain and won't let it go. Some of us can even get stuck in this pain and never again come close to a real chance for emotional freedom."

"What you're saying is beginning to make a lot of sense, Robert." I glanced at my watch. "Oh, my god," I said getting up from the table. "I really hate to end this—I'm learning so much—but I have to get back to the city to get ready for an audition."

"Hope I didn't keep you too long," he said, escorting me out the door. "Just trust your feelings, Nora; listen to them and let them guide you. Soon you will see how accurate they really are."

"I will." I reached over and kissed him on the cheek. I was surprised at how freely I did that. An Aquarian turning into a mushy, touchy human being!

"I'll see you next Saturday," he said. "We'll work on some more character profiles if you would like."

"That would help a lot." I waved good-bye, danced lightly down the steps, and headed home.

By the time I arrived for my reading on Saturday south of Market Street, I felt I knew my character, Tanya, better than anybody. Robert had helped me create an imaginary chart with all her planets in place. Now I had some very good reasons why she reacted the way she did and I felt I could explain her to anybody. With Robert's help, I softened her up by giving her a Moon in the sign of Pisces right next to Jupiter in Pisces. This would make her a big caring mother to the world. Jupiter was for big and the Moon was for mother or nurturing.

I checked in with the receptionist and took a seat along with two other women. One of them played nervously with her car keys, the other one mumbled her lines, and I just sweated. Finally, my name came up.

"Nora Lakewood?"

"Here," I answered.

"You can go up now. Upstairs, second door to your left."

"Thanks."

When I walked into the room, there was a tall, thin woman standing at a table with her back to me. "Are you Nora Lakewood?" the woman asked, turning around. She looked overworked.

"Yes," I replied cautiously.

"I'm Mildred Sword, the casting director. We talked on the phone."

I nodded. She looked liked Ms. Dexter, my high school English teacher, who was an old maid and a real nag. Dexter really hurt my feelings one time when she made fun of my poetry in her English class. I called her "horse-face Dexter" after that.

"Have you ever done a lead before?" she asked.

"Yes, off Broadway. I played the lead as a rock musician for almost two years—that was a long run. I also had the lead in a summer stock performance at White Horse Lake in Massachusetts. I did some TV work in New York."

"Uh huh. Please have a seat," she said, pointing to the only chair in the middle of the room. "Could I see your portfolio?"

"Sure," I said, handing it to her.

She thumbed through my history. "I see that you've done some recent work with Marcia Kimmell at the Next Stage."

"Yes, that's where I met Lenny. We were taking the Actors and Directors Class, and I did some scripted work with him. We had a great time—he's such a funny man."

"Uh huh," she mused. "Are you ready to read?"

"Yes."

She picked up the phone and punched in some numbers. "We're ready whenever you are, Lenny," she said.

Lenny came in the room eating a pizza. He sat down at the table next to Mildred. He is a short, bearded man with dusty black hair and thick eyebrows; he reminded me of Perry Mason on TV, who was a Taurus with a hearty appetite.

He sat down at the table next to Mildred. "Excuse my lunch, Nora, I'm on the run. How are you doing today?"

"Fine, Lenny. It's good to see you again."

"I talked this part over with Marcia Kimmell and she thought you should read for Tanya."

"Thank you," I said.

"Do you have a script?"

"No, Lenny, I don't need one."

"You don't?" he asked.

"Nope," I replied, shaking my head.

"Oh, that's right. I remember from the class, you have a photographic mind. I could use one of those myself." He picked up the script. "Let's do that emotional scene between Tanya and her father."

"You mean her grandfather? I believe her father is dead."

He gave me a puzzled look and then flipped through the script. "Yes—okay," he said finally. "You seem to know the characters better than I do," he laughed. "Anyway, we'll do that scene on page 36. I'll be your grandfather."

We went through about three pages of dialogue and he raised his hand. "That's enough, dear. I have a feeling for what you can do."

I had the feeling it wasn't enough, but I wasn't going down sniffling. "Lenny," I said. "I hope you don't mind, but there's something wrong with Tanya's character. Could I make some suggestions that will make her a lot more interesting?" A hot silence hung in the air. I imagined being ordered out of the room.

"Ms. Lakewood," Mildred said, raising a voice full of annoyance. "You're not here to rewrite the script. We've heard your reading so you can—"

"Let her finish," Lenny said, raising his pizza hand. "Go ahead, Nora."

"Well, to be honest, Lenny, the writer has made Tanya too much of a bitch. When a character is all bad no one cares much about her. She has to have *some* good qualities. . .you know, to create empathy."

"Right," he said, taking a bite from his pizza. "What would you suggest?"

"Tanya could be a financial genius—something she inherited from her wealthy grandfather, and she could help poor people make money. This could be one of the changes she finally goes through before the story ends. She discovers the importance of helping other people and changes into a very giving person."

"Not bad," he said. "I'll talk it over with the writer. But you did very well showing her as a bitch—do you think you could portray a softer side?"

"Oh, yes. I can show that as her real strength when she goes through her changes. I feel I really do understand this character, Lenny."

"You *could* be right." There was a subtle wave of doubt in his voice, but then he said, "I think Marcia was right. I'm going to give you the part." He got up from the table. "I'll see you in two weeks. Mildred will give you the details on the shooting."

"Thank you so much, Lenny," I said.

He smiled back at me and said, "De nada," as he walked out the door.

"You're one lucky girl," Mildred said as she gathered up her papers. "That's the first time I ever saw Lenny do anything like that."

"Like what?" I asked.

"Take advice from an actor."

"Do you think I was too blunt?"

"Apparently not. In fact, I thought you did very well. But I was sure he was going to throw you out when you wanted to change the script—especially since his wife wrote it."

"She wrote it?" I looked at the title page. "Oh, my god!"

"Not to worry. He obviously liked what you did, so count your blessings."

As we walked out into the parking lot and over to her car, I saw that Mildred didn't really look like Ms. Dexter. She certainly didn't have a horse's face. I saw that I had been overreacting from all the rejections I had suffered in the past two years. Actually, I felt warm towards her. "Thank you for giving me a chance, " I said, extending my hand.

She shook my hand and then said, "That's okay, Nora. I admire a woman who can stand up for what she believes. The important thing is that you've got the part. I'll call you tomorrow and let you know when we'll start." She slid into her car and waved as she drove away.

The next morning Mildred called to tell me to meet with her and the assistant director on October the 9th to go over the schedule. "By the way," she said, "Susan Pace, Lenny's wife, liked your suggestions, and said she was sending you a revised script."

"She really made some changes?"

"Looks like it. Poor woman, she's gone through so many rewrites and is still willing to redo it if it makes a better script. I'm very curious to see how you're going to play it."

"Me, too," I said. "Do you have any last minute suggestions?"

"Not really. Just follow your instincts, you'll come out fine."

"Thanks, Mildred."

"Meet me at the office on October the 9th at ten o'clock and I'll introduce you to the assistant director."

"I'll be there," I said, and hung up.

8

    Someone Who Cares turned out to be a miniseries, which put a lot of cash in my pocket. One of the first things I did with that money was to send Robert a $5,000 bonus and a long letter. I hoped he wouldn't send it back. No telling what he'd do with it considering that he'd spent so many years as a renunciate. I thought he would probably give it to Lelia. But anyway, that was the least I could do.

    I wrote Richard a quick note thanking him for the loan and paid him off, but I didn't send him a bonus. In fact, he didn't even need what he said I owed him. He had gotten a permanent part in one of those soap operas like *Days of Our Lives* that runs forever, and I haven't even seen or heard from him—except I did notice when I got my bank statement that he had cashed the check.

    Mildred was right. Everything worked out okay. I would probably get residuals on the miniseries for many years, but I was still anxious to do a major film, something closer to my heart. Television chews up so many stories. I was certain *Someone Who Cares* would also fade into the dust to join all those other films in the basement archives. In the meantime, I kept gaining a deeper understanding of the planets and vowed that if I ever would get another major role, I'd do all the planetary patterns of all the characters I had to work with. Already I had a file of the charts of prominent producers and directors. In fact, other people in the industry were beginning to hound me for some inside information on the people they wanted to work with, but I sent most of those people to Robert.

    Finally, I got a call from my new agent, Mark Ravenwood, to contact Mildred again to try out for the lead role in *The Chords of Heaven*, a script based on a novel by Noel Alexander. I had heard it was being produced by Metamorphics, a new age film company. This is one of my favorite books because it's about a musical therapist who used music to heal people and it shows how she was harassed by the medical profession. I called Mildred for an appointment to do a reading, and she said she'd send me the script.

This time when I arrived for my reading on south of Market, only one woman was waiting in the reception room. When she was called in, my heart jumped up against my rib cage. But it stopped jumping when I saw her come back down the stairs shaking her head.

"Ms. Lakewood?" the receptionist called out. "You can go up now. Second door to your left."

It was like I was reliving my past. I hadn't been here in more than a year—this time I felt more confident. I looked forward to working with Lenny again. But when I opened the door, I felt like I was thrown into a nightmare. Instead of Lenny, it was my old enemy David Delcroix. He was sitting right next to Mildred.

"What's *this* woman doing here?" he asked, jerking his beaky head toward Mildred.

"David," she said looking perplexed, "this is Nora Lakewood. She's reading for Kathryn."

"I know who she is," he snapped. "She's not reading for anybody."

"But Pace recommended her for the part."

"Leonard Pace?" he asked, looking surprised.

"Yes."

"But he's not directing this film. I am."

I stood there totally stunned. I had assumed that Lenny was directing the film and Mildred hadn't told me.

"I'm sorry, Nora," Mildred said shrugging her shoulders.

I could see there was nothing that she could do, and I still felt there was nothing I could do to change Delcroix's mind about me. "So what's new?" I said, as I turned around and marched out of the room.

The next morning, Mildred called me. "I'm sorry for what happened yesterday, Nora. I didn't know Delcroix disliked you so much. What happened between you two?"

"It's just karma. He thinks I'm an angry bitch who doesn't know how to play sensitive roles. He's always turning me down and I'm always trying to avoid him."

"Maybe you should get Lenny to talk to him," she suggested.

"Do you think he could change Delcroix's mind?"

"It's worth a shot. There's just one problem, though, Lenny's on vacation in Europe and I don't really know where he is. You could call Nancy Fox, his secretary. She might know. I'll get her number."

"Thanks, Mildred."

After Mildred gave me the number and we hung up, I called Nancy and asked her where I could find Lenny. Nancy's a nice lady who had brought me sandwiches while we were shooting the last film.

"He's in southern France someplace," she said, "but I'm not sure where. It may take me a few days to find him. Is it important?"

"Life and death. I need you to tell him David Delcroix doesn't want me for the part of Kathryn in *The Chords of Heaven* and I need him to help change Delcroix's mind. This is a once in a lifetime shot for me, Nancy."

"Why don't you write a letter to Lenny and fax it to me? If I can get a hold of him, I'll fax your letter to him. But I can't promise you anything for sure, Nora. As you probably know, Lenny is very hard to track down sometimes."

"I know, I understand—just do the best you can. What's your fax number?"

After she gave me her fax number, I said that I'd send her the letter in about a half hour.

"I'll be looking for it."

"Thanks."

I sent Nancy the fax, but when I didn't hear back from Lenny, I figured he was unreachable. About a week later, I was surprised to get a call from Mildred telling me that Delcroix was willing to hear me read and that I should come to his downtown office.

When I arrived at Delcroix's office, the memory of me throwing the script at him the year before surged back into my mind. "Did I really do that?" I asked myself. It seemed like something that was done by another person in another century.

"I got a call from Leonard Pace," Delcroix said. His mousy mouth tightened as if poised to lash out at me. "He twisted my arm to give you a reading. So, this is an act of professional courtesy. Do you know what I'm saying?"

I wondered if he had a lot of picky Virgo planets. "All I want is a chance," I replied.

"Where's your script?" There was a bite in his words.

"It's all up here," I said pointing to my head.

"The whole script?"

"Yes."

"Really?" he asked. He picked up the script, thumbed through the pages, and then stopped. "Tell me. What's the scene on page 99?"

I looked in my head. I saw the page number and then the dialogue. It reminded me of how I had remembered piano scores. "That's the scene where Kathryn is confronted by the medical researcher, Doctor Herder. Herder starts out by saying, 'Your idea that music can replace medicine is one of the most stupid notions I've ever run across.' Kathryn replies, 'There's a great danger in making false assumptions from research when there are certain energies that your scientific instruments have no way of . . .'"

"Okay, okay," Delcroix interrupted. "Let's see what you can do with Kathryn. How are you going to play her *emotionally*? As I recall from your past readings—even with my lousy memory—you've had some trouble projecting feelings. Go to page 61 where Kathryn is saying good-bye to her mother for the last time. Mildred will read your mother's part.

I glanced over at Mildred. She gave me a supporting nod. I thought about how much she had helped me on the *Someone Who Cares* set. "You'll do fine, just follow your instincts," she used to say when I had doubts.

The cold and empty feeling of the room faded as I reached into myself to feel Kathryn's last words to her mother. Then I thought of my own mother and plunged into an emotional well. My feelings overflowed. It seemed like I re-cried all my tears again. I don't know how much time had passed, but I thought Delcroix should have stopped me by now, saying something like, "That's all, Ms. Lakewood, I see nothing has really changed." But the room hung still long after I had finished. As I slowly emerged from my crying place, I looked up at Delcroix. His eagle face seemed softer in the light that was shining in from the bay.

"What's happened to you?" he said, slowly rising from his seat.

"Oh, no," I thought. "I might as well pick up my bag and head for the door."

"Well, whatever happened to you, Nora, don't change it—you really let your feelings carry the words this time. I want you to play Kathryn exactly the way you did just then."

"Really?" I asked, hardly able to speak. "You mean the part's mine?"

"You got it."

I lost all awareness of restraint, rushed over to the table, flung my arms around him, and kissed him on his beaky cheek. "Thank you so much. I guess I owe you an apology—for breaking in here that day and calling you a nerd."

"Don't worry about it. I had a good laugh with my secretary after you flung that script at me—besides, I admire spunky women. I'm not known for being sensitive to other people's feelings—maybe I had you pegged in the wrong hole. Anyway," he said, releasing my hug, "we need to get together to work out the changes. Lenny said you were good at that."

"You mean it?" I asked.

"Yes—here's my card. Give me a call tomorrow and we can arrange for a meeting with the script people."

9

After three rewrites, gobs of retakes, and 300 lattés later, *The Chords of Heaven* was finally released. Shortly thereafter, I began to spin in outer space. Wonderful reviews flooded my fax machine. Here's one I especially liked that was written by Sandra Brenner of the *Times*:

NORA LAKEWOOD LANDS HEALING ROLE — DIRECTOR PRAISES HER UNDERSTANDING OF CHARACTER

by Sandra Brenner
Special to the Times

After struggling for more than five years to do a film close to her heart, Nora Lakewood finally lands a role that is so moving and heartwarming that she could be nominated for an Oscar. She portrays Kathryn in The Chords of Heaven, a story about a courageous woman, a musical therapist who discovers how to heal people through music. This remarkable film opens tomorrow at the New Vision Theater.

"David Delcroix, the director, gave me a lot of freedom to explore the emotional levels of Kathryn's life," Lakewood says. "He allowed me to express the depth of her intense caring side. It was deeply transforming to be so absorbed in her character. I found out who I am through Kathryn."

"Nora did what I felt she would do," says Delcroix. "She had far more insight into Kathryn than I did. She gave all of herself to the effort and came in with a tremendous performance."

The role was especially appropriate for Lakewood because she was trained as a classical pianist at an early age, studying diligently with her mother. "But," she says, "I couldn't make any money with classical music. The competition at that level was so fierce—and I didn't want to teach at the conservatory like my mother did. So, I went into playing rock with Rene's Renegades, and then into theater."

Lakewood cut her acting teeth off Broadway and at summer stock theaters in Massachusetts. When asked how she was able to project so much feeling in The Chords of Heaven, she replied, "Someone broke my heart, and I'm not the same person since that happened. I don't have to be in control anymore—I'm not afraid to show my feelings. Whenever a character demands that I let loose, I can go deep into my emotions. Besides, I have a very special method for exploring my character that is not used by most actors."

When asked what that was, she smiled slyly and said, "You would laugh if I told you; so, maybe I should tell you and let you laugh. The planets and their positions at the time a person is born show who that person really is. I create a fictional chart for my character's planets. By simply exploring their planetary energies, I immediately understand who they are. Of course it takes some time to play it out, but I always try to find the best planetary mix to reveal my character's hidden side according to the script. This hidden side may not be obvious to other people but it is to me, and this helps me play them on a much deeper level."

"So, you're using astrology?" I asked.

"Well, yes and no. Astrology means 'study of the stars,' but this system has more to do with the study of the planets. My teacher calls it planetary psychology."

Whatever she's doing with the planets, it must be working. Nora Lakewood is already headed for the stars, even if she's not really studying them.

Movie offers came in from everywhere, but the one from Kingstar Pictures was the clincher. They guaranteed me $2 million to star in a thriller that was set in Salzburg, Austria—Mozart's birthplace. After reading the script, I knew it had been written for me. The deal was sealed when I talked to the director on the phone and got his birth date. Robert helped me compare the chemistry of our planets and said there was a natural harmony between us. "But," he winked, "I'll leave that discovery to you."

The day before I was to leave for Salzburg, I called Robert to say that I wanted to tell him "good-bye" in person. But there was no answer. I decided to drive over to Marin and see if I could find him. As I drove on the Golden Gate Bridge, I passed the north tower where Rachel had pulled me away from the rail. My heart made a big leap and filled up with a warm fire. I wanted to kiss her again for saving me from that terrible fate.

When I reached Robert's house, I rang the old cowbell several times. No answer. I walked down to the white cottage and knocked on the door. Nobody. My heart went heavy. *After all he's done for me, and I can't say good-bye?* I took out a pen and paper and started writing.

"Nora," a voice said coming from behind me. "So good to see you." It was Robert. He walked up to me and gave me a hug. "I was going to call you and tell you how magnificent your film was."

"Thank you so much. But it wouldn't have happened without you, Robert. I just came by to tell you I have to go to Austria for a while. I'm short on time, but I really didn't want to say good-bye on the phone."

"You'll be coming back, won't you?"

"Yes, in about three months."

"Don't forget to call us when you return. We can have dinner. Lelia would love to meet you. We cried in your movie—your performance was very powerful, and so much from the heart."

"Thanks to you and the planets, Robert."

We stood there looking at each other for a moment, then hugged and kissed good-bye. I gave him one last look and walked toward the gate.

"Robert," I said turning around.

"What?" he asked smiling.

"Something's been bothering me. In your book, you quote Raman as saying, 'Only by becoming a fool will you ever discover true wisdom?'

What did he mean by that?"

"Well, first there's knowledge," he said, walking closer. "You've gained a lot of that. Then there's love. Your heart was broken, so you know what love is. Then comes wisdom. In order to find wisdom, you . . ."

". . . have to become a fool," I said, finishing his sentence. "I think I've already been a fool," I laughed, "but I still don't feel very wise."

"The fool that Raman was talking about is the constant practice of losing who we are. Letting go of our face. If we spend our life protecting our position, we stay as we are—limited. We protect our beliefs, our self-image, our place in the world. Raman is saying that as long as we do that, we will not awaken to who we really are. Our true spiritual nature remains hidden. A real fool is willing to leap into the unknown. If a wise woman is afraid, she confronts her fear, pushes her boundaries, and discovers a new awareness of herself. It's as simple as that. It is traveling into an unknown place without a guide. That's one of the things Raman taught me. Emerson, another great man, said the same thing. 'Do the thing you fear and the death of fear is certain.' But you've already started being a fool, Nora."

"How's that?"

"You brought an end to your relationship with Andrew even while you loved him. A sensible person, one less foolish, would have held on a lot longer. But you knew in your heart that it wouldn't work. So, you became a real fool. You gave Andrew back to himself—the part he only pretended to give to you."

I shook my head in disbelief. "Robert, how do you know all this stuff?"

"Let's just say I've lived most of my life with egg on my face. Fools learn a lot. By the way, I've been waiting for you to tell me about the secret you've learned."

"Well—I think you gave it to me a long time ago, but I just didn't understand it then. Isn't it about giving our heart away?"

"What about that?"

"It's when we give our heart away that we find it!" I said, surprising myself. "I found out what I'm really like on the inside— and I know more how I really feel about things. I believe I'm stronger, too—more sure of myself." I really didn't know that I knew this until I had said it. Somehow, his asking put me in touch with what I already felt.

"That's wonderful, Nora. Can you see why real love remains a mystery to so many people?"

"Sure. If we don't give our heart away, we'll never understand what love is—but I don't know of anyone who would deliberately choose to give their heart away, Robert. I certainly didn't. But fortunately, it was something that was done *to* me. It was like you said—I had no choice but to feel it."

"You've also learned something else."

"What's that?"

"In an absolute sense, we really don't know what anything is. But in a relative sense, human beings can be completely understood by studying the position of their planets at birth. In this sense, you have learned that no one is a mystery."

At that moment Robert's black and white cat came springing out of the woods and leaped into my arms. My body flooded with feeling as I embraced her graceful form. Her eyes were full of infinite space—a look I had never seen before.

"She seems to like you," Robert said.

"I love her," I said, placing her face against mine. I walked over and hugged him with the cat still in one arm. "Thank you for all your wisdom," I whispered. "I won't forget what I've learned from you." Then I handed him the cat. "Tell Lelia I would love to meet her, too. She must be a great lady to be with someone like you."

"That she is, Nora. Thank you for that."

"Well, I guess it's bye for now."

"Don't forget to be a fool," he said, dancing playfully through the leaves.

"Only a fool would forget that," I said, smiling back. "See you in June." I turned around and walked down the path toward the outside world, wondering what kind of fool I was going to become next.

The Secret Chemistry

of

Relationships

by

Robert Christos

Introduction

So many of us are suffering from psychic starvation because we are out of touch with the subtle world that feeds the heart. This book's purpose is to help awaken this intuitive awareness so that we can once again be fed from within and commune with that which breathes us.

By discovering the psychic meaning of the planets, you will contact the hidden side of human nature and gain a profound understanding of why human beings act the way they do.

As a mother or father, you will be able to understand your children from the first day they are born. By using the principles in this book you will know what is really best for your children and learn how to guide them to their goals.

As a lover, you will know another person upon first meeting and determine if they are your true mate. This knowledge alone will help you avoid making serious mistakes that usually lead to much heartbreak.

As a student, you will be able to understand your relationship with your teacher and determine whether your minds can work together. You will also see how your mind functions and learn how to use it to your advantage.

If you have a business, you will discover when to promote your product and when to pull back. You will also find out whether you should have a partner or work alone.

If you are a therapist, you will be able to take shortcuts into the mind of your clients and help them remove the obstructions that pervade their psyche. You will be able to pinpoint their major issues with great accuracy and save years of trial and error.

As an actor or writer, you can portray or create stimulating characters by giving them planetary patterns that make them rich in contradiction and motivation. This technique will enable you to give depth to an otherwise boring portrayal.

If you are a musician or an artist, you will be able to determine the best time to perform and when the planets are going to support your creative process.

As a spiritual seeker, you will be able to understand your capacity for self-transcendence and discover your talents that enhance, as well as your obstructions to, the spiritual process. You will learn which path is best for you and what to focus on to awaken a deeper awareness of the living presence.

Whomever you are or whatever you do, you will be able to live your life more creatively and learn how to work with the energies of the planets to find your place in the world.

Please see the section beginning at Appendix A-12 to obtain your personal planetary information.

I hope this new journey brings you many satisfying discoveries.

Robert Christos

Your Journey Through Planetary Psychology

You don't have to know anything about the signs or stars or the Moon or Mars to reap the wonderful rewards from this book. Just travel along with me for a while and you will learn how to see into the heart and soul of any human being. By exploring the amazing secrets hidden in the planets, you will discover superior knowledge that you can use for the rest of your life. Listen in on the lessons I gave Lelia and you will find the answer to your own mystery.

"Only by becoming a fool will you ever discover true wisdom."

Raman

Lesson 1

Let's Meet the Planets

How can I really use the planets to understand anybody?

Sounds strange, doesn't it? But it's a lot easier than you may think. To get you started, Lelia, let's take a trip to the heavens. Imagine that we are riding a giant ball right up there with the planets as they travel along their celestial highway. You will soon discover that this celestial circle—which is traveled by all the planets—is full of many esoteric wonders that will help you look right into the heart of anyone you meet.

Speaking of meeting, let's look in on the planets. Just ahead of us is Saturn and the Moon. The Moon is traveling very fast, trying to get past the old man Saturn.

Why does the Moon want to get past Saturn? Why do you call him the old man?

Because Saturn is a dark character—such a Scrooge. He tends to depress any smaller planet that comes in contact with him. That's just the way Saturn works.

This is an intriguing fantasy, Robert, but what do Saturn and the Moon have to do with me? They are just planets, physical objects out in space. Aren't you just repeating the myths of the Greeks and Romans? They too gave the planets human qualities.

Ah, but that's where we have made a great error—by assuming that the planetary gods were myths. The Greeks and Romans were smarter than that; to them, the planets were metaphors.

What do you mean by "metaphors"?

Thousands of years ago, ancient Vedic astrologers taught that human beings are psychic replicas of the planetary patterns formed at the time they were born.

> Human beings are psychic replicas of the planetary patterns formed at the time they were born.

This means that if a man or woman was *born at the same time* as the Moon was traveling next to Saturn in the heavens would have a tendency towards depression and would feel as if a shadow was hanging over them. Their childhood might end up being depressing, and they could become shut down emotionally or feel abandoned by their mother. They'd probably find self-nurturing difficult to learn because they feel separated from their heart. This was an amazing discovery the ancient observers made. Obviously they understood each other on a far deeper level than most of us do today and felt that they were closely connected to the heavens. They realized that the planets are not merely material objects traveling through physical space; they are also moving *psychically* through our inner space. Therefore, they are full of psychological meaning.

> They realized that the planets are not merely material objects traveling through physical space; they are also moving *psychically* through our inner space. Therefore, they are full of psychological meaning.

This understanding emerged from thousands of years of observing how the reactions and attitudes of human beings coincided with specific planetary patterns. People realized that they were deeply connected to the planetary cycles because they discovered that the daily motion of the planets *reflected* the events in their lives. For them the planets were pregnant with meaning, just as psychic space itself is full of meaning. But today most men and women still think of the Moon and Saturn as only material objects. This brings up a challenging question: "Why should we go out into physical space to explore Mars and the other planets when we have not even explored the planets that live within us?" Most people have not yet awakened to a psychic awareness of their own inner planets. If they had, they would be living their lives quite differently than they do.

With the Age of Reason—when scientific materialism became god—the loss of awareness of this subtle world within us accelerated because people started depending on science to interpret their reality. Now it has come to the point that the average man or woman no longer hears the voices of the planets. To learn the psychic meaning of the heavens is considered by many to be superstition. The ears of these critics are tuned to the voice of modern science who is still only a young brat hardly 200 years old. Yet, psychically immature science remains the sacred cow of the many. This is because too many of us rely on science to dictate our reality.

So, what do you suggest?

Simply test everything for yourself and you will soon come to understand this mystery. If you stay with me, I will show you how it all works. Let's continue to meet the planets.

Just below us are Venus and Jupiter, having a great time together. Jupiter is such a happy fellow that his enthusiasm rubs off on Venus.

But I still don't know what these planets have to do with me, Robert. They are not real to me because I haven't had any experience with them. I'm trying to be open, but I must confess I'm not convinced.

It's good that you don't accept something just because I say it, Lelia. You have a very penetrating and challenging mind. That's why it will be easy for you to understand how these planets relate so intimately to your life when we look at your own personal patterns.

As I was saying, everything that Jupiter touches turns positive. Here he is dancing with Venus and she is very happy. What this means in human terms is that any person born at the time Venus and Jupiter are moving next to each other along the celestial circle (astrologers call this a conjunction) will express a happy state of being. They will be very positive, generous, outgoing, loving, and most likely will have lots of friends and money. These are the fortunate few who feel full inside, and they have the "touch of gold." Maybe this is because they feel that they deserve the good things of life. But if old Scrooge, Saturn, was passing next to sweet little Venus at the time this person was born, they would feel totally unworthy—like they didn't deserve any wealth. Saturn would rob Venus of any feeling of self-worth. In a little while, you will be able to check this out for yourself. Then you will begin to see that almost everything we do in life hinges on when we were born.

> Almost everything we do in life hinges on when we were born.

Let me give you another example, perhaps one you can relate to. Imagine that you are looking at the fiery planet Mars further along the circle, just beyond Jupiter and Venus. Mars is having a bad time with Pluto this week.

Why's that?

He's really hot because the coercive Pluto won't let him rest. Maybe Pluto's going to burn Mars out of the sky one of these days. He's such a pushy character. Fortunately, these two planets only run into each other like this every year or so.

But where is Pluto now?

He's about 90 degrees from Mars. This means that Pluto is one-fourth the distance of the circle away from Mars.

But what does that really mean in human terms?

Well, when any two planets are traveling 90 degrees from each other, they are at war. It's like that phrase the Americans use when two people get in a fight: they call it "squaring off." As you probably know, a square is a 90–degree angle. But thank heavens the planets are always changing their relationship to each other. At one time, they are conjunct (0 degrees apart); at other times, they are square (90 degrees apart), or trine (120 degrees apart). Good or bad, the planets transmit their energies and reveal our human character and destiny. We will be studying these angles in greater detail in Lesson 5.

To give you an example, not too long ago there lived this great martial artist. He was a very fierce and angry young man who was born in San Francisco at a time when Pluto was "squaring off" with the Moon, Venus, Mars, Jupiter and Saturn. These energies made him an outstanding martial artist and compelled him to crush his enemies. Pluto gave him that power. He was an archetype or model of the fierceness of Pluto when it is agitating or frustrating other planets. You could see this intensity in his eyes as well as in the movies he made. He waged a great battle within himself that was expressed overtly in the outside world. Even though he should be honored for his great control and masterful discipline, I suspect that his aggressive response to life was his way of dealing with his own demons—an innermost rage.

What was his name?

Bruce Lee.

Oh yes, I remember him. A remarkable young man.

Lelia, I know you're anxious to learn about your own planetary patterns, but let's meet a few more planets before we do that. This will give you a deeper understanding of your own situation when we come to it. Now, imagine that we have arrived at Neptune's position along our circle. He is truly an *out of this world* planet. profound connection to the subtle side of life. At this mo. happens to be right next to Mercury.

What kind of effect does that create?

Neptune tends to make Mercury feel lost when he's so close that planet. Mercury is normally a planet of reason, but when Neptune is nearby, Mercury functions more from intuition and less on logic. If someone were born when these two planets were next to each other, they would be very intuitive. But every time this person would try to be logical or use reason to think through a problem, they would most likely become confused or spaced-out. They are not linear-minded people. They should always rely upon their inner voice to solve their problems because Neptune imparts very strong psychic impressions. However, this planet can also lend some negative effects to the mind.

Like what?

Well, whenever this person drives a car, they will tend to go in the wrong direction or get lost. To some people they seem fuzzy-minded. They usually have difficulty with the hard sciences—like mathematics. The reason for this is that they do not reach their answers in the same was as most people. If they are pressured to be reasonable, they will become confused. A parent or teacher may misjudge and make a critical error here by assuming that a child with this pattern is not very bright, especially when it comes to math. But they may not realize that this child is highly intuitive. I find that if intuition is allowed to function freely, it is actually superior to reason. You will often find a great artist or an excellent musician born with this pattern. They might fall into the ocean of the mind without a rope and emerge with great insights. The great master musician J.S. Bach had Mercury conjunct Neptune. However, as I said, there can be some negative effects upon the mind—this is especially true when Mercury is square Neptune, 90 degrees away. Remember the square we talked about?

Yes.

A person who was born when Mercury was forming a square to Neptune has difficulty facing the reality of most situations. They often lie to themselves or to others when confronted with the truth and, instead, create their own truth. But when their "truth" collides with the real truth, they may find it too painful to face up to. Therefore, they tend to make up a reality to suit their own perception of it. This is more comfortable for them. Most people would simply call this lying.

....aczynski, has this position of Mercury square
.... pattern in a woman who was the wife of a
.......vas introduced to me by some of my clients
.......r. But every time I came close to helping
.......tuation, she denied that such a condition even
.......ed her to a recent time when she had felt unsupported
....usband and emotionally cut off from him, but she said she
...ad never experienced those feelings. In several different ways I tried
to help her see what was behind her continuing frustration. It was
very clear to me, but she would not accept my insights. In fact, she
rejected all of my suggestions regarding her situation. Later, her
friends told me that I was right in my perceptions. They had pointed
out to her that she had previously complained to them about not
getting any emotional support from her husband. Apparently, she had
chosen to block those feelings from her memory.

Maybe her experiences were too painful for her to face at the time.

Yes, no doubt you're right. But that's the nature of Neptune's
negative effect upon Mercury. However, I never forced the situation.
After trying many different ways to get a person to feel or understand
the reality of where they are or what they are working with, I usually
back off if they are not ready to feel it or take a look at it.

Does Neptune affect other planets this way?

When he is squaring off with the other *personal* planets—which
are the more ego-oriented planets (Sun, Moon, Mercury, Venus and
Mars)—Neptune tends to distort an individual's perception of reality.
Most people born with any of these patterns are very sensitive to life's
unpleasant experiences. In one way or an other, they have had painful
childhood experiences and seem to have a deep need to create their
own perfect world from within. They have real conflicts when their
inner world clashes with their outer world. For instance, a woman
born when the Sun or Mars was squaring Neptune almost always has
a childhood where her father abuses her, abandons her, or dies when
she is very young. She acquires a deep unconscious need to rescue
men, believing that they will be there to love her after she has helped
them through their own trouble. However, the man she attracts rarely
ends up loving her. She tends to sacrifice her own needs for his needs
in an attempt to make him whole so that he can eventually love her.
The point here is that her own inner male is not strong. She feels
helpless to change things because she feels no support from within

herself. Sooner or later she realizes that her strategies of trying to save men are fruitless. If she matures emotionally and refuses to be a victim, she will become free of throwing her own life away for the sake of weak and irresponsible deadbeats.

From another viewpoint, a man who was born at the time that Venus or Moon was forming a square to Neptune will have deep fears of being abandoned by his mother (the Moon) or the feminine (Venus). He will go to great extremes to make sure the woman is there to sustain and nurture him. He may be manipulative and push all of her guilt buttons to get what he wants. On the other hand, he may fall into the hands of a dominating woman who maintains control over him by taking the role of his mother. This can also be a trap for any woman if she allows herself to fall victim to her own mothering instincts. But there are many positive effects of Neptune often revealed by the conjunction and the trine.

When the Sun, Moon or Venus are conjunct Neptune (0 degrees), or when they are 120 degrees apart (trine), there is a potential for spiritual or artistic greatness. Here the higher energies of Neptune are allowed to manifest creatively through an inspired intuition. I sometimes find very successful artists or sincere spiritual seekers with these patterns. Of course, if these planets are squared by Saturn, Uranus or Pluto, we have a different situation altogether. It would take a lot of pain releasing for this person to become free of childhood traumas. I would like to add that normally you would have to calculate these squares and trines, but by using The Sign Table in your appendix, this becomes unnecessary. You will learn how to use this table later.

That's good to hear. You mentioned the planet Uranus. How does it affect us?

I like your curiosity, Lelia. Uranus is a real character and gives whatever it touches an extremely independent desire. If you were born at the time when any of the ego-oriented *personal* planets—Sun, Moon, Mercury, Venus, or Mars—were next to Uranus, you would express a highly individualistic style. The energy of Uranus imparts a strong urge in human beings to do their own thing. Let's look at a few examples to see how Uranus affects these personal planets.

When Uranus is in the same space as the Sun at the time we were born, it makes us very independent and unwilling to conform to rules, regulations, or tradition. You can check this out for yourself. You will find that anyone with this position loves their freedom above all. They are often called a "character." Freedom is their lover and their song—they really desire to follow their own drumbeat. These people are attracted to strange friends and tend to associate with people who have odd and unusual habits. Ted Kaczynski, the Unabomber, has his Sun conjunct Uranus in Gemini, which is the mark of someone who rebels against the traditions of society and goes his own way. However, this is an extreme example. There are many very creative people with this position who blaze their own trails but never harm other people. Obviously, many people are born on the same day when the Sun was conjunct Uranus but have not committed any crime against others.

A person born when Uranus joined the Moon sometimes displays erratic emotions. They can be willful and often have sudden reactions that surprise people. This particular planetary chemistry indicates that they have strong emotional reactions towards the mother and have a deep desire to be free of the mother's influence.

If Uranus is next to Venus, it imparts the spirit of free love. Someone with this combination finds it difficult to commit to one person because they are forever in search of love thrills.

When Uranus is joined with Mercury, this energy imparts a very perceptive and intelligent awareness; though the person is sometimes arrogant and quick to show off how smart they are.

Uranus conjunct Mars gives a wild and risky nature. The person should take great care to control the tendency to live on the edge and push situations too far. Special respect should be given to safety measures when racing cars or motorcycles, or flying airplanes. The famous martial artist Chuck Norris has Mars conjunct his Uranus, but he uses his flying feet creatively to club villains on television.

Detailed information on all these and many more planetary patterns can be found in the Chemistry section that I gave you. Therefore, you do not need to remember them or worry about how to calculate their positions. You will soon learn how to read them quite easily by using the *Planetary Profile Card* and other helpful tools. But more about this later.

Now it's time to check out the patterns of your own planets. To do this, I will need your date, time, and place of birth. Let's go to the computer and put this information into the program. Years ago, with my teacher Raman, I had to do all these calculations by hand. It used to take me an hour or more just to set up a chart, and I had to use some technical books to get it right.

How does this chart work?

We don't need to go into much detail about the mechanics of the chart here, because most of it is technical information that you don't need to deal with—the computer takes care of it. In simple terms, an astrological chart is a picture of the planetary patterns at the time you were born. With your date, time, and place of birth, the computer calculates the position of the planets and their relationships. Then the computer creates a wheel full of astrological symbols, which is a celestial shorthand that the astrologer uses to interpret the planetary patterns. Fortunately, you do not have to worry about any of this shorthand. These lessons are presented in a special way to make your discoveries exciting and painless, and you will be able to read anybody with a minimum amount of effort. I see that the printer has finished your chart, so let's take a look at it. . . .

Oh, my goodness! How can you make any sense out of all of that? It looks like hieroglyphics.

It takes many years of constant practice, but all the work is worth the effort. Every person is different, totally unique. I never tire of discovering new things about people. You don't need to worry about how to do this, however; as I said, I will soon show you a way to get your answers easily. For now, let's take a look at what some of your planetary patterns tell us.

There is a standout cluster that I see right away: You have three sets of conjunctions, which is quite unusual. The obvious question is, "What does this really mean?" It will help if you think of a planet as a desire or an urge to express a need. All the planets and their desires are provided in your Chemistry section starting on page 137. I see that you have it with you, so let's look at the descriptions for Mars and Neptune. Notice that on page 174 Mars is described as the desire to take action and a planet of passion. On page 204, Neptune is described as the desire for blissful experience and a planet of the subtle. Since a conjunction is where two or more planets are next to each other, they add extra energy and emphasis in that area. Because you have these two planets conjunct in your chart, we can simply conclude that you have rapturous desires. You have a longing to express something beautiful that will bring you delightful experiences. You can do this through many channels—art, music, and graphics are three possibilities. Another one would be in seeking spiritual experiences that would awaken you to a greater awareness of being. You are in pursuit of ecstasy.

At one time in my life, I played the viola in an orchestra. Music was a great passion of mine. Sometimes, when sight-reading a new piece, it felt as if someone else was taking over—it seemed like a man—someone with very mature musical experience. He would show me the heart of the piece by using my body to play it. I don't know who he was but I received little pieces of memories of his daily life.

That's remarkable.

At present, I'm really happy with my plants and flowers. The flowers bring a lot of hummingbirds and they are such a great joy to watch. I also love the trees. You know, a friend once told me that a single tree creates enough oxygen for one person to live on.

Thank god for people like you, Lelia. I also notice that you have Mercury conjunct your Jupiter, which indicates an expansive mind. Look up Jupiter on pages 186-187, and you will find that it imparts the desire to acquire and to expand—it is a planet of infinite possibility. Mercury imparts the desire to think, gather information, and disseminate it through writing and speaking—it is a planet of communication. (See page 156.) So, in simple terms, you are big on communication. It seems that you like to talk a lot, and you put across your ideas with great enthusiasm. Jupiter's bouncy and restless nature compels you to talk or write out your ideas. He is the dominant planet here. It is a wonderful position for becoming a successful storyteller. Some well-known writers have this pattern. Margaret Mitchell, the famous author who wrote *Gone With the Wind* had Jupiter and Uranus right next to the personal planet Mercury in the sign of Sagittarius. These two larger, less ego-oriented, impersonal planets had a tremendous influence on her thinking.

All of this seems to be a very accurate interpretation, but how can I ever come up with such clear insights like yours? If I were trying to read these patterns on myself or for another person, I would be totally lost. You have so many years of experience, and I certainly wouldn't be able to make sense of all those symbols the way you do.

I can understand your doubt, Lelia, but you don't have to worry about that. I have made it very easy for you to get the same kind of insights by following a simple procedure.

That sounds too good to be true. What is this procedure?

Let's take your third conjunction—where your Uranus and Moon are together—and I will show you. Pages 199-200 provide you with a description of this pattern. After you read that description I will continue. I'll wait here until you finish.

Have you finished?

Yes.

Does this description make any sense to you?

Yes, absolutely.

There is something other than Uranus affecting your Moon. Pluto is 90 degrees away from your Moon, which indicates a square, and as you know, a square indicates frustration. Now, simply look up "Pluto frustrates the Moon" on page 215.

Are you saying that all I will have to do is look up page numbers and gather information?

Mostly, but the real fun begins when you see how it all flows together to give you a complete picture of yourself and others. It is much more fruitful than just the computer printouts that are available these days. This way, you can gain a personal relationship with the planets and establish a psychic awareness of them.

But isn't there more information about my life than what you have given me regarding three conjunctions?

Oh, yes, much more—we have hardly opened the book on your life. We still need to understand a lot of your experiences relating to your father, mother, children, and relationships. But rather than take your time by doing that now, I will spend some quiet time with your chart and give you the information that will help you put together your own Planetary Profile.

What's a Planetary Profile?

We will get to that in Lesson 5. Next time, however, we need to explore the secret chemistry of relationships.

Lesson 2

The Secret Chemistry of Relationships

The moment you took your first breath, Lelia, you became a vital planetary system composed of earth, air, fire, and water. Because the planets are contained within you, you are a one-of-a-kind solar system, moving and breathing through time and space. I know it may not appear that way, because here we sit sipping our tea and everything seems so ordinary; but we need to embrace and use the planets more in our daily life and make them ordinary. So much wonderful help is available to us if we will only turn our attention to the planets' psychic world within us.

Each of us is born into an extraordinary situation, and the planetary energies that we inherited from birth are uniquely our own. Even if someone else was born the exact date, time, and place as we were, our own soul would use the planetary energies differently. As we orbit through life, our own planetary energies will naturally harmonize or collide with those of other people around us. Whether this is good or bad is determined by the choices we make.

How does that work?

Almost everyone has walked into a room and felt an instant attraction or hostility toward someone. We certainly don't have to know them to feel the reaction—we are immediately aware of whether or not we want to be with them. As is obvious from this common experience, we express a planetary chemistry or energy field that other people pick up. Their own personal planetary chemistry is either attracted to, or repelled by, our physical presence. This chemistry is created by the planetary patterns in effect when we were born, and you are learning how to read this chemistry. Our personal solar systems either flow in harmony or else repel each other through fear of contact or instant hostility. If you can accept this fact, you will discover many startling things about people—even those whom you are very close to.

The good news is that, in a matter of seconds, our computer can give us the planetary patterns of any person before we even meet them. Of course, we could figure out their planetary patterns by hand, but as you know it would take a lot longer. There's no need to worry about not having a computer; you will be able to get all the information you need without one.

I'm beginning to understand what you are really talking about, Robert. It's starting to sink in.

Good. Our very first obligation to ourselves is to know who we are—to explore the hidden nature of our own planetary chemistry. Once we have discovered this, we can understand how other people affect us. Rather than becoming confused by thinking something is our fault when it isn't, we know what causes certain experiences and will find ways to work with them. We will understand *why* one person reacts to a certain situation while we react to another. The understanding and clarity will be there. You are already moving toward this clarity.

Maybe you could explain why my daughter, Sharyn, gets depressed so easily. We get along so well, but I can't seem to help her out of the slumps she gets into.

Sure. We can use your situation to show how the planets work for or against each other, but first we will need to determine how each of you is affected by the other. Obviously, our first step is to enter Sharyn's birth data into the computer and explore her planetary patterns. Let's do that now.

I'm amazed at how fast the computer calculates the position of all those planets.

Yes, you can see it only took a few minutes. Whenever a person has trouble with depression, I check out their Moon. Let's take a look. Yes! See? Look at that.

What?

Look closely at the computer printout. Have you seen this symbol before?

Uh huh. It looks like a crescent Moon.

Exactly. It is the symbol for the Moon. Now, look closely to the symbol next to the Moon.

What's that?

It's the symbol for old Scrooge Saturn. He's right next to your daughter's Moon. Do you remember in the beginning when we took an imaginary journey to learn about the planets?

Yes, I remember what you said about Saturn—the Moon was trying to get away from him because Saturn depressed her.

Well, Sharyn was born at the exact moment when the Moon was passing near Saturn. This planetary pattern is explained on page 193 under "Saturn Frustrates the Moon." We have already learned that when Saturn is next to a personal planet, it is a negative energy—it indicates an obstruction that we have to work through. It would have been a lot easier for Sharyn if you could have delayed her birth for a few more hours, because the Moon would have moved past Saturn. But that's not the way things work out in life. Obviously, we just have to take what we get. Sharyn was born with the feeling that a shadow is hanging over her. It's hard for her to shake the feeling that life is always going to be depressing, because she feels there will always be a cloud somewhere in her life. There also must have been a situation in her earlier childhood that reinforced this tendency to melancholy. Did she have a lonely childhood?

Yes, there was one time—I'm sorry to say—when she was a small child. I had to have my mother take care of her because her father had run out on us and I had no money. I went to work as a hotel clerk at night and to computer school in the daytime. I couldn't do all this and take care of her at the same time. I wanted to finish my computer training so I could get a higher-paying job, but I saw her as much as I could. It was a very difficult thing to do—to leave her to my mother and to be away from her that much. I had no choice, though. The sacrifice had to be made.

I didn't know it at the time, but later I found out that she really didn't like my mother—I guess their planetary chemistry didn't work out that well. My mother is a somewhat emotionally detached person. I think Sharyn may have felt that I had betrayed or abandoned her, but she has never said so. She has always been such a sweet person, never a whiner. She did cry sometimes when I had to leave her to go to work at night. I wish I could have been there for her more, but it seemed impossible at the time. I was having some heavy money problems.

Eventually I did get a high-paying job as a troubleshooter and had more time with her, but I guess the damage was done by then. We are very close now . . . all the same, I can't seem to help her with her depressions.

So, it appears that not only was she born with a tendency to sadness, but her feelings of loss were magnified by her separation from you. This is what I call a *karmic condition*—the things we are destined to experience. The planets show that we are set up to have specific positive and negative experiences because of the inherent reactions we bring into this world. These reactions are already ours at the very moment of birth and our life conditions seem to reflect and reinforce our responses. But we have to take the attitude that we are not bound to dance to the tune of the planets or feel stuck with our feelings. What I'm saying is that we are greater than our reactions. We cannot stop the rain, but we can wear a raincoat. We can transform and transcend our reactions through understanding. This is how we change a karmic condition.

What can I do to help Sharyn?

This is a question that a lot of mothers ask. Maybe we should take a few moments to show how knowing the planets can help us understand a child. Even though your daughter is already grown, I have some specific techniques to give you that may help her, but let us digress a few minutes to talk about children in general.

It is a very joyful experience to look into the heart of a child by using the planets. Most people read books on child psychology, consult a therapist, talk with other parents, or cultivate their own observations—but as you have probably guessed by now, the quickest and most accurate way to understand a child's inner life is to look at his or her planets at birth. Unfortunately, most parents don't realize this.

Everything and everyone that is born is born within a cycle. The secret to understanding that cycle is to learn to read the character of the moment in which it began.

The planets reveal the quality of this moment. There is a wonderful truth about our birth planets: *They do not lie.* While we may lie to ourselves or be misled by the latest fad psychologist, the planets will tell us the truth. They are neither subjective nor biased, nor do they take sides. Without this esoteric information, we may be "dead wrong" when making assumptions about a child's emotional and mental condition. Fortunately, the planets reveal what these emotional and mental states are precisely.

For instance, when applying discipline, one child may have to be treated very directly and quite strongly while another cannot be treated in the same manner. As you probably know by now, we cannot treat a child with Aries planets the same way we treat one with Scorpio planets. You never want to mince your words when you discipline an Aries type; you have to be very direct. But a Scorpio type does not respond to this kind of approach. They will respond to suggestions and subtlety, but you must never accuse them directly. Direct accusations will earn you an enemy for life. For instance, did you know that you should never point your finger at a Scorpio or attack them for a mistake?

Yes, I know that one very well, being born with four planets in Scorpio!

Oh, I forgot, you do have a lot of planets in Scorpio. Excuse me! You certainly would know what I mean.

Yes, I do. There is this man who does a television commercial. At first, when he would finish his spiel, he'd point right at the audience and say, "I guarantee it." I used to get annoyed at his pointing his finger at me like that, but I have noticed that lately he points off to the side. Someone must have told him about the threatening implications of pointing his finger at the audience to make a point.

You're probably right. Well, as you have learned so far, a mother does not need to take a long time to get to know her child, read a lot of books on child psychology, or risk making a lot of stupid mistakes through trial and error—nor would a child psychologist or therapist. By studying the meaning of a child's planetary positions at birth, she can gain an instant understanding of who her child really is. Their planetary patterns show why they react the way they do.

Another important point to remember: If you find a child who seems uncooperative, has a tendency to withdraw, or displays outbursts of anger, think about the fact that he or she was *born that way*. As you now know, children come into the world *with* these tendencies and parents often seem to reinforce them by their own reactions. If we understand who our children are and what they were born with, however, we have a better chance of helping them and freeing ourselves of any potential guilt about it being our fault.

Finally, we need to understand the attitudes and tendencies of our own celestial chemistry so that we can determine how we will respond or react to the emotional and psychological needs of our children and everyone else.

The good news is that you don't really have to know very much about setting up charts. As you will soon learn, there are no charts to calculate—there are only a few descriptions to assimilate from the material I have given you, and you bear no risk of making wrong predictions. For the most part, all you need to do is use a condensed chart to locate the specific planetary information, compile it and then read it.

Well, let's get back to Sharyn.

After all these years of studying the effects of the planets and the psychological states they manifest, I have found some methods to be useful for people who have a depressed Moon like Sharyn does.

One is that you may need to help her go back and feel some of the emotions she felt when you were working and going to school. You could begin by telling her how much you love her and explaining what was going on with you at the time when you had to leave her with your mother.

But she says she knows that I love her. She's never blamed me for her depression.

But some reaction may still be hidden, and you may need to make her feel safe in exploring this. This feeling of safety may help her access some of the emotions she has not allowed herself to express. Nice people seldom give themselves the privilege of honoring their own feelings, and your invitation to help her live out some of them consciously may help her relieve her depression.

Next, there is a way to go back to the past and change it. At first this sounds strange, because we can't *really* go back to the past. But we can go back to the past in our memory and through our imagination change that memory into any picture we want. Through guided imagery, Sharyn could go back to those childhood scenes and change the dark pictures into other pictures of light. She could make them happy scenes through her imagination—where you could be home playing with her, baking her favorite desserts, sharing her life with a pet, and having wonderful birthday parties. This form of guided imagery has helped a lot of people change the pictures in their unconscious.

One other option that might work: There are antidepressants that help people who have chronic depression to reconnect to life in a positive and creative way. If the first two suggestions don't work, she might try consulting a psychiatrist who may recommend these remedies. I've seen this help a lot of people, because sometimes the problem is simply organic.

I would also like to say that you are not to blame yourself for what happened to your daughter. The relationship of your planets together is quite good. Your Jupiter is conjunct her Venus, and she certainly feels that you love her. In fact, she may be puzzled if she ever gets depressed in your company. While her reasoning mind probably knows that you will always support her, her unconscious mind may still hold memories of those lonely years and feel the loss of your nurturing. Her feelings of depression may even appear to be illogical to her at times.

You could be right. She has a very good marriage and her husband is just as sweet as she is.

On the other hand, *your* relationship to Sharyn would be entirely different if your Saturn were on her Moon.

My Saturn? I'm not sure I know what you mean by that?

Well, Sharyn was born with Saturn on *her* Moon. If she did not have this pattern, she would not get so depressed. But if the position of your Saturn was in the same position as her Moon, your Saturn would be on her Moon, and you would function as a depressant to her. You would be like Saturn. She would find you cold and critical and would not want to be around you. Even though you are her mother, you would be one of those people she would tend to avoid.

I can't even imagine that.

But you see, the relationship between you would be different. Something about her emotions and habits would annoy you, and you would always have to work at not criticizing her. That's why being around you would depress her. But fortunately, your Saturn is not in that position. You have some very good energies between you. It is my guess that she knows in her heart that you are not the cause of her depression.

I'm amazed that you can see this in people simply by understanding where their planets are.

Yes, but what is really more amazing is that almost anyone can learn to do this. You can see how it helps in understanding our relationships—it is simply a question of whether any two people are in harmony or in discord. The planetary patterns immediately show the real situation. This is why it does not take a lot of time to get to know someone. When you have their planetary patterns in hand, you can look right into the core of their nature and understand them. It is my life's purpose to show people how to do this.

Why isn't this knowledge of the planets taught in schools? So much misunderstanding could be resolved, and people would truly be able to help each other.

Yes, that's very true, but the problem is that most educators are afraid they will be ridiculed for using such a so-called pseudo-science as astrology. This situation reminds me of the time when President Reagan and his wife Nancy were made fun of nationally because people learned that she had used an astrologer to schedule the timing of his activities. Many people who will spend five years and a tremendous amount of money with a therapist to try and understand themselves would recoil in laughter if you told them to go see an astrologer. Yet, I have counseled thousands of people (including therapists) who have been very grateful for the profound insights the planets have given them. Astrology is not a scientific matter—it relates to the psychic/intuitive world within us that the scientific community cannot accept.

I know one woman who thinks that astrology's "The work of the devil." Others think of it as some kind of superstition, or an amusing entertainment that they read about in the newspapers or explore on the Internet.

I'm glad you brought that up. As you know, the daily newspapers only deal with the Sun in its sign. We will be getting to the signs shortly, but for now think of a sign as a specific attitude that a planet is found in at birth. The Sun is only one of the ten planets—as you know, we consider the Sun a planet in this approach. So, what about the other nine planets? What about the sign Venus is in? The sign Mars is in, etcetera? The newspaper writers cannot possibly know how those other planets are related in each person's life, because they would have to interpret everybody's chart individually. Newspaper astrology is a very shallow, inaccurate, and misleading practice that only perpetuates the myth that astrology is a mere party or computer game for Friday night fun.

Well, I guess I got on a soap box there, but it seemed necessary. I don't suppose you have the birthday of Sharyn's husband?

Oh, yes. I've been collecting everybody's birth date since I started coming to see you.

Good. What's his name?

Karl.

Let's enter him into the computer and see what we come up with.

What can you tell me about Sharyn and Karl's relationship? I'm sure she would be curious.

Their relationship is very good because his Neptune is on her Venus. Venus represents the desire within both sexes to love and appreciate. Here, Karl's Neptune arouses Sharyn's love feelings to the point of ecstasy (Neptune)—a love that is very deep. They loved each other the moment they met.

That's what she said. How could you tell that?"

When a man and a woman have this kind of planetary connection, they seem to have loved each other before.

Really?

Well, usually when I have seen this pattern, the lovers say that they already felt that they knew each other. What is implied is that they knew each other in some previous time, but I have no way of proving this.

There are two more patterns that support their relationship. One is that his Jupiter is trine her Moon. You remember, the trine is where two or more planets are 120 degrees from each other? You will be learning more about this in Lesson 5, which I will be giving you in a few weeks. This pattern shows that Karl supports Sharyn's emotional needs. Jupiter makes the Moon happy, which means that when Sharyn is down or feeling depressed, Karl has a way of getting her out of it.

You're so right—that's exactly what she said.

You will recall that Sharyn has Saturn on her Moon, which creates a feeling of not being nurtured. But the position of Karl's Jupiter shows that he gives her the support she needs. Even though she has periods of depression, she knows that Karl is really there for her, and his actions always show this. They have a natural expression of harmonious feelings between them. Sharyn is very fortunate to have both a good mother and a good husband.

The other supporting pattern I see is that her Uranus is right next to his Venus. We talked about Uranus briefly; look on page 198 for a review of Uranus—it gives a full description there. Venus is described on page 165. As you can see, when we combine these two planets, we have a heightened love relationship. Sharyn and Karl have intense moments of sexual rapture, which is another reason that their relationship will never be boring!

You can actually see that?

Yes.

They are so fortunate that their chemistry really works. Others are not so fortunate.

In what way?

What often seems true between men and women is that they are confused about their relationship. For example, many women have told me that they love a particular man but don't really like him. They don't understand how this could be. I usually explain that you have to be clear on what part of this man you love and what part of him you don't like. The answer is made clear by looking at the relationship between their planets. I recently did a chart of a woman who had this problem—she loved this man but didn't like him, and she was confused about what to do about it. I explained why she loved him. His Jupiter is on her Venus and her Neptune is on his Sun. Well as you know, contacts with Jupiter are very supportive, especially when the contact is with Venus. He behaved like Jupiter toward her—very generous and always wanting to give her what she liked. Remember, Venus relates to value. With her Neptune on his Sun, she saw him as a kind of "god man," someone who could do no wrong. This shows that she has a very deep love for him despite his other faults. But her Saturn is conjunct his Mars and his Mercury.

If you look at pages 194-195 and 197 of the Chemistry section, you will find a description of Saturn frustrating Mercury and Saturn frustrating Mars. Always keep in mind that Saturn's *conjunctions* are non-supporting. She complained that he was too impatient sexually, and had no finesse in that area even though he was very kind in other ways. She also said that he was mentally scattered and had no ambition. I told her that her Saturn functioned as a critic of this part of his nature and he felt this criticism. Consequently, he felt very inhibited by her. I explained that she needed to concentrate on better communication there and to talk it out with him.

My explanation helped her understand what parts of him she loved and what parts she disliked, and she could still allow herself to enjoy the harmonious side of their relationship.

I come across such problems all the time. Sometimes, it is very obvious that certain people should not be together, yet they seem bound through karma to grind out that piece of their destiny. But I consider Sharyn and Karl to be very fortunate.

Does Karl have any problems?

Yes, like all of us, there is always something. He has Saturn square or frustrating his Mars.

What can you say about that?

From what I can tell, I don't think he and his father got along very well. This pattern in a man's chart shows that his will (Mars) was blocked by an authority figure, represented by Saturn, his father. His father had too much control over him. This creates an inner feeling of frustration. Karl might hold a lot of anger against his father—a repressed rage. Mars in a man's chart shows his aggressive power. If Saturn is blocking it, he could be subject to angry reactions at times. This would most likely happen if he feels frustrated when trying to accomplish something. His frustration is not likely to be projected towards Sharyn. It probably arises in relation to a boss or with other men. He does not work well under any kind of restriction. He needs to work by himself, be in charge, or feel that he is in control of his own work. To resolve this conflict, he would find it helpful to retrace the experiences he had with his father or other men. He could use the same approach recommended for Sharyn.

So much of the reactions we have toward people are due to those feelings we have suppressed. It is important to go back and relive them, to feel and know them consciously. We must let the body re-experience them so that we can release them.

Do you have any questions on what we've covered so far.

I probably do, but my brain feels like rubber right now. I think you've stretched it out of shape.

I'm sure you can use a break. When you come back next week, we will explore the signs.

Okay, thank you.

Lesson 3

Signs of the Times

We hear so much about the signs, but what are they, really?"

The word "sign" has been inked to death in newspapers across the world. Signs are simply attitudes people express through the energy of their planets. All the particular planetary patterns and sign positions that were in effect when a person was born reveal the inner world of that person. This is why people use the phrase "their signs and their planets." The signs show us the kind of attitude a planet uses to fulfill its desire. I realize this makes the planets sound like separate beings, humanized by a romantic astrologer, but to look at them in that way helps us because that's how they seem to function *psychically*.

Each 30-degree segment of the circle that a planet travels through charges that planet with a specific attitude.

You will easily understand the signs if you remember the circle we talked about in the beginning. This circle is the path of all the planets, which travel counterclockwise through the signs starting with Aries in Figure 1 on the next page.

Figure 1 below presents the signs (or attitudes) in different colors to make them easier to remember. Because there are twelve signs, we have twelve different colors: Each color or sign covers the distance of 30 degrees of the circle, which is one segment—1/12th of the Sun's 360-degree path. In simple terms, if Mercury was traveling through the red sign of Aries when you were born, you would express a different attitude in fulfilling your intellectual purpose than if Mercury was moving through the yellow sign of Gemini at the time of your birth.

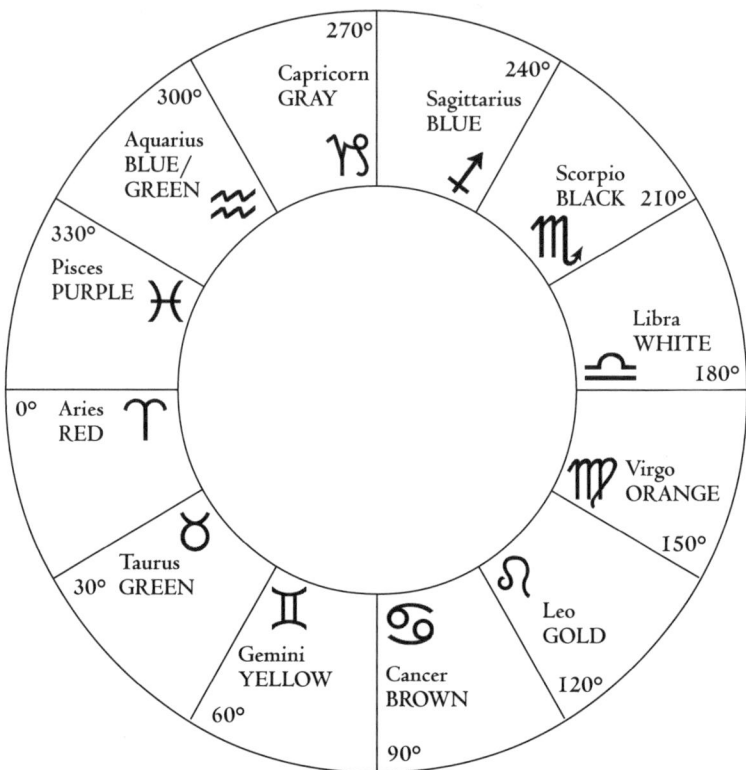

Figure 1

We also need to look at the signs as attitudes. Here is the way you would describe a planet in a sign: "My Mercury is in Aquarius. Therefore my thinking, which is shown by Mercury, is influenced by the blue-green attitude or the attitude of Aquarius."

From my long experience with the planets, I have personally chosen specific colors to reflect the meaning of the signs. Use of the colors in this way is not part of the astrological tradition, but they will help you get an immediate *feeling* for what the signs are like. For instance, the sign of Aries is like the color *red*. People with personal planets in Aries are active, impulsive, aggressive, and sometimes foolish risk-takers. It has been said that people with red cars tend to attract more trouble than people with cars of a different color, because we seem to react to red as a challenge. Remember how the red cape of the bullfighter incites the bull? The color red seems to arouse these feelings in us. With this method, you don't have to spend a lot of time learning about the abstract names of the signs and what they mean. Of course, some colors are much more subtle than red, but with a little reasoning everything will become clear to you. The concrete imagery of the colors will stay in your mind much longer than an abstract description like "Your Mars is in Aries." However, you will notice that I have included the symbols for the signs in the circle in Figure 1 if you want to know what signs these colors represent. The **Master Table** found in your appendix (A-2) will help you translate the symbols for the signs (or attitudes).

Also, you have probably noticed that I don't give sign descriptions for the bigger *impersonal* planets—Jupiter, Saturn, Uranus, Neptune and Pluto. Because these planets are less personal in their meaning, their sign descriptions are unnecessary to learn the work we are doing together. When the impersonal planets are considered alone—not in relationship with the personal planets—they are best seen as being inconsiderate of the ego. They have been called "ambassadors of the galaxy" and relate to more powerful evolutionary forces hidden deep within the psyche. They will kick us out of a lifeless job that does not serve our purpose, or bruise our ego when we have become too proud, or bring loss so that we can connect to the deeper feelings of love and compassion. The impact of these planetary forces upon our lives compel us toward a deeper understanding of our existence by shattering the expectations of our human ego; whereas, the personal planets tend to support the ego and its desires. Think of the *personal* planets—the Sun, Moon, Mercury, Venus, and Mars— as the more human or ego-oriented planets. The impersonal planets are the dominating planets, and they have tremendous, important effects upon the personal planets. For example, as you may remember, Venus is a happy and graceful planet by herself, but when she is squared (90 degrees away) or joined by the Old Scrooge Saturn at birth by conjunction (0 degrees), she will feel miserable. Any person born at this time would have a low self-esteem and would often become the victim in their relationships. Usually they feel they are worth little, and people tend to treat them that way. Let us now explore some more signs to see how they function in actual practice.

Let's look at Taurus. I call Taurus the green sign attitude because it relates to money as well as the good things of the earth that are green like grass. This is enough imagery to lead you through a basic interpretation of a personal planet in Taurus. Let's say a man's Venus is in Taurus. On page 165 Venus is described as a planet of pleasure and value. So, this man would be very interested in money and the sensual enjoyments of life. Also, in a man's chart, Venus always shows the kind of woman he is attracted to. This man's feminine ideal is Taurus, because Venus, the planet of the feminine spirit, was in Taurus when he was born. If he were to use this information as his guide, he would soon discover that almost any woman he is attracted to would have a planet or two in Taurus in their own chart. Actors Orson Wells and Raymond Burr were two individuals who symbolized the sensual enjoyment of the good life. Both had Taurus planets.

What do you feel about yellow?

I find yellow very uplifting, positive, full of movement, bright, and happy.

If you know people with planets in Gemini, you will find they have these qualities. Consider Gemini as the yellow sign attitude. The problem here is that some other signs are similar in expression—we need something more concrete to recall the Gemini energy. One way is to think of the word "Gemini" as "Jim and I," which obviously always means two people. People born at the time planets were moving in Gemini are always into two or more things. They will engage many projects at once, but they have a hard time completing them. Most Gemini people live in their head and are obsessed with new ideas. I chose yellow because it makes me think of pure intellect, and the mind of the Gemini often works so fast it reminds me of light—the sometimes yellow light of the Sun. These people have the capacity to see two things at once. For example, you might recall when Joe Montana, a Gemini, was the quarterback for the San Francisco 49ers. He could look in one direction and throw the ball in the other, and he was famous for getting rid of the football with lightening speed. His mind is as fast as the flight of a hummingbird and can change direction just as fast. A true Gemini will often sit under a bright yellow light polishing his clever ideas.

A woman whose Sun is in Cancer has her heart in the home. I call Cancer the brown sign attitude for several reasons. Chocolate is brown. On a cold winter day a cup of hot chocolate or warm brownie makes us feel loved and nourished. Cancer is the mother sign. They love the home and family and they like to feed people. They are also interested in houses and real estate. Dirt or land is also brown. These images of brown are very helpful in understanding Cancer's desires and attitudes. Mother Wright, who feeds thousands of homeless people every year in Oakland, California, has *four* planets in Cancer. She completely demonstrates the nurturing principle of Cancer—a World Mother.

I once saw a woman's boyfriend who had Mercury (thinking) next to his Jupiter (expansion) in Cancer (home). The woman asked me to tell her something about him. I said, "He loves the home, family, and real estate; he thinks about these things all the time."

"That's unbelievable. He owns a real estate company!" she said.

Think of Leo as the gold sign attitude. Gold is a symbol of wealth. It is associated with kings, queens, and power. Leos feel themselves as a source of love, full of inner wealth and strength. Even though the actor Sylvester Stallone has his Sun in Cancer and his Moon in Libra, he is fierce on the inside—with Pluto in Leo on top of his Mercury in Leo. Another actor, Arnold Schwartzenegger, has his Sun, Saturn, and Pluto in Leo, making him something of a "bonecrusher." Sometimes, people with planets in Leo have gigantic egos and are self-glorifying. That seemed to be the case of Benito Mussolini, the Italian dictator of World War II, whose ego got in the way and led to a quick demise. But usually people who were born with "happy" Leo planets—not stressed out by squares—have "hearts of gold." They are often very generous, and their outgoing, positive energy tends to make others feel good just being around them.

I recall that Mars was moving through the sign of Virgo at the time you were born, Lelia. Virgo is the orange sign attitude. Traditionally, orange is associated with service and harvest time. Think of all the orange pumpkins being harvested in the fall. Since Virgos have a need to help others and organize information, they harvest ideas and set them in their best order. The aggressive and action-oriented planet Mars was in Virgo when you were born, so you have a passion (Mars) for helping others and placing things in order. Princess Diana had her Mars conjunct Pluto in Virgo which gave her an intense passion for helping others. (She was killed at the time visiting Pluto was making a square to these two planets.) Tibetan and Indian monks who wear orange robes symbolize service and renunciation. These symbols of the color orange will serve to anchor in your mind the basic meaning of the attitudes of Virgo.

You can also associate the quality of a sign with the activities of a person or an event to help you remember. For instance, earlier we talked about your Mars in Virgo being close to Neptune—which indicates a passion for ecstasy. Mars is the desire to pursue

101

aggressively and Neptune is the desire for ecstasy. You have sought to fulfill this ecstasy through music and spiritual practices. The well-known Italian opera singer Luciano Pavarotti has Venus in Virgo next to his Neptune; this gives him a great need to experience ecstasy by serving perfectly the god of music, Neptune. Because you were born with planets in Virgo, you are an expert on the attitudes of Virgo.

It is very revealing to note that while the late astronomer Carl Sagan belittled astrology, his Sagittarius Moon gave him a desire for truth. His Mars in Virgo squared his Moon, however, and apparently interfered with this deeper impulse of Sagittarius by compelling him to go through the linear part of the mind in search of that truth. Therefore, it appears that he could only accept his truth if it was scientific. Perhaps he had an absence of psychic awareness. This leads me to wonder how science limits itself with its own linear methods.

What would you say about white?

White to me is very neutral, full of potential, but with nothing definite—like a blank canvas.

Libra is the white sign attitude. Librans find it hard to take sides because they see value in both. People with planets in Libra can exasperate us when they act indecisively and fail to take a stand. They have a great capacity to neutralize any situation where there is conflict by raising the white flag to negotiate a truce, which makes them excellent mediators or arbitrators. Libra is also the "waffling" sign. President Clinton has Venus and Mars conjunct Neptune in Libra and was accused of "waffling" by George Bush. But Mr. Bush has his Moon in Libra. So, what we have here is a "waffler" calling a "waffler" a "waffler." Libra types believe in togetherness and hate to choose a path that closes off choices. In fact, they don't like choosing at all. They have the most amazing capacity to rationalize any attitude they may have despite how false or unrealistic it may be. They seem to have a great distrust of the particular—anything that is one way.

For example, I had a client who had a lot of planets in Libra and had difficulty accepting the reality of the specific conflicts that were shown in her chart. She would always counter with, "Well, everybody has that," or "but I'm not like that very much." In short, she would always find a way to rationalize everything I pointed out to her—as if these things were true of everyone.

People who inherit Libra planets are surrounded with the white blanket of possibility but may fail to act decisively.

Tell me, what color would you choose for Scorpio?

I only know one Scorpio other than myself. He was very secretive and unable to talk about his feelings—kept things hidden. I would choose a dark color.

I consider Scorpio to be the black sign attitude. As the absence of color, black can be nothing and everything. It represents night—the unknown, what is not seen. As you say, "hidden." People born with planets in Scorpio often appear other than they really are because they prefer not to be known. We often see the mask rather than the real person. The Scorpio planets give the desire to remain fiercely private, proud, independent, emotionally in control, and unknown. The actress Jaclyn Smith seems to be an emotionally in control person in her TV performances—she has three planets in Scorpio.

It is also interesting to gaze upon a Scorpio person when they wear black. They exude an intensely mysterious quality that makes them very seductive and they sometimes appear threatening. The planet Pluto is a close friend to them, and we know what that planet is like. Do you remember our discussion of Bruce Lee?

Yes.

He was born with the Moon, Mercury, Venus, and Mars all in Scorpio and square Pluto. He was awesome in black! Well, let's go on.

How about blue?

Blue is the sky, a symbol for the heavens. There is something spiritual about it—otherwise, I'm not sure.

Well, that makes sense because blue is an ethereal energy, so it is hard to pin it down in concrete terms. I consider Sagittarius to be the blue sign attitude. Think of the "wild blue yonder." Shoot a blue arrow into space. Those born with planets in Sagittarius have wanderlust and a passion for discovery. It is the realm of law, justice, teaching, writing, religion, and philosophy. People with strong planets in this sign seek to understand by probing the deep, blue space of the mind in search of answers. Sometimes they are simply looking for information, for example, lawyers seeking to discover facts. The classical composer, Beethoven, had three planets in Sagittarius. He hated hypocrisy in religion and pretenders in high positions. He brought forth great music from the blue place.

Robert, you make it sound so simple, but I'm still not sure I can do this as easily as you can.

You will, trust me. Let's explore the rest of the signs together, and I will ask you some more questions. Let's continue with another color. How would you describe the color gray?

Gray is kind of depressing, empty, wintry, lonely.

Good. Capricorn is the gray sign attitude. Capricorn is serious and matter of fact—all business. But people with Capricorn planets really try to be humorous. Perhaps you have seen the actor Mel Gibson who always manages to crack a smile and make clever, offhanded remarks. His Sun and Mercury are in the gray sign of Capricorn. When a person has Mercury in the gray sign, they tend to think seriously. (Remember, Mercury relates to thinking.) To offset this wintry state of mind, they look for humor. The 1950s comedian and musician Danny Kaye had four Capricorn planets. Capricorns seem to be in search of something light-hearted because they don't really feel that way. If a person has three or four planets in this gray sign, they will be very serious and therefore take themselves too seriously.

Your brief description of Capricorn is certainly quite adequate. It is said that this gray sign is ruled by the leaden planet, Saturn. Maybe this is why these individuals practice being light-hearted. They may feel dull to themselves and want to get rid of the serious mood they carry around inside of them.

Would you say something about the other signs? Their attitudes?

Yes, what about blue-green?

Blue-green feels intense to me, different—unusual beauty.

Aquarius is the blue-green sign attitude. The Aquarian attitudes are radically different from all the other signs. People who have planets in this sign are charged with charisma. You will find many people with planets in Aquarius on TV and in the movies—Paul Newman for one. Sharon Stone has Venus in Aquarius, and Marilyn Monroe had her Moon there. Mel Gibson has Mars in Aquarius, and Cybill Shepherd has four planets in Aquarius. True Aquarians possess unique qualities of self-expression, yet are often detached emotionally.

It is very interesting to note that three of the world's greatest composers had planets clustered in Aquarius. Mozart had four planets in Aquarius. Saturn was next to his Sun and Mercury, so his father—representing Saturn—played the roll of Scrooge. He was very heavy on Mozart and made him perform all the time. Because his father had Scorpio planets, I'm sure they didn't get along. However, this did not obstruct Mozart's true Aquarian genius—he was a musical wonder.

The Austrian composer Franz Schubert had Aquarian planets in conjunction—Mercury, Sun and Pluto. Remember how Pluto pushed Mars? Well, here he is pushing Schubert's mind (Mercury), which gave the composer tremendous perception. His was a very special voice: The exalting effect of his Ave Maria endures through time.

Then there is Frederic Chopin, who had Mercury right next to Venus in Aquarius; this led his mind to focus on Venus, the goddess of love and beauty. He sought to crystallize a romantic ideal in his music, but found it hard to actualize it in human terms with his lover, Georges Sands. He hated being called a romantic but this may be because Aquarians prefer to remain detached. They seem embarrassed to show deep emotions.

So, when you think of Aquarius, think of some of these giants. It is the sign of difference, uniqueness, and the voice of originality.

How many more signs do we have left?

One. What do you think of purple?

Purple feels intense to me—something special. It seems to be royal—maybe honorable, ritualistic, or stately. It's definitely not an ordinary color. Purple draws my attention.

I consider Pisces to be the purple sign attitude. Think of a deep ocean of consciousness when you think of Pisces. Those born with a lot of planets in this sign are considered far-out, very psychic and attuned to the subtle world within them. Edgar Allan Poe, who had four planets in Pisces, was a writer and poet of great imagination who certainly lived in a purple world—sometimes in a euphoric world of opium. Pisces types live in deep inner space. Not liking the world as it is, they seek to create their own world to live in. Often Pisces have a deep desire to bring forth something beautiful into the physical world. The great painter Michelangelo had his Sun and Mars in Pisces. He certainly had a passion for the sublime, which he expressed in his paintings. A Pisces who has too many disappointments might try to merge into the deep purple by drowning themselves in drugs or alcohol—they need their ecstasy one way or another, even if it is only temporary.

You may think that the signs of Sagittarius and Pisces sound similar, but actually they are quite different. Sagittarius is a fire energy and Pisces is water. Sagittarians seek to understand the blue sky of higher awareness, but Pisces tend to fall into it—they want to live there. Sagittarians are more intellectually connected to this higher awareness; Pisces are more emotionally connected. Yet, these two signs seem to understand and have compassion for each other.

While we are speaking of signs, let me give you some examples of how the personal planets of the Sun, Moon, Mercury, Venus, and Mars work through them. As I mentioned earlier, the planet picks up the energy of the sign it is passing through at the time of our birth. From then on, we use the planet's energy to express that sign's particular attitude.

For example, the other day a lady came to me for a reading, and I noticed that she was born with her Moon in Gemini, the yellow sign. The most outstanding feature of a strong Gemini person is their restlessness and endless flitting from one subject to the next. It was a real challenge to hold this woman's attention on the point I was trying to make. Then I realized I was working too hard to get her to understand. I thought I would try something different: Every time she would jump off the subject, I would jump off of it with her.

We went here and there and everywhere, and I finally guided her back to what we were first talking about. Just as I began to get to my point again, she went off on another tangent—and I went with her. Again we went here and there and everywhere, and I gradually brought her back once more to the point. This second time she said, "You sure jump around a lot." "Yes, that's true," I said smiling. Then she suddenly jumped back. "Oh, me, that's what I've been doing. I'm the one who's been jumping around. I've always had such a problem with focusing. How can I stop doing this?"

I told her that understanding her tendency to grab "two of everything" was already half the battle.

What do you mean by "two of everything"?

Well, remember the Gemini attitudes we talked about? Geminis always need to do two things at once. So, their challenge is to be able to concentrate on one thing at a time. This woman finally realized that it was okay to do two things at once, because that was her nature, but that it would work out better if she agreed to finish whatever she started. She called sometime after our session and told me it was still very hard for her to stay focused, but she had realized that she would never accomplish anything if she didn't.

To carry this a little further, it is interesting to note that a woman who has her Sun or Mars in Gemini may have trouble choosing one man. Like Libras, people with planets in Gemini hate the word "one." A man with his Moon or Venus in Gemini might always find himself chasing two or more women.

I once had a male client with Venus, Moon, and Mercury in Gemini who was going with three women at the same time! One day he called me in desperation—he wanted to know how to solve his problem. After checking his planets, I told him it would be resolved by next Sunday. When Sunday evening came around, he called and told me that one of the women had caught him in bed with another one; as a result, he had lost both of them and went back to the only one left. But I wonder how long it will be before he re-creates a similar situation.

I mention these stories to illustrate how strong these attitudes (signs) are in our nature. You can see why people are more predictable than we think; how wonderful it is to be able to understand them through the planets! However, it is very important not to judge. With our understanding of the planets, we can look through another person's eyes and know why they do the things they do. We will know how to work with them and communicate with them on a deeper level of intimacy. You may soon hear people say, "You're one of the few people who really understands me."

Here I have shown people using their energies to express the tendencies of just one sign, Gemini. Yet there are eleven more signs! You can see that there are endless combinations available to explain the complexity of human nature. Knowing how this works will enable you to cut through all the "psychobabble" that's present in the world today.

> You can always rely upon the planets to lead you to the heart of any human condition. Astrologers may make mistakes, but the planets never lie.

Summary of the Signs

The Red Sign Attitude (Aries): Aggressive, competitive, impulsive, courageous, dangerous, challenging, energetic, fiery (fire engine), foolish, egotistic, indiscriminate, and arrogant.
    Things: Cars, knives, guns, iron, steel, muscle, penis, hammer, weapons.
    Function: To initiate.

The Green Sign Attitude (Taurus): Possessive (green with envy), tenacious (like crab grass) sensuous, earthy, bullheaded, loyal, avaricious.
    Things: Banks, bulls, stock market.
    Function: To produce.

The Yellow Sign Attitude (Gemini): Dualistic, flighty, clever, restless, bright, adaptable, and unfocused.
    Things: Birds, letters, keys, messages, telephones, documents, speeches, and agreements.
    Function: To communicate.

The Brown Sign Attitude (Cancer): Nurturing, motherly, thrifty, clannish, traditional, moody.
    Things: Baked goods, land, stomach, grains, property, houses, and plumbing.
    Function: To sustain.

The Gold Sign Attitude (Leo): Proud, generous, dramatic, creative, warmhearted, entertaining, self-centered.
    Things: Gold, jewelry, theaters, sports, gambling, children, and the arts.
    Function: To create.

The Orange Sign Attitude (Virgo): Helpful, efficient, economical, patient, and critical.
    Things: Small animals, food products, health products, service organizations, statistics, plants, efficiency systems.
    Function: To serve.

The White Sign Attitude (Libra): Artistic, friendly, harmonious, people-centered, indecisive.
> **Things:** Cosmetics, design, beauty, partnerships, and marriages.
> **Function:** To relate.

The Black Sign Attitude (Scorpio): Intense, secretive, strong-willed, passionate, seductive, proud, thin-skinned, tenacious, and vindictive.
> **Things:** Reproductive organs, mines, assets, concealed weapons, insurance, death, and taxes.
> **Function:** To transform.

The Blue Sign Attitude (Sagittarius): Straightforward, blunt, opinionated, fiery, philosophical, judgmental.
> **Things:** Legal matters, religion, travel, universities, and philosophy.
> **Function:** To understand.

The Gray Sign Attitude (Capricorn): Honest, ambitious, traditional, hardworking, pragmatic, responsible, cold, and matter-of-fact.
> **Things:** Corporations, business, science, and doctors.
> **Function:** To lead.

The Blue-Green Sign Attitude (Aquarius): Independent, unique, unpredictable, intelligent, creative, friendly, charismatic, insensitive, futuristic, and detached.
> **Things:** Computers, airplanes, television, astrology, psychology, new age therapies.
> **Function:** To change.

The Purple Sign Attitude (Pisces): Sympathetic, sensitive, mystical, spiritual, escapist, imaginative, self-effacing, irresponsible.
> **Things:** Hospitals, drugs, film, photography, monasteries, nunneries, mysticism, healing, meditation, Nirvana, and communion.
> **Function:** To care.

Lesson 4

When the Planets Come Visiting

Good to have you back, Lelia. We're going to have some fun today with the visiting, impersonal planets.

I'm really curious about the visiting planets. When you say "visiting" you don't really mean visiting do you?

I know it does sound strange. Obviously, if I say that Neptune will be visiting your Venus next week, I don't mean that this planet will visit you physically. If you were to look at Neptune through a telescope, you would not see him coming down towards you. What Neptune will be doing is making contact with your psychic Venus, the Venus within you. Even though we were born with fixed planetary patterns, the patterns of the planets in the actual solar system are always changing. We need to know where they are going today because, psychically, the planets are always traveling through our inner space and affecting our reactions, feelings, and impulses.

Psychically the planets are always traveling through our inner space and affecting our reactions, feelings, and impulses.

I see that your Venus is in Scorpio, the black sign attitude. If I say that Neptune will be visiting your Venus, you need to know in what way. Will he be joining your Venus in the same sign—which would be a conjunction—or will he be moving toward a square or trine relationship with your Venus? Does this make sense to you?

Can you give me another example?

Sure. Do you remember how in Lesson 2 we talked so much about the effect one person's planets have on someone else?

Yes.

Well, simply think of a planet in the actual solar system as another person coming into your life. While an actual person may come and go in your life, a planet is always visiting you in some way or another. They never leave you, but their effects seem dormant when they are not triggering the power points. We will be looking at the power points in Lesson 5, but don't worry about that for now.

The actual planets are always moving through us psychically, but their effects upon us change as their patterns to other planets change.

Does this help?

Yes, I think I understand it now. By calculating where the planets are, I can tell when they will affect me in a particular way.

That's it.

How would Neptune affect me if it were to join my Venus in a conjunction?

In Part 2 of your Chemistry section I describe the kind of effects the *visiting* planets have upon the personal planets. Neptune supporting Venus is described on page 208. Here is what it says about Neptune visiting Venus:

As a visiting planet: This is a visitation of inspiration, a time to create something beautiful. Love that comes to you during this time can be of the highest kind. If you are in the arts, it is a great time to make things happen—a very creative period.

Sounds like a nice experience. How often would Neptune join my Venus?

After it made a conjunction, it may make contact two or three times within a year or so. But once it moves away from the conjunction for the last time, it will never join your Venus again in this lifetime. Later down the road, however, it could form a square or possibly a trine relationship to your Venus.

Can you give me some actual living examples of how the visiting planets have affected other people's lives?

Sure. I have literally hundreds of situations in my files, but I will simply chose a few that stand out in my mind.

There was this nice lady who had a dog-grooming business—but nothing was working out for her, business was drying up. She said that people didn't seem to care much about their dogs anymore. At the time of her troubles, visiting Saturn was frustrating (squaring) her Sun and Uranus was frustrating her Mars. This amounted to obstructions from her banker who would not extend her loan payments, an ex-husband who was threatening to sue her if he didn't get the money she owed him, and harassing situations with difficult customers too hard to please.

When she came to see me, she was thinking about giving it all up. After a complete analysis of the planetary patterns affecting her life, I told her I had good news: Everything would straighten out within a week or so and she would be headed in a much better direction. She gave me this funny look and said, "I can hardly believe that. Are you sure?" I said, "It's a very unusual situation. The best way I can explain it to you is that the planets show that you are about to leave a bad situation and move into a better one. Everything will turn around for you and you will be in a much better place." She was very happy to hear this, but she had experienced such a hard time in those past six months that she could barely accept the good news. She thanked me anyway and left.

Sometime later she called me and told me that she had just gotten this lucrative contract with a wealthy woman who breeds dogs for shows, movies, and special sales. She could not praise me enough and said she was going to send a lot of people to see me. I was very happy for her. Once again the planets had showed the way.

But what happened? What did you see that told you everything would turn around for her?

It was an unusual situation. Just as Saturn and Uranus were leaving their square positions, they began forming supporting positions or trines to her Venus and Moon. Since these were the two planets that were behind most of her trouble, I saw that their change to a trine relationship would bring a better situation. While I couldn't tell exactly what would happen, I knew the negative conditions would leave her and something more positive would come into her life. It was even better than I had expected. It is interesting to note that Venus rules the world of money, while the Moon rules the world of women, and here it was a wealthy woman who had brought good fortune into this nice lady's world. She was so happy that she had discovered the planets and promised again to send all her clients to see me.

One thing puzzles me. You mention that Saturn helped bring a better situation by forming a trine to her Venus and Moon. I thought Saturn was basically a Scrooge planet and has never brought anything good to anybody.

Well, a trine is about the only situation in which Saturn can be beneficial. In this position, he brings solid results. Otherwise, he always tests us and makes us work for everything we get. Who knows, he may have been obstructing our nice lady to develop her character by forcing her to hang in there. Just when she was about to give up, he did turn around and help her. I'm not trying to humanize Saturn here, but if this lady was meant to abandon her business, her destiny might have been for Saturn to hang around frustrating her Sun a little longer until she gave up. This only shows more of the mystery in how the planets work. When we truly engage them, they always offer the gift of profound understanding of the human condition. I am so glad you have decided to pursue this marvelous way of understanding human nature.

I'm glad I did, too. Can you give me more examples of the visiting planets? I really find this an eye-opener.

I have seen a particular situation occur many times when Neptune is in conjunction to the Sun. As you know, Neptune is a planet that relates to the psychic or spiritual world, but when it joins a person's Sun, it can be devastating. For some reason that I can't explain, it tends to make the person very weak, which is strange because a lot of conjunctions by Neptune are very inspiring.

A woman who was experiencing this conjunction over her Sun asked me to explain what was happening to her. I told her about the time that Neptune had visited my Sun. I had experienced a bone-tired feeling, nervous exhaustion, loss of self-confidence, and a strange confusion. She said those were her experiences exactly. She asked what she could do about it. I told her it was very important for her to see a doctor, get lots of rest, and simplify her life until this period passed—I took regenerating herbs, myself. The problem is that this condition comes and goes for a couple of years because it usually takes Neptune that long to completely leave the Sun. The Sun is the center of our vitality, and Neptune seems to drain our energy.

Even though this woman was very discouraged, she was glad to know what was happening to her, and that she wasn't really losing her mind. Sometimes people can handle life better if they understand what's affecting them. By hearing my story, she knew that there were probably a lot of other people out there who had gone through the same thing and survived. So, she felt she could do the same.

I must have had something like that—I remember having similar experiences. Can you tell if that happened to me and when?

Let me call up your chart on the computer. Here we are. Let's see, yes—Neptune did conjunct your Sun in 1968 and 1969. Do you recall what went on with you during that time?

My god, in 1969 I got divorced and started losing a lot of weight. I was exhausted. They thought I had Leukemia, but everything started getting better in 1970. This is truly remarkable to see that you can read all these things in the planets. Have you ever been wrong?

Oh, yes. A friend of mine wanted to take a woman friend of his to Europe and cycle through France together. He wondered whether she was attracted to him and if they would have an exciting love affair together. Because he was so enthusiastic and anxious for the right answer, I did a special chart on the situation to see what I could find out for him. I looked at the chart and told him it would work out fine. A few weeks later, he called me from Paris to tell me that it wasn't working out fine. She was flirting with every guy they ran into and kept holding him at arm's length. I was surprised and apologized. I had thought it would work out for him, but it didn't. I went back to review the chart: The answer was staring me in the face. Two planets in their charts had strong frustrating squares between them. It was very obvious from hindsight. I remember actually looking at this obstruction when I first did the reading, but I unconsciously overlooked it, or rationalized it away, because I wanted him to be successful. Also, during their trip Pluto was passing over her Venus, which gave her an increased sexual drive and moved her to engage other men. I had thought she would spend all of her flirting on my friend, but the two obstructed planets were between them. Apparently, she just wanted to see Europe and this was her chance. My friend kidded me for a while and then laughed it off, but it took me some time to forgive myself for making that kind of blunder.

We're all human and make mistakes.

Yes, it keep us humble. I had egg on my face.

After learning of the effect visiting Pluto has upon Venus, I have seen this position in the charts of many people. It seems to heighten sexual desire in everyone—even to evoke a kind of sexual compulsion to go after whoever is available. Such a visitation could be upsetting to someone who feels they ought to have better self-control. But this is another example of the intensity of Pluto. Whatever personal planet he touches, we experience a heightened impulse to act excessively. He seems to compel us to get to the bottom of things. Sometimes, when Pluto conjuncts Venus, he compels us to pursue love or lust intensely.

Have you ever found a situation where you've predicted a bad situation from the visits of Pluto?

Not really, but I did come close once.

Can you talk about it?

Actually, I was very upset over what I had discovered. This casual acquaintance had asked me to check out his life. He didn't make an appointment, but I looked over his planets anyway—just as a favor. He had Saturn frustrating (squaring) Mars in his chart, which indicates heavy karma with men at some time in his life. Pluto was about to make a visiting conjunction with his Mars in Scorpio. For me, this meant a possible explosion of anger and violence with some kind of serious consequence, because Pluto was stimulating the Mars/Saturn square pattern in his chart. He had hinted that he was having trouble with some business associates who were accusing him of ripping them off. Actually, he did seem a little shady to me. It looked so bad for him that I didn't even want to discuss it, but he kept prodding me to tell him what I saw. What I saw wasn't good. I actually thought he might be killed or end up in prison. I felt there was no way I could help him, and I didn't know how to tell him what I saw. Finally I said, "I think the best thing you can do is to get out of town." He actually did leave town but I never found out what happened to him. I must confess that I really didn't want to know.

Pluto is strange: When he is frustrated, he can do terrible things; yet I've also seen him bring about wonderful transformations in some people's lives.

A young woman came to me very upset because she thought she was going to die. Her heart was breaking in two. She had given her heart to a man who was married and had no chance of fulfilling her dreams with him. The moment she told me her birth date, I knew exactly what was happening to her—her Sun was in Scorpio and Pluto was visiting her Sun. A woman's heart is represented by the Sun in her chart—the male within her, her other self. When visiting Pluto hits a woman's Sun, it completely opens her heart to the man she desires. But this situation often occurs when she is unable to be with the man who has stolen her heart. Pluto forces her to feel her own heart. This can be very excruciating. Almost every woman I know who has had this experience says that they are stronger and more capable of loving because of it. They are more in touch with their own heart, their own power. By truly loving a man, they have discovered their own inner strength and capacities. Thus, they rely more upon their inner strength because they are more aware of who they are. Mysteriously, this is how real love changes us.

On the other hand, I have seen some women experience a great personal loss during visiting Pluto's conjunction to their Sun. Sometimes her father or a close male friend dies. The loss seems to be necessary to awaken this person into more feeling.

I told this young woman that she had to allow herself to feel the pain she was going through and try not to deny it. I explained that even though it hurt, it was a process in which she was destined to recognize her own power and come to love herself even more—and that love itself would heal her.

Pluto seems like a very powerful planet.

Yes, he really is—he cannot be denied. I might add that we don't really know that the visiting planets do these things to us, but we do know that these events occur during the times they make their contact in the way I have described. The planets tell us what is happening, and this is good enough for our purpose. This system of analysis and prediction is very effective and you can always rely on it.

Well, I guess that's enough for today. When you come again next Saturday, I will get you started in creating your own Planetary Profile.

I'll see you then.

Lesson 5

How to Create Planetary Profiles

Well, as I promised you, Lelia, you are going to learn how to create Planetary Profiles. Take your time in learning how to do these and you will be very happy with the result.

It is very important that you first do a Profile for yourself; then it will be easier to do the Profile for someone else. Your Profile will give you a clear understanding of who you are, and it's necessary to know your own reactions for you to understand the reactions of other people. Your own personal viewpoints can serve as a reference point that will help you see how other people differ from you. You will be able to understand their differences by using your knowledge of the signs (colors or attitudes) and planets they have inherited. Let's call up your chart on the computer. Simply go with me step by step and we will create a Profile.

Notice that the computer has listed the sign positions of all your personal and impersonal planets in symbols in the *condensed* chart below. This is your **Planetary Profile**.

Lelia Thore's Planetary Profile

Your Personal Planets

Sun	☉	25 ♏ 29
Moon	☽	22 ♈ 27
Mercury	☿	06 ♏ 05
Venus	♀	25 ♏ 22
Mars	♂	17 ♍ 56

Your Impersonal Planets

Jupiter	♃	08 ♏ 19
Saturn	♄	21 ♒ 56
Uranus	♅	28 ♈ 26
Neptune	♆	14 ♍ 20
Pluto	♇	25 ♋ 58

You may be wondering what is meant by *personal* and *impersonal* planets. The Moon, Mercury, Venus and Mars serve to support the Sun, which is or "reflects" the personal ego and instinct for survival. This is why I refer to them as personal planets. The impersonal planets are indifferent to our personal ego. They may support it or they may not, depending on how the impersonal planets relate to our personal planets at birth.

I suggest you copy the appendix and place it in a binder or a protective folder. You will refer to this information for all of your future work. Of course, if you do not want to copy the appendix, you can flip back and forth through the pages to get the information you need.

The first step to creating your Planetary Profile is to note the signs your personal and impersonal birth planets are in. For example, reading the condensed chart on page 117 from top to bottom, you can see that your first planetary symbol is a circle with a dot in the center (☉). Look up this symbol in your Master Table, which is found in the appendix. Note that it is the symbol for the Sun and (♏) is the symbol for Scorpio shown here at 25 degrees and 29 minutes of the sign. Therefore your Sun is in the black sign of Scorpio. As you continue to read from top to bottom of this condensed printout, please take note that the first five planets are the **personal** planets and the remaining five planets are the **impersonal** planets. For the sake of our analysis, we want to list these separately. Let us first take your five personal planets.

The Master Table in the appendix enables you to translate all the symbols that were generated by the computer and listed here. In Lesson 3, you found detailed information on the signs, and Part 1, the Chemistry section, describes the planets in the signs in more detail. Let's look at the basic attitudes of your own personal planets, Lelia.

How to Create Planetary Profiles

The Basic Attitudes of Lelia's Personal Planets

1. **SUN** (ego, survival instinct, desire to survive) is in Scorpio, which is the black sign attitude. Refer to pages 144-145.

2. **MOON** (feelings, habits, desire for security) is in Aries, which is the red sign attitude. Refer to pages 149-150.

3. **MERCURY** (thinking, communication, desire to think) is in Scorpio, which is the black sign attitude. Refer to page 161.

4. **VENUS** (values, feminine, desire to relate) is in Scorpio, which is the black sign attitude. Refer to page 171.

5. **MARS** (passion, masculine, desire to act) is in Virgo, which is the orange sign attitude. Refer to page 179.

The next step is to group together the planets that are in the same attitude (sign). We can see here that your Sun, Mercury, and Venus have the black sign attitude of Scorpio. This is a lot of Scorpio energy.

Now select the page with the appropriate sign description for each of these planets and copy them. A detailed description of the Sun in the black sign of Scorpio is found on page 144-145. Mark these pages for copying. Next, we find your Mercury in Scorpio described on page 161. You have Venus in Scorpio, which is described on page 171. Now locate the Moon in the red sign of Aries and Mars in the orange sign of Virgo. Copy all of these sections to collect a detailed description of all of your personal planets, and put them aside.

How the Impersonal Planets Impact Your Personal Planets

Now, we need to go further and see how the five impersonal planets impact your five personal planets.

It is necessary to understand that each of the twelve signs is composed of either Fire, Earth, Air, or Water and it is by relating these elements to each other that we can determine whether two signs are naturally in harmony or in discord.

Figure 2. Elements of the Signs

Fire Signs	Earth Signs	Air Signs	Water Signs
Aries	Taurus	Gemini	Cancer
Leo	Virgo	Libra	Scorpio
Sagittarius	Capricorn	Aquarius	Pisces

All signs of the *same element* seen above are in harmony. Aries, Leo, and Sagittarius are compatible because they all express fire energy. All of the earth signs are in harmony with each other. The same is true with all of the air and water signs. Now we need to ask ourselves a few reasonable questions. Are the fires signs in harmony with the water signs? The answer is "no" because fire and water don't mix—they are incompatible with each other. Are the earth signs compatible with the fire signs? Again, the answer is "no," because earth and fire don't work together. What about the water signs with the earth signs? Yes, they are harmonious because water and earth work in harmony. But water and air are discordant. Do the air signs go with the fire signs? Yes. Use the **Element Chart** from your appendix (A-4) to help you determine quickly whether two planets are in signs that support or frustrate each other. However, they must be within a certain distance of each other to activate the **power points**.

There are four major **power points** formed between planets that tell us whether they are functioning in a friendly or hostile manner: the **conjunction, sextile, square,** and the **trine**. Power points are areas of space that release positive or negative energy when two or more planets are related to each other in a specific way. They are determined by measuring the actual distance between the personal and impersonal planets. We will now use the **Sign Table** from your appendix to determine these power points. Let us see how these major power points are formed.

CONJUNCTION: Any impersonal planet is conjunct and harmonious with a personal planet if that personal planet is *in the same sign* and within orb (see note below) of the impersonal planet. An *exception* to this occurs when the impersonal planet is Saturn. In this case the conjunction is negative. Remember: Planets are conjunct only if they are in the same sign. The following

HOW TO CREATE PLANETARY PROFILES

examples will help you see how the conjunction is formed.

Note: An orb is the range of plus or minus 10 degrees (or less) from exact conjunction, sextile, square or trine. Do not read the pattern if the two planets are more than 10 degrees from a power point relationship with each other. Simply skip it.

The Rule: If a personal planet is frustrated by an impersonal planet in the birth chart, then a conjunction to that personal planet by any *visiting* impersonal planet or the *impersonal planet of another person* creates a negative reaction. If a personal planet is supported by an impersonal planet in the birth chart, then a conjunction to it by any visiting impersonal planet or impersonal planet of another person creates a positive reaction. However, Saturn's conjunction of a personal planet is always negative regardless of the positions of the birth planets.

Examples

→ If your Jupiter is at 10 degrees of Gemini and your Mars is at 20 degrees of Gemini, these two planets are conjunct because they are no more than 10 degrees apart and are in the same sign. Because these two planets are conjunct, they work harmoniously together and support each other. This would also be true if Mars were at 0 degree of Gemini.

→ If Jupiter is at 28 degrees of Gemini and Mars is at 3 degrees of Cancer, these planets would not be in conjunction even though they are only 5 degrees apart (count forward from 2 degrees left in Gemini to 3 degrees of Cancer, which is the next sign). This is because Mars is not in the same sign as Jupiter. Note that Mars is in a water sign, which is not compatible with Jupiter in an air sign. You would not read this pattern.

→ Uranus is at 1 degree of Aries and Mars is at 29 degrees of Pisces. (Aries follows the sign of Pisces.) Even though the impersonal planet Uranus is only two degrees away from

Mars, it is not conjunct Mars because Mars is not in the same sign as Uranus.

Don't forget to think of the Sign Table (on page A-6) as a circle of signs. This will help you realize, for example, that Aries is only one sign away from Pisces not eleven. (See Figure 1, page 98.)

Always change the word "sign" to "attitude" and it will be easier for you to understand. Remember, do not try to relate the impersonal planets to each other—relate them only to the personal planets.

SEXTILE: Any impersonal planet is sextile and therefore harmonious with a personal planet if that impersonal planet is in a compatible sign with the personal planet and is within plus or minus 10 degrees of the 60-degree power point. Remember: There is no sextile relationship if one of these planets is in a sign that is hostile or incompatible with the sign the other planet is in. Use the Element Chart from your appendix (A-4) to keep you on track.

Examples

→ If the impersonal planet Neptune is at 24 degrees of Cancer and your Venus is at 21 degrees of Virgo, these two planets are sextile. As you can see from the Element Chart, the signs Cancer and Virgo are compatible because one is water and the other is earth. Now look at the Sign Table from your appendix to get a visual picture of how this works.

Locate the sign of Cancer, which is under the fourth column of the Sign Table, and run your finger down to the 24th degree in that column where Neptune would be located. Now look at column six where the sign of Virgo is located, and run your finger down to the 21st degree where Venus would be. Now go back to Neptune at 24 degrees of Cancer and count forward from there to the 24th degree of Leo in column five. This is a distance of 30 degrees. Now go to the 24th degree of Virgo and you will see that you are 60 degrees from where Neptune is located at 24 degrees of Cancer. (Keep in mind that every sign consists of 30 degrees.) Since Venus is at 21 degrees of Virgo, it is only 3 degrees away from the exact power point of the sextile.

of column one, which is Aries, we are 120 degrees away from Neptune's position. From 20 degrees of Aries we move forward to the 29th degree, where Venus is located. This shows that Venus is only 9 degrees away from an exact trine with Neptune (120 degrees). Therefore this is a trine pattern, and because both Leo and Aries are fire signs, it is very harmonious. Don't forget that, even though this pattern is read as an "S" (sustained) in your Element Chart, it cannot be considered if the two planets are not within the 10-degree orb of an exact trine.

Do Not Read Oppositions

When two planets are in opposition, do not read their pattern. An opposition occurs when two planets are 180 degrees apart, e.g., Aries is opposite Libra, Taurus is opposite Scorpio, Gemini is opposite Sagittarius. For the sake of simplicity, this pattern is not used in this method. While there are many more power points between planets than those shown in this book, we are only using four for simplicity of interpretation: the conjunction, sextile, square and trine. These four power points will give you a solid reading without having to confront the overwhelming complexity that would arise if we included the other patterns.

Now you know how to determine if an impersonal planet supports or frustrates a personal planet. Armed with this understanding, you are ready to put together the rest of your Profile.

Your condensed chart on page 117 shows what signs your impersonal planets are in. For your convenience, I have listed these signs below. Remember that if the minutes following the degrees are less than 30, we use the lesser degree. If greater than 30 minutes, use the next higher degree.

Sign Positions for Lelia's Impersonal Planets

Jupiter (expansion/optimism) in Scorpio at 8°

Saturn (contraction/restriction) in Aquarius at 22°

Uranus (radical change/independence) in Aries at 28°

Neptune (inspiration/escape) in Virgo at 14°

Pluto (transformation/extreme pressure) in Cancer 26°

NO ONE IS A MYSTERY

The computer printout shows that your impersonal planet Saturn (♄) is in the blue-green sign of Aquarius (♒) at 22 degrees and your personal planet Venus (♀) is in the black sign of Scorpio (♏) at 25 degrees. How would you know whether Saturn supports or frustrates the planet Venus? Simply locate Saturn in column eleven in the Sign Table and count backwards to the 22nd degrees of Scorpio, which is the square power point. Because your Venus is only 3 degrees from an exact square, it is within the orb of a square with Saturn. You read this as a frustrating pattern because Saturn and Venus are in incompatible signs, which activate the square relationship.

After discovering this, you place a "post it" or marker on the page that describes the relationship of the specific impersonal and personal planet. In this case, you copy page 196, which describes Saturn's frustration of Venus. You also have Mercury and the Sun in the black sign of Scorpio; thus, Saturn also frustrates the Sun, but it is too far from Mercury to frustrate that planet. Mark Saturn's frustration of the Sun on page 192 for copying.

It is important to mention that when using the Sign Table to determine the pattern between planets, you choose the shortest distance from the impersonal planet to the personal planet. Take, for example, relating your Saturn to your Moon in Aries: With Saturn in column eleven in Aquarius, rather than count backwards ten signs (300 degrees) to Aries in the column, you can simply go forward past Pisces in the twelfth column and on to Aries at the first column. Keep in mind that the signs form a circle and you can go backwards or forwards at your convenience. (However, the planets always move counterclockwise.) Anyway, it is helpful to realize that the sign of Aquarius is not 300 degrees away from Aries—it is only 60 degrees away. If this is still unclear, refer to Figure 1 which is found in Lesson 3. Aquarius (air) and Aries (fire) are compatible, so they are in a favorable sextile relationship. Now, let us continue with your planets.

I will help you with one more example before leaving you on your own. Note that your condensed chart on page 117 shows Jupiter in Scorpio. As you can see, Jupiter supports Mercury by conjunction because they are in the same sign and only two degrees apart. Note that Jupiter also supports Mars. I will leave you to determine why. As usual, find the appropriate sections under Jupiter supports Mercury and Jupiter supports Mars, and mark them for copying.

How about Uranus? What is his relationship to your personal planets? Your condensed chart tells us that Uranus is in Aries at 28°.

Going to that position in column one of the Sign Table, notice that your Moon is in the *same sign* as Uranus and within 10 degrees of it. This means that Uranus is conjunct the Moon. Remember to consider The Rule that was given in Lesson 5 when you see a conjunction.

Complete your analysis of your impersonal planets' effects on each personal planet with Uranus, Neptune and Pluto. Then copy all the pages you have marked. You now have enough information for a basic reading of your life. But there is more!

Creating a Summary with Analysis Forms

Let's now take the material that you copied for your chart, Lelia, from the other sections of this book and we'll organize it. The same procedure will apply for all future charts. You have already compiled the various descriptions for each personal planet and copied the effects of your impersonal planets. We will go through this together so that you can see how it is done. The next step is to synthesize the information to summarize it. Use the five Analysis Forms found in the appendix that you recreated. Notice that each form shows an example of how to fill out that form. Here is an example:

Descriptions of Lelia's Personal Planets

1. **Descriptions of the Sun**

    The _____(_____) is in the _____.
    Therefore the _____ is influenced by the _____.

    Example of how to fill in the above sentence: The <u>Sun</u> (ego, survival instinct) is in the <u>black sign</u>. Therefore the <u>ego or survival instinct</u> is influenced by the <u>black sign attitude</u>. My Summary Analysis of the ego and survival instinct (the Sun) after studying the text descriptions I have compiled is. . .

    Here is an example of what you might say:

    I can see how my tendency to privacy has been reinforced by how I was treated by my father. I never realized before how much he damaged my ego. I can see now that this may be why I have always felt that I had to fight for everything I wanted. Nothing has come easy. But now I am beginning to see that I was just set up that way. Somehow I've got to find a way to feel better about

> myself, in spite of my karma with my father. Robert says I need to take more chances in relationship, but I'm really afraid of losing control. By having control, I feel like I can work from a secure place. Control is my survival.

After completing this form, attach it to the descriptions of the personal planet you have copied and are analyzing. So, you would attach the above form to the description of your Sun shown below that you copied.

Sun with a Black Sign Attitude (Scorpio)

Summary Statement

> "I am intense, possessive, and critical. I love being my own boss and need to be in control of my life and feelings. Remember this about me: Don't ever blame me for anything."

You are a person who lives in subtlety. You usually look over your territory and see what the situation is before you make a commitment. You never want to take a chance of being a fool, so you're very cautious. You certainly wouldn't go leaping into things—who would want to be as foolish as that? Your pride is deep and intense and you do not want anything to get away from you. To make sure nothing surprises you, you seek to control your world. Sometimes you feel that if you reveal too much about yourself, other people will take advantage of you. So a big lesson in your life is to learn to trust. Once you have given your trust, you can be very loyal. But you find it hard to forgive if anyone ever betrays you. In your book, betrayals are simply unforgivable. Your awareness of the subtle can be your greatest talent, because you understand what's really going on behind the scene. Some of you make great investigators, detectives, doctors, financiers, or mystics. Once your goal is set, you are very tenacious. You can express unusual powers of endurance and might even fight to the death just to prove that you will never give up. You uphold the rights of the underdog and will go out of your way to help someone who has been treated unjustly. Although open to suggestion, you tend to ignore those people who try to dictate to you. As far as you are concerned, you don't take orders. You will cooperate fully if well treated, but subservience is one thing you cannot endure. You do better as a manager, free from the controls of any direct authority. It is very important for you to do your own thing, your own way, and in your own time. Wouldn't that be nice?

Now attach the description(s) of the impersonal planets that support and frustrate this personal planet. In this case, the description is from page 192.

Saturn frustrates the Sun: Because the Sun expresses the desire to survive (the ego), negative effects of Saturn can really hinder the ego's freedom of expression. This usually results in a lack of self-confidence, as well as self-doubt and fear of pushing forward. This situation can be traced to this person's relationship to their father, mother, or to the principal authority in their childhood. This person may have to work very hard to get what they need—when they do, they will have earned it. They do not feel like anything is going to be easy and expect to put out a lot of effort for everything they achieve.

Here is a second example of how to organize the information you gathered on a personal planet, the Moon.

1. **Descriptions of the Moon**

    The _____(_____) is in the _____.
    Therefore the _____ is influenced by the _____.

    Example of how to fill in the above sentence: The <u>Moon</u> (feelings, habits, and desire for security) is in the <u>red sign</u>. Therefore the <u>habits, feelings, and desire for security</u> are influenced by the <u>red sign attitude</u>.

    My Summary Analysis of the feelings, habits, and desire for security (the Moon) after studying the text descriptions I have compiled is. . .

The Moon With a Red Sign Attitude (Aries)

Summary Statement

"I gain security from starting new things, and embracing new challenges, and I like being impulsive. I like to change my surroundings occasionally."

You gain your security and nurturing from new adventures. You love to try new things and be with people who can make quick decisions. Since these are the energies that you were associated with from birth, they are the most comfortable for you. You may have trouble finishing things because it is more important for you to start them. You are a "doer" not a "finisher." But you can inspire others to take action by taking the lead yourself. You are attracted to strong and aggressive people who are not afraid to make things happen. You are not emotionally "mushy" and seldom look back—you are more interested in what is happening now or what lies ahead of you. Your mother could be a fiery and aggressive person.

Uranus frustrates the Moon: This person could have a hair-trigger temper and surprise us with their reactions. They may explode when they are pressured to do something they don't want to do. They do not take kindly to any form of domination from others, and you will certainly hear from them if you attempt to tell them what to do. They are fiercely independent and sometimes quite volatile. As the Moon is involved here, this anger could relate to reactions to the mother or to women. Violence could result.

Pluto frustrates the Moon: This pattern presents an altogether different picture, which includes some form of emotional loss. Even though the mother may not have literally abandoned this person, they feel like she did. The person has a deep emotional fear that they will be forsaken. This is usually not conscious, yet it plays out in daily life. Therefore, with any hint or threat of loss of security, they go into a panic. Driven by fear and anxiety, they are intensely emotional and very demanding in getting their needs fulfilled.

This is the end of one portion of your analysis. Follow the same steps to complete the other forms found in your appendix: Descriptions of Mercury, Descriptions of Venus, and Descriptions of Mars.

After you have gone through all of someone's personal planets in this way, you will have a basic understanding of that person.

Lesson 6

How to Explore the Hidden Chemistry in a Relationship

As you have learned from our lesson on the "Secret Chemistry of Relationships," you can compare the planetary positions of any two people and discover how they relate to each other. To do this, you need the positions of all of their planets, which you can get from their condensed chart.

Let's say that you want to compare the relationship between your daughter and her husband. We will use a fictitious chart for each of them to protect their identities. You find out his time, date, and place of birth, and print out the condensed chart information and place it along with hers. Usually any astrological program will print out several sheets of information, but you will not need all of this for your comparison. I have selected only the condensed portion from my own computer printout that we need to illustrate the relationship between your daughter and her husband.

Let's assume that her condensed chart is on the left and his condensed chart is on the right. Here's what their fictitious charts look like.

		HERS		HIS
Sun	☉	08 ♋ 03	☉	22 ♌ 29
Moon	☽	26 ♐ 48	☽	07 ♎ 39
Mercury	☿	21 ♋ 24	☿	23 ♌ 30
Venus	♀	04 ♊ 01	♀	13 ♋ 38
Mars	♂	16 ♈ 11	♂	29 ♍ 05
Jupiter	♃	21 ♎ 56	♃	29 ♑ 38
Saturn	♄	21 ♐ 14	♄	24 ♑ 39
Uranus	♅	09 ♌ 52	♅	25 ♌ 54
Neptune	♆	02 ♏ 03	♆	08 ♏ 43
Pluto	♇	00 ♍ 21	♇	07 ♍ 19

To determine how she affects her husband, we will take *her impersonal* planets and relate them to *his personal* planets. So we will start with her Jupiter, which is her first impersonal planet. By using the Master Table to translate the symbols, you can see that her Jupiter is in Libra at 21 degrees and 56 minutes. Remember that every sign has 30 degrees and Jupiter (♃) had moved to almost the 22nd degree of Libra at the time she was born. We will round the number to 22 degrees.

Relating her first impersonal planet, Jupiter, to his first personal planet, the Sun, you can see from his readout on the right that his Sun is at 22 degrees and 29 minutes of Leo. If the minutes are more than 30, we go to the next number. Here it is 29, so we use the lesser number of 22 degrees. In this system, 60 minutes equal 1 degree. Turn to the Sign Table in your appendix and locate Jupiter's position in column 7, which is Libra. To determine the relationship of her Jupiter to her husband's Sun, count backward to the sign of Leo in column 5. This position tells us that her Jupiter is almost exactly sextile his Sun, and because Libra is air and Leo is fire, this is a favorable pattern. You will find this described on page 187 under "Jupiter supports the Sun." If these were real charts, you would mark this section for copying or simply make a list of the pages to copy later.

We next relate her Jupiter to his Moon, which is found at 7 degrees and 39 minutes of Libra. We will round off the position of his Moon to 8 degrees because 39 minutes is more than one-half of a degree. Here his Moon is in Libra and in the same sign as her Jupiter. But this is *not* a conjunction because there is more than 10 degree difference between the two planets' positions in the same sign. Subtract the 8 degrees of the Moon from the 22 degrees of the Sun = 14, which is too far. So, according to our rule of no more than 10 degrees, we do not read this pattern.

You continue with this procedure until you have compared all of her impersonal planets to her husband's personal planets (Sun, Moon, Venus, Mars and Mercury). After you have gathered all of your copied pages, you would read them thoroughly and summarize what you feel her relationship is to her husband and how she affects him by using the Analysis Forms from your appendix. As you would do in constructing an individual's Profile, use them to add your own insights to the analysis. Of course, since these charts are fictitious, you will not need to do this work to complete them.

The exception of The Rule found in Lesson 5 also applies to relationship analysis.

Obviously, the next step is to relate all of her husband's impersonal planets to all of her personal planets, following the same procedure we discussed. This analysis will tell her *how he affects her*.

The Relationship Table in the appendix (A-8 and A-9) serves as a quick reference guide, providing you a summary insight of the relationship between any potential lovers once you have determined which impersonal planets support or frustrate the personal planets of the other. The planet on the left side of each set in this table is an impersonal planet of an individual with the affected personal planet of the other to the right. We use the impersonal planets of a person because they have the greatest impact on the personal planets of the other. Under the heading "Positive Attraction Indicators" in the table, please note (as an example) that when the Neptune of one person supports the other person's Sun, they have "deep soul connections." The positive attraction indicators are all favorable because the impersonal planet of one person is either conjunct, sextile or trine the personal planet of the other. If you have determined that the attraction between you and another is negative, then you would read the Negative Attraction Indicators section. In this case, the negative pattern of Neptune to the Sun shows that they "will not support you."

How to Avoid Fatal Attractions

The question is "How can we recognize a fatal attraction so that we can avoid getting involved in one?"

Fortunately, we have the planets to guide us. Once we see how to work with the Relationship Table, we can recognize a fatal attraction immediately and avoid it altogether.

Fatal attractions are always possible when you have negative connections between you and another person. If this is the case, you would read the Negative Attraction Indicators found in the Relationship Table.

There are two types of fatal attraction that are shown by the adverse relationship of the major planets Pluto and Neptune to one or more of our personal planets Sun, Moon, Mercury, Venus, or Mars. Neptune relates to the world of illusion, deception, seduction, idealism and spirituality. Pluto relates to the world of unconscious desires, sexuality, possession, coercion, and self-transformation. The energies of these two planets arouse the most intense and the most seductive desires between the partners of any sex. Therefore, we have:

The *Pluto Types* of fatal attraction and the *Neptune Types* of fatal attraction.

Pluto Types of Fatal Attraction

The adverse relationships created by the planet Pluto relate specifically to emotional, sexual *possession* and *coercion*. When another person's Pluto relates to your Sun, Moon, Venus or Mars in a negative way, the Type A fatal attraction dominates. When Pluto in the charts of both people are related negatively to each other's Sun, Moon, Mercury, Venus or Mars, the Type B fatal attraction is present.

Type A: This is where a person is obsessed with you and makes impossible demands for you to fulfill their needs. The impulse of Pluto drives them to extract more from you than you may want to give or are capable of giving. You may find their behavior coercive and overt, because you do not have the same obsessive desire for them.

Type B: This is where you both are obsessed with each other and make impossible demands upon the relationship. You both seem to become different people when you are together. The intense sexual and emotional energy between you may turn into an addiction that would be very difficult to live with.

Neptune Types of Fatal Attraction

The adverse relationships created by the planet Neptune relate specifically to emotional, sexual *deception* and *seduction*. When another person's Neptune relates to your personal planets in a negative way, Type A fatal attraction dominates. When Neptune in the chart of each person is negatively related to the other's impersonal planets, Type B fatal attraction is possible.

Type A: This is where the other person can manipulate you emotionally or sexually to gain control over you. They will play upon your guilt and your need to be needed. It may be difficult for you to see what is happening because you may be seduced by their so-called good intentions.

Type B: This is where you both tend to deceive each other and create confusion and distrust in your relationship. You seem to depend too much on each other to explain what the relationship really means. Accusations, lies, and intrigue tend to grow like a disease and can create an impossible situation. The reliance upon each other for emotional support and sexual thrills can be based totally on an illusion. Your dreams about each other could turn into a nightmare because they are built on quicksand.

Code Red: A dangerous combination exists when both parties are possessive, coercive, deceptive and seductive. Remember, such a condition can occur when both parties' Pluto and Neptune are related negatively to each other's Sun, Moon, Mercury, Venus, or Mars. This type of relationship should be avoided with all the resistance you can muster because it is very destructive.

The Chemistry

Dear Reader:

The information in this section was used by Lelia to set up planetary profiles. It is divided into **Part 1, Descriptions of the Personal Planets in the Signs,** and **Part 2, The Effects of the Impersonal Planets**. As you follow her through the lessons, you can look up the same information that she did. Use the information in the Chemistry section and Appendix for all of your future charts. (See page A-12 on how to obtain chart information.)

Part 1

Descriptions of the Personal Planets in the Signs

THE SUN (Ego/Survival Instinct)

The Desire to Survive

The Sun gives us the desire to survive. It is outgoing and masculine in nature and rules the force behind all our creative activity. It represents authority and those in power. It is sheer energy without complication. It is strongly connected to the ego because it manifests as the desire to be alive, to survive, and to be recognized by others. Since the Sun is masculine, it is the heart of a woman. This is because the heart of a woman is a man. The Sun in a woman's chart shows the male energy she is attracted to. Its location at the moment of her birth reveals her heart nature, the man inside.

It is important for the Sun to be free of frustrations at the moment of birth, because it is our ego and sense of strength felt within. Since our Sun is the source of our life, we are very unhappy when a planet casts a shadow over it. We have to struggle for recognition, to emerge from the darkness, and to be honored for who we are. The Sun is the place inside of us that we point to when we say "Me." It leads to a most sacred place.

Sun with a Red Sign Attitude (Aries)

Summary Statement

"I am aggressive, arrogant, and adventurous. I like to try new things and want to be first. Remember this about me: Put me in charge and I'll be happy."

You were born under a very powerful color that strongly resembles fire-engine red. A red Sun imparts a very aggressive spirit and dominant attitude. (Do you love red cars?) Not only do you want to be in charge, you also want to be first. You were born with the impulse to try new things, even if it gets you in trouble. While you are not aggressive out of malice, you can stir up strong resistance against you. But it is the nature of red to stir things to action. Red hates stagnation, inactivity, or indecision. Action is a word that beats forth from your heart: To do. To conquer. To achieve. To be first. To take up the challenge and charge ahead. This is you. You are not interested in thinking and pondering. You want to be up and doing; to go over the hill and find the next adventure that will test your courage and your will to prove to yourself that you are someone to be recognized. Others may accuse you of being "a big ego" but you don't care. The adventure of being first is a joyful experience for you. You mean no harm, but you have to be there in the middle of the action to test yourself against the opposition. In fact, you go looking for opposition just to prove that you can and will meet the challenge. Sometimes, you "go where angels fear to tread" and need to learn discrimination from the Orange (Virgo) and Black (Scorpio) Signs. However, you are not prone to listening or taking advice from others, so you usually learn the hard way. But you are not a brooder. You don't sleek away into the night, lick your wounds, and feel sorry for yourself. You usually say, "To hell with it," and are off to the next adventure, leaving the past behind.

Your spirit of adventure can be an inspiration to the dullards of the world. You have the energy to make things happen and the courage to get others to follow you. Set yourself a goal and a plan and turn on your engine. You are one of the great doers of the world.

Sun with a Green Sign Attitude (Taurus)

Summary Statement

"I am tenacious, sensual, and earthy. I love money and all the good things it can buy. Remember this about me: I need to take my time and I cannot be pushed."

Green is a very earthy color. You live in a different world than that of the red Sun. You like to keep things as they are and want to take time to make your projects bear fruit. You like to latch onto something material and work with it until you have shaped it through your own tenacious desire. You don't like giving up on anything, but you need to do it in your own time—which, to others, may seem forever. But you are reliable. You are no fly-by-night. You are enduring, steadfast, loyal and productive. You are moved to find money, to create wealth, and enjoy the best restaurants of the world. Food, drinking, sex and song are dear to your heart and you want them all. You are sensual, loyal, and honor tradition. Your feet are placed solidly on the earth and you savor the green fields of opportunity that are spread out across the world. Sooner or later you will find something that works and do it for the rest of your life. However, it may take you a long time to get there. But you cannot be prodded into doing things too fast. You don't take kindly to pushing and shoving, and will resist the demands of others to meet their deadlines. In fact, you will meet no deadlines before your own time. It is said of you that the more they push you, the more you resist. You feel that they should understand that you only respond to kindness and gentle nudging. Those who place ultimatums upon your shoulders or shout in your ears will only receive the wrath of your quiet resistance, or rage, if you are pushed too far. You may be accused of being lazy, lethargic, or lounging on the couch too long. But you will spring to life if the words "money, food, or sex" are whispered into your ears.

Your tenacity of purpose and steadfast desire are helpful to people who live in the air. You are well-grounded in results. Therefore, people will consult you on practical matters when they want to know how to get something done. You are capable of showing them the direction they need to take to realize their dreams. Thank God, you have such good, common sense.

Sun with a Yellow Sign Attitude (Gemini)

Summary Statement

"I am clever, quick-witted and restless. I need to communicate and keep busy. I have a hard time finishing things. Remember this about me: I always need to do two things at once."

Your purpose is to get the words in your brain and on your tongue onto paper or into the air. You long to get your ideas across to somebody. In fact, you're always looking for someone who will listen. You want people to really understand what you know. So you have a great desire to communicate. You could be a writer, a speaker, a journalist, a newscaster, a poet or artist. Your nervous energy drives you here and there like a great yellow warbler who cannot stop in one place long enough to survey the scenery. There is not enough time for you to do everything that you want. Therefore you rarely finish what you start. Patience is not something you can live with. You are a glutton for new ideas and are always soaring higher than your wings will take you. You often tumble from this sky of inspired knowing, unable to capture your fleeting inspiration. If only you could endure the sustained fire of repetition or stay on one subject long enough to tap the depths—you would be great indeed. Yours is truly a great gift that can be harnessed by the will to complete every project that you start before you begin another one. You owe this to yourself. If you do this, you will be amazed at what you can achieve. By holding the reins of your restless mind, you can capture the inspiration that runs silently through you. You may even surprise yourself. Of course, you always need to nurture the desire to do two things at once. This is a gift that few possess. If you hold your racing mind in check, rather than letting it go in too many directions, you will become a great communicator.

You were blessed with flashes of knowing that can be uplifting to others. You can see things quickly and know how to handle situations that require instant decisions. You are very clever and function mentally faster and farther than most people. If you can harness your mind, your ideas will bring you much success and recognition. Learn to do two things well.

Sun with a Brown Sign Attitude (Cancer)

Summary Statement

"I am sensitive, nurturing and crabby. I need a home and family. I have to feel safe and secure. Remember this about me: My feelings are very personal and my moods are always changing."

Your emotions follow the Moon as she makes her monthly journey across the sky. Since the Moon weaves through a different sign (attitude) every two and a half days, your emotions seem to follow her and change just as swiftly. One day you may be the most caring, nurturing person in the world, and the next day you can appear to be very detached, as if you were completely submerged in your own feelings. You can appear to be emotionally unresponsive and seem to be on a very private journey of your own as if you did not want to be bothered. This mood seems to be related to the changing signs of the Moon. (The word "mood" is spelled like the Moon and the word Monday came from the Moon ("Moons' day"). We all have heard of "Blue Monday," a time when we leave home and turn our attention back to the world. Moon is also the mother who gives milk and nurtures the world. She feeds the family. Your emotional self is centered on the family, even though you do have your "moods." You do things that relate to the color *brown*. You can cook or bake the good things of the earth (brown bread, brownies, or hot chocolate) or work with the land and property to make a secure place for your brood. Like a brown squirrel who stores up food for winter, you want your pantry always full of good food for a rainy day. The home is truly your castle.

You are loyal to your nest and will fight to sustain the traditional values of your forefathers. Your family is your rock, your piece of the world, and you will protect them with all your strength. You have a gift for helping others feel at home. You hate to see people suffer the loss of food or shelter and will reach out to help them. Whether male or female, you will always be the great mother. When others need food or shelter, you will awaken from your self-absorbed mood and come running.

Sun with a Gold Sign Attitude (Leo)

Summary Statement

"I am proud, creative and romantic. I like being at the center of attention and have to be in charge. Remember this about me: I need to be treated with respect."

You are very proud and want to be honored for who you are. Who are you? You are aware of being full of life and energy. You sense a strong presence of self in your body. Menial jobs or subservient positions are intolerable to your proud spirit. You can be bossy and domineering because your male self is very strong. Therefore you tend to "lord" it over others. You consider yourself a very special person and will not take kindly to people who treat you otherwise. You love to express love and generosity. Small minds disturb you and can be "a thorn in your paw." You are full of vital energy and are a life-supporting and life-giving person. You can be lordly, queenly, kingly and never think small. You want to live on a grand scale and desire to outweigh or outshine others. After all, you are the Sun, the center of all life. Why shouldn't you be treated as a unique individual? After all, your very presence should be felt as a gift to those around you. You expect to be recognized for who you are, a person with a great lineage, an enduring clan. If you go unnoticed or unrecognized, you will sulk, withdraw and show your claws. This is an insult. An honored look of appreciation will make you purr—you are easily flattered. You will pay back adoration with generosity of energy and money if you have deep pockets. But above all, the king or queen must be treated with true respect.

Sun with an Orange Sign Attitude (Virgo)

Summary Statement

"I am helpful, picky and efficient. I love a job well done and am very hard on myself. Remember this about me: I really think everything should be done right."

You are born with a very practical eye. Other people think you have it together, but you never feel that you do. "Neat," "proper," "efficient," "helpful," "dutiful" and "organized" are words you get excited about. But why are you so hard on yourself? Nobody is perfect. Nothing is ever really right. Everything needs to be corrected and done skillfully. But where is the emotion? The feeling? The heart? Are efficiency, order and perfection more important than human relationships? Too many planets in this sign can lead to obsession with perfection at the risk of losing feeling. Nevertheless, to you, the form is the thing. Sometimes you may wonder over such things as a staple. Should it be inserted horizontally or vertically in a document. You seem to be in search of a need to fulfill. Service could be your middle name. Order is your song. You sing it night and day. You love the song of birds and the sound of animals, plants and little things. Sometimes it helps to just look up at the sky and lose touch with the endless trivia that can bury your heart. Feeling and relationship can balance out your need for perfection. Seek to hold hands, speak words of love and forgive those who are not in search of perfection. Forgive yourself, too, for falling short of an ideal that is seldom attained. No one knows better than you do that nothing is ever totally right. Still, you won't stop trying.

Sun with a White Sign Attitude (Libra)

Summary Statement

"I am social, artistic and indecisive. I love being with people and want harmony and beauty in my relationships. Remember this about me: I don't like taking sides."

You are drawn to the beautiful, the artistic, the just, the fair, and the ideal loving situation, because this is the way you envision yourself in your heart. But there is some tendency to pretend that everything is perfectly all right even when the evidence shows otherwise. One reason for the distortion is that you hate discord and conflict. You are motivated to look at opposing viewpoints and seek to bring them into balance. It is difficult for you to stick to one side of an issue, because you feel the other side could be right. You can usually find a case for both. But this tendency can cause problems in relationship because you don't really seem to take a strong stand for anything. This wavering can lead others to break off with you. The group, belonging, and sharing with others are of primary importance to you. Solitude is not something you can live with unless you are engrossed in the creative act of making music, designing, decorating, writing or painting. Beauty and harmony are very necessary to your sense of well-being. If these elements are missing in your life, you can become miserable. You seek the middle path, which may be strewn with broken dreams, because real treasures are found in deeper places. You will often settle for a false harmony bought at the price of convenience. Take care not to compromise everything or your life will become a meaningless existence. Seek peace and harmony through sound and color, and come to realize that some things really are black and some things really are white.

Sun with a Black Sign Attitude (Scorpio)

Summary Statement

"I am intense, possessive and critical. I love being my own boss and need to be in control of my life and feelings. Remember this about me: Don't ever blame me for anything."

You are a person who lives in subtlety. You usually look over your territory and see what the situation is before you make a commitment. You never want to take a chance of being a fool, so you're very cautious. You certainly wouldn't go leaping into things—who would want to be as foolish as that? Your pride is deep and intense, and you do not want anything to get away from you. To make sure nothing surprises you, you seek to control your world. Sometimes you feel that if you reveal too much about yourself, other people will take advantage of you. So a big lesson in your life is to learn to trust. Once you have given your trust, you can be very loyal. But you find it hard to forgive if anyone ever betrays you. In your book, betrayals are simply unforgivable. Your awareness of the subtle can be your greatest talent, because you understand what's really going on behind the scene. Some of you make great investigators, detectives, doctors, financiers, or mystics. Once your goal is set, you are very tenacious. You can express unusual powers of endurance and might even fight to the death just to prove that you will never give up. You uphold the rights of the underdog and will go out of your way to help someone who has been treated unjustly. Although open to suggestions, you tend to ignore those people who try to dictate to you. As far as you are concerned, you don't take orders. You will cooperate fully if well treated, but subservience is one thing you hate and want no part of. You do better as a manager, free from the controls of any direct authority. It is very important for you to do your own thing, your own way, and in your own time. Wouldn't that be nice?

Sun with a Blue Sign Attitude (Sagittarius)

Summary Statement

"I am straightforward, blunt and restless. I love to travel and look for new adventures just over the mountain. Remember this about me: I hate dishonesty."

With the heart of an adventurer, you seek and love truth and honesty. You have an intense aversion to weakness because you are forthright, speak your mind, work hard and play hard. Yours is energy for action. You love to travel and explore distant countries and foreign cultures. Learning, education, publishing, law and philosophy interest you. You have a restless spirit. You're not much for sitting, dreaming and pondering. You are a "now" person who responds to immediate action and activity. You probably love to walk and you find sports challenging, stimulating and entertaining. You could be a lawyer simply looking for facts. If you are intuitively advanced, you will look for understanding and probe the greater mysteries of life. You will search far and wide for the meaning of life and explore the spiritual realms through meditation and contemplation. Never pretentious and hating hypocrisy, you have a strong taste for telling it like it is—you don't mince words. Sometimes this throws you into hot water, but somehow you come out all right. Others would say "It was an honest mistake." With you, what we see is what we get. We always know where we stand with you. You could be foolish at times, taking unnecessary risks just to prove that you can go the farthest the fastest. You are basically fearless—never bowing to others as if they were superior: To you, that's just not right. You will fight for your principles—for honor and for truth.

Sun with a Gray Sign Attitude (Capricorn)

Summary Statement

"I am serious, dedicated and sensible. I love tradition and am ambitious to find my place in the world. Remember this about me: I prefer being the leader."

This is the attitude of the father archetype, an earthly energy. It gives practical and pragmatic tendencies. "If I can't use it, throw it away." This is the symbol of the goat who loves to "go at" things that are a challenge. You don't back down easily and are often quite firm in your convictions. The group is more important than the individual, and if an individual offends or is irresponsible toward the group, company or association, you are willing to act ruthlessly to get rid of him. You identify with tradition, ambition, achievement, social status and power. You honor integrity and responsibility and are very conscientious of the work at hand. This influence tends to make you want to uphold the norm. You try to build on what went before but usually within the same mold. There may be a strong attachment to the father or memories of an austere childhood where you were expected to handle responsibilities that were beyond your maturity. If this is the case, you don't expect things to be given to you. You probably feel that you have to earn everything you get. You are the one person who knows that you don't get something for nothing.

You could use a few thousand dances to lighten your spirit. Reality really is not always just what you see in front of you. You consider people who live on the edge to be quiet foolish. That would be risking too much and very impractical. You love parameters, rules, regulations, law, propriety and the status quo. You like to deal in certainty. But you need humor and lighthearted people around you to help you get more into your feelings. After all, there is more to life than just hard work and duty. You really need to listen twice to those people who tell you, "Lighten up."

Sun with a Blue-Green Sign Attitude (Aquarius)

Summary Statement

"I am opinionated, cool and detached. I love my friends, but I love my freedom most of all. Remember this about me: I don't like being attached to anyone."

You are unpredictable—a free spirit who follows his own drumbeat. You may not possess a very deep emotional nature. You are mostly interested in friendship and the thrill of exploring new possibilities in science, technology, sex and relationships. It is always the future that holds the greatest promise for you, so you try to make sure that your options remain open for you to take advantage of any new opportunities. It is probably true to say that you are the one person who does not look back. If you do, then it is probably only briefly. The next experience, relationship, goal or possibility is what holds your interest. You have no sentimentality or gushy feelings. Everything is rather cut and dried—it either is or it isn't, there is not much in between. You are extremely honest and sometimes brutally frank and cruel without meaning to be. You might speak abruptly without discrimination and offend those close to you. You cannot endure any demands or restrictions that others may try to press upon you. It is difficult to form lasting bonds with one person because of your need to remain free, detached and uncommitted. You like your friends but you don't want to be bound to them. Others often find you very magnetic and attractive, challenging, exciting and interesting, but too often unreachable. You may have to get used to people not understanding you. They may consider you unreliable and unpredictable. Some people may think that your actions and reactions are "off the wall," as if there is no logic to how you live your life. But you'll always do your own thing, anyway. If you can be an individual who has created something special in the world, you will probably be happy. You place a high premium on being your own person, not attached to anyone.

Sun with a Purple Sign Attitude (Pisces)

Summary Statement

"I am sensual, sentimental and sacrificial. I feel deeply about other people's pain and have a need to escape from the world. Remember this about me: I have a need to help others."

As they say, "deep as the ocean." That's you. Mysterious, sensuous and sensitive. But you carry so much on your shoulders. You are often burdened by a past that you know nothing about. There is a natural trigger of guilt that can go off at any time inside you. Must you always help everybody who asks for it? Are you responsible for the whole world? Sometimes it does seem so. Sometimes you really feel like a misplaced person, like you don't really belong here. You would prefer to live in your dreams, your art, your romance or in your sanctuary. But you can find your place in these realms. Great writers and musicians have had this sign. You soar in the art and film world where you can find a place to spread your wings and be your creative, imaginative self. You can even show great saintly qualities through your service to others. If you don't find your niche here, you could drink yourself into an illusion. In fact, you don't really like it here on earth. You would rather escape. Sometimes the world as it is with all of its demands and responsibilities just seems too much for you. Then escape becomes your song. Be careful, though. Having gained a physical body, you need to take care of everything that the world requires of you. You probably know it won't just go away. If you must escape, make your dreams produce solid results in the material world and you can be happy.

THE DIFFERENCES BETWEEN THE MOON AND VENUS

It is important to understand the differences between the Moon and Venus, because their descriptions sound similar. The Moon is the great mother, giver of the milk. Venus is the goddess of the feminine—she rules all that is beautiful, delicate, refined, as well as love and relationships. The Moon is a man's heart and Venus is his feminine ideal. Both reveal the kind of woman he needs and desires. Without these very human planets, he would have no food or love.

A woman's feminine self is shown by Venus and the Moon. While the Moon relates to the mother, Venus relates to feelings of self-worth. The Moon and Venus work closely together because they show our feelings and work to sustain us on earth. They are feminine energies because they embody nurturing, sustaining, preserving, caring, and relating. These two planets are more externalized in a woman and internalized in a man. However, they show the emotional relationship to the mother in both sexes. These two planets hold the key to a man's feminine self. The Moon is his heart and Venus is the woman he desires or idealizes.

THE MOON (Feelings/Habits)

Desire for Security

Mother Moon is the great nourisher, the food-giver. She owns the cookie jar. Her position in the sky at the moment of our birth shows where we seek security and nurturing. She reveals our relationship to our mother, our family, where we look to be protected and sustained, and our emotional response to others. Because the Moon is a man's heart, its sign position shows the kind of woman he looks to for emotional nurturing.

The Moon rules the stomach, home, family, mother, and real estate, and it relates to emotional and material comfort. Her daily motion through the sky shows the general mood of the people on earth any given day. She is very important for predicting the outcome of an event or enterprise.

The Moon with a Red Sign Attitude (Aries)

Summary Statement

"I gain security from starting new things, embracing new challenges, and I like being impulsive. I like to change my surroundings occasionally."

You gain your security and nurturing from new adventures. You love to try new things and be with people who can make quick decisions. Since these are the energies that you were associated with from birth, they are the most comfortable for you. You may have trouble finishing things because it is more important for you to start them. You are a "doer" not a "finisher." But you can inspire others to take action by taking the lead yourself. You are attracted to strong and aggressive people who are not afraid to make things happen. You are not emotionally "mushy" and seldom look back—you are more interested in what is happening now or what lies ahead of you. Your mother could be a fiery and aggressive person.

The Moon with the Green Sign Attitude (Taurus)

Summary Statement

"I feel nurtured and sustained by plenty of money, good food and great sex. I like to keep a comfortable home with plenty of everything I need."

Taurus is a very green earth energy. If your Moon is here you have a strong practical sense and are probably good at handling money. You love the good things of the earth. Usually you can cook well, create a garden or build a house. You need time and space to move around because you cannot be pushed into anything. It is best to coax you into something—you are more likely to respond to gentle nudging. You are fixed and stubborn but loyal in your feelings to your mate, home and family. You are also very sensuous and love to touch, unless some other planetary pattern interferes with this. You find it hard to forsake your mate even if your relationship is not working.

Sometimes it will be like having to pry open a clam with a knife just to get you to talk about your feelings. This seems to be due to the natural stubbornness of the Taurus nature. People should not push you or make any kind of authoritative demands. If people want your help, they need to ask and suggest. Being vulnerable is not easy for you but you can show your love in many ways. Was your mother into finances?

The Moon with the Yellow Sign Attitude (Gemini)

Summary Statement

"I feel nurtured by good books, great ideas, living in two places at once, and having lots of choices. I really prefer two bedrooms."

Here the Moon is expressed through the mental world, moving like a swift warbler, with restless intellectual habits. There is always a need to be in two places at once, to do more than two things at a time, an impatience for detail, distaste for finishing long projects, and a tendency toward being emotionally indecisive. Here, the feelings tend to be in the head unless other planets are in water energies that express more emotions connected to the heart. There is a natural emotional detachment.

You seek comfort in new techniques, new methods, and change in your surroundings. You love the feeling of moving around and are attracted to change. You may even like to live or sleep in two places, going back and forth whenever you feel like it. Your mother could be a teacher or writer.

The Moon with the Brown Sign Attitude (Cancer)

Summary Statement

"I feel nurtured by my home, my family, and money in the bank for a rainy day. My home gives the feeling of comfort and security."

Here the Moon is in a very emotional position that lends fluctuations to the emotions. There can be marked mood changes and sensitivity to the environment. Since the Moon changes to a different sign every two and a half days, a person born with their Moon here seem to reflect these changes in their attitude. With women in particular, there seems to be a deep attunement to the lunar cycle which reflects emotional withdrawal from others during the menstrual cycle. In general, people with the Moon here tend to be moody.

You are a certainly a homebody. A man with his Moon in Cancer can be strongly attached to his mother and place his own wife in a mother role. You love the family, your hearth, and a cupboard full of goodies to feed those in need, and your sensitivity extends to other people's feelings as well as your own. You could cry in a moment, as emotions are full within you. You can be possessive and overly motherly to those who look to you as the mother hen. Men with this position tend to be homebodies and even motherly themselves. Your mother could be a good cook.

The Moon with the Gold Sign Attitude (Leo)

Summary Statement

"I feel nurtured by attention from others, love experiences, being creative, and expressing myself emotionally. I like a warm and loving family with a big heart."

This attitude gives an intense and dramatic expression to the Moon. There is usually a strong desire for romance, creativity, and the arts. You love to create an emotional impact on others while being at the center of attention. While others may avoid the limelight, you love to be at the center of the action. Of course this could be nullified if your Moon is "afflicted" by unfriendly planets. In general, you are very positive and can't stand moody or depressing people. In fact, you are usually the one who lifts other people's spirit because you always see hope and light where other people do not. You love expressing the energy of life and inspiring people to do their best. You are often found at the theater, on stage, or in the movies. You have a deep love nature and enjoy the whole realm of romance. You could be strongly drawn to acting or music because these areas provide you with a channel for creative self-expression. One way or the other, you are going to find ways to get noticed. Your mother could be a very dramatic person and very bighearted.

The Moon with the Orange Sign Attitude (Virgo)

Summary Statement

"I am nurtured and sustained by order, perfection, beauty and helping others. I prefer a home that is in perfect order."

Here the Moon falls into a box where the feelings are kept in a neat and tidy place. Emotions are kept under control due to an overt need to maintain order, efficiency, accuracy and perfection. The habits are particular, patient, and show great capacity for boring and tedious work. You can endure long hours of repetitive endeavors as if you had a machine in the back of your brain that could go on forever. The problem with this is that the feelings are mentalized—not really felt. Romantic feelings may be considered "mush." Let us hope that other parts of the nature can balance out this passion for efficiency with passion for love.

You may have trouble knowing your feelings and expressing your emotions. You are usually a very responsible and caring person who knows how to carry out duties effectively. But why not let your life hang loose a little more? A lot can be discovered by not knowing so much ahead of time. You could be critical of women, or have a mother who is very critical.

The Moon with the White Sign Attitude (Libra)

Summary Statement

"I am nurtured and sustained by harmonious surroundings, beautiful music and loving friends. I have a special talent for making the home beautiful."

Libra is an attitude that draws us toward relationship and cooperation with others. You like to be with people and to be known as a person who is very friendly and helpful to others. People tend to like you because you know how to charm them and get them to like you. You are interested in the beautiful. A pleasant, colorful atmosphere in your home is very important to you and you seek harmony with everything you relate to. You could assist women in making their home beautiful because you have a natural attraction for making your nest pleasant and congenial. You could be the person to choose to set up a great party because you are a people person. There is something special about how you decorate your place. Others will tend to admire this gift and even seek you out to do this kind of work for them. Your mother could be a beautiful woman or someone in art, design or fashion.

The Moon with the Black Sign Attitude (Scorpio)

Summary Statement

"I desire to be in control of my world, intensely sexual, nurtured and sustained by a loyal lover."

Here the Moon is in the mysterious black sign. What we see is not what we get. You are a "still water runs deep" person. Your inner life is not well known by others and you like to keep it that way. You are extremely sensitive to accusation or blame. No one should ever point their finger at you if they wish to remain your friend. Once you are hurt, you do not forgive easily and you may look for a way to get even. Your private life is very important to you, which is why you usually have many secrets. You like to probe into the causes of things and have a strong awareness of people's hidden motives. You could be a researcher, detective, psychologist or mystic. You are not easy to know. Therefore your greatest challenge will be to practice the willingness to be known, because this is the true path to intimacy. Your mother probably had secrets that she kept hidden from you.

The Moon with the Blue Sign Attitude (Sagittarius)

Summary Statement

"I am nurtured by the outdoors, far away places and the feeling of traveling. I have fast emotional reactions. I like to have an RV and am at home wherever I go."

This blue sign lends a fiery impulse to the emotions. You have a great interest in mobility. Traveling and wandering are very strong habits of yours. You have a strong need for adventure, to find out what is beyond the horizon, to connect with distant lands, people and foreign cultures.

You could be very interested in spiritual matters, law, writing, publishing and teaching. You are usually a very open person emotionally, uncomplicated and forthright. You despise deception and could never keep a secret. Although you may not be conscious of it, you are seeking to understand the greater picture of your life; you are in search of meaning. Some people may say you are never home, but you tend to be at home wherever you are. Your mother could be religious, a publisher or teacher. She is probably very forthright and honest.

The Moon with the Gray Sign Attitude (Capricorn)

Summary Statement

"I am nurtured by my family, tradition, ancestors and my standing in the world. My home is like an anchor in the community. I like to preserve the past there."

Your feelings are cooled by this position. They are colored with ambition. You tend to be serious and carry that mood with you wherever you go. This indicates that you were conditioned by an austere childhood—at least emotionally. Your feelings may be predictable because they function within the boundaries of what is the proper and correct thing to do. You need to be around people who are lighthearted to help you laugh at yourself and keep up your spirits. But you tend to associate with business people or people who are older. You are usually a very responsible person and feel that duty is a very important principle to follow. You are usually honest and forthright about your feelings because you wear no illusions about your emotional self. All the fluff is removed from your expectations—your outlook toward your world is practical and realistic. Sentimentality is certainly not in your vocabulary, but you could use some intimate strokes to warm up your insides. Your mother may be a business woman who seldom shows much warmth through her feelings.

The Moon with the Blue-Green Sign Attitude (Aquarius)

Summary Statement

"I am nurtured by my friends, new experiences and the unexpected. I like to invite unusual people to my home. It may seem like an eccentric place to other people."

This blue-green sign is full of surprises, brilliance and the unusual. Your emotions have a marked difference from the rest of your nature—unless, of course, you have a lot of other planets in this same sign. This is a radical energy and quite unpredictable. Therefore, your emotional reactions will always surprise people—sometimes even you. Certainly your habits are unpredictable. You recognize the rights of others to be free and certainly demand that for yourself. You love living on the edge of experience, open to new influences if they offer you an opportunity to discover something new. Your friends may complain that you are too detached emotionally, that you don't seem connected to others with your feelings. Your mother is possibly very emotionally detached from you, more like your friend than motherly.

The Moon with the Purple Sign Attitude (Pisces)

Summary Statement

"I am nurtured by caring for others, escaping into my dreams, and finding peak experiences that fit my inspirations. My home is my place of escape."

Here, your habits and feelings wander in the world of imagination, dreams, and tears. Where other people may fall short in emotions, you overflow and can be quickly moved to tears. You are in tune with the suffering in the world and may carry a deep sense of sorrow or loss without knowing why. Trying to help fulfill the needs of others might be a way that you try to squash your own needs. Remember with your great capacity to care for and to love others to feel enough for yourself. It may take you some time to accept that your needs and self-nurturing are also important. Try not to overdo your sympathy; you could drain your own energy and be used and abused if you don't draw the line on the side of safety. You have a far-reaching imagination and the power to create an effect or illusion. You could act, dance, or write. The best way to use your intuitive and psychic talents are in the arts. Avoid alcohol or mind-expanding stimulants because you could open psychic doors that would be hard to close. If you have a need to escape this "cruel world," then do so through creative self-expression. You may come from a family where you had to take care of someone—possibly your mother. Your mother may be a martyr, an artist, or inclined to drink.

MERCURY (Thinking/Communication)

The Desire to Think

Mercury is a planet that shows us how we think and how we communicate. It seeks to communicate what the ego needs to say, write or express. Since Mercury is very close to the Sun, the desire to survive, it is closely connected to the ego. Mercury seeks to organize information and help fulfill the ego's purpose. The Greek god Mercury was the "messenger of the gods." It seeks to connect the desires of the other planets and translates their feelings and impulses across to others. Mercury is the planet of speech, thought and logic. It connects one part of our psyche with another through these processes. Its primary function is to make sense out of what it receives from the planetary energies connected to it. If you wish to know what a person thinks about, simply look at the sign position of their Mercury and look up the meaning of that sign in this book. The impersonal planets seem to have protocol or dominance over these personal planets. Favorable energies from other planets enhance the communication skills between people; unfavorable energies obstruct them.

DESCRIPTIONS OF THE PERSONAL PLANETS IN THE SIGNS

Mercury with the Red Sign Attitude (Aries)

Summary Statement

"I think fast. My mind is on fire. I sometimes wear myself out with so many ideas firing away in my brain. I sometimes bite off more than I can chew."

As you can see from previous descriptions, the fire of the Aries sign can excite the mind. The person with this placement could have a mind that runs like a motor with the switch always on. The mind works fast and constantly—always thinking, always thinking, until it tumbles into exhaustion. A person with this position may have headaches because their mind is often on fire and their brain can get overheated. They need to keep a cool head and a calm mind. They can be blunt and inconsiderate in their speech because they are so quick to react. They often do not take time to consider the consequences of their words. This is a mind of great enthusiasm and it has the potential to be very creative, but the fire needs to be harnessed. They usually communicate well with people who have fire and air energies in their nature: Gemini, Leo, Libra, Sagittarius, and Aquarius.

Mercury with the Green Sign Attitude (Taurus)

Summary Statement

"I think slowly because I need time to work out my projects. Don't push me for a decision—I will only resist you. They say my mind is slow and hard to change."

Here Mercury is influenced by the earthly attitude of Taurus. The emphasis is on finances, banking, stock market, commodities, trading and wealth. The mind is in a sign that is just the opposite of the effect of Aries. The mental functions are very slow, methodical, deliberate and predictable. A person with this placement needs to have a lot of freedom to do their own work in their own time. They cannot be pushed to "get the report out." They will get it done, but they need a lot of time on their own. These people tend to be good researchers because they do not miss details, and they are excellent builders. They love form and structure and may spend hours going over an idea persistently until it bears fruit. They are very tenacious mentally and communicate well with the earth and water energies of Cancer, Virgo, Scorpio, Capricorn and Pisces.

Mercury with the Yellow Sign Attitude (Gemini)

Summary Statement

"I think extremely fast and can handle two things at once. It is hard for me to finish projects because I get bored so easily. Sometimes I get confused with too many options."

In this yellow sign, Mercury truly races in the head. This person is very mental, quick-witted, silver-tongued, and clever as a crow. They are in the realm of air, living in the lofty space of ideas and sometimes in the depth of clever evasion from the truth. They can be double-minded, double-tongued (or forked tongue, as the Indians used to say), and a weaver of tales. To get out of a fix, they will tell little lies of convenience. They are always seeking harmony but have so much interest in so many things that they have a hard time living up to promises to themselves as well as to others. They can come forth with the most clever and bright ideas but may have a difficult time using them because they get bored too easily and therefore fail to capitalize on them. Their greatest lesson is to learn to finish the projects they start, which they can learn this from the Mercury-in-Taurus people. They communicate very well with the air and fire energies of Aries, Leo, Libra, Sagittarius and Aquarius.

Mercury with the Brown Sign Attitude (Cancer)

Summary Statement

"I think with my feelings. Therefore, my thoughts are influenced by my emotions. Objectivity is hard for me. I concentrate on security. They say my desires are influenced too much by my feelings."

Here the mind falls into water, which is the realm of feeling and mood changes. The thought process are more psychic or intuitive than logical. Their thinking is centered on the home, family and security. They can be good at selling any products that have to with the home, family or real estate because they naturally understand the needs of parents and home buyers. Having given a great deal of thought to these areas, they are well qualified to persuade others to their choice. They may have interests in architecture, carpentry, landscaping, baking, or managing a restaurant. Since their mind is centered on the home, they know how to plan good meals, feed everyone well, and make them feel comfortable and secure. They like the whole idea of mothering, nurturing, and being nurtured. They can express some crabby or picky attitudes at times because of the changing moods of their thought processes. They usually communicate well with the water and earth energies of Scorpio, Pisces, Taurus, Virgo and Capricorn.

Mercury with the Gold Sign Attitude (Leo)

Summary Statement

"I think proudly, creatively and artistically, and I like to be honored for my ideas. I have a stubborn mind and I don't like to change my opinions. I really do feel that my ideas are the best."

Leo imparts the attitude of importance and being right. The mental attitude is usually one of superiority and basic dominance. There is a great deal of mental pride: the person often describes his or her achievements as if the world revolved around them. This could be described as mental arrogance. But behind this arrogance is a basic insecurity. If this person does not get to keep the center stage, you may find them sulking or refusing to participate in any joint effort. They feel their ideas are of great importance and tenaciously cling to them. However, they can speak with great eloquence and be very persuasive because of the energy that radiates from their speech. Their voice can persuade the listener to great emotion. This could be the golden-tongued orator.

They may be very good at theatrical performances, art, music, radio or television. They think about love affairs and emotional expressions of the heart, but the attention and thrill of an affair could be more important than real love. They can appear to be very romantic, spinning words like fine silk, but depth of intimacy may be lacking. They usually communicate well with Aquarius, Gemini, Sagittarius, Aries and Libra.

Mercury with the Orange Sign Attitude (Virgo)

Summary Statement

"I think in detail. I am thoughtful, particular, efficient, and know how to organize my life. I can't stand disorder. I like to do things right. They say I'm too nit-picky."

Mercury is very much at home in this earthy field because it is strongly influenced by the tendency to think critically. The mind is usually absorbed in detailing, organizing, discarding, weighing and analyzing in the pursuit of the perfect method. Of course the perfect method is never reached—but the process goes on anyway. Where others may make foolish and poorly timed decisions, this person has already thought everything through. They seem to have a sixth sense of how to function best in any practical endeavor. Therefore, they can be excellent at law, chemistry, medicine, or other fields that require detailed analysis. They are often highly intelligent. Sometimes they lose sight of the bigger picture and can be critical to a fault. Generally, they will fuss unduly over any little mistake on their documents or become very upset if something is out of place. They usually like to help other people solve problems because they have a deep need to be of service, and if approached from this angle, they will be the first to volunteer. They are usually very dependable and will "get the job done." They communicate well with Capricorn, Taurus, Scorpio, Pisces and Cancer signs.

Mercury with the White Sign Attitude (Libra)

Summary Statement

"I think in terms of harmony, cooperation and sharing. I like to express artistic ideas. I often have trouble making decisions because my mind vacillates."

The energy of Libra is expressed in working with opposites. Mercury here finds itself expressing beautiful words and sounds, and seeking harmonious relationships. Songs may be created and sung with great emotion. Peace and harmony between two opposing parties may be achieved through the convincing words of a Mercury in Libra, or a great romantic novel may touch the hearts of dreamers everywhere. They may be effective marriage counselors because of an ability to see both sides. Intensely interested in the group and its joint achievement, they can be effective at public relations or in handling large gatherings. Although there is a need to find harmony with everyone and everything, the search is not always successful because a basic idealism or pretense may not match reality. They can also play both ends against the middle and be accused of being two-faced. Some types can be tormented by having to make decisions, if they have to take a stand for one side over another—a very difficult position for a Mercury-in-Libra person to accept. The energy fields of Gemini, Aquarius, Leo, Sagittarius and Aries are most harmonious with their mind.

Mercury with the Black Sign Attitude (Scorpio)

Summary Statement

"I think deeply, secretively, and I like to be in control of my own ideas. I like to work out my plans in solitude and make independent decisions. They say I have a sarcastic tongue."

You may think that with their Mercury in a water sign, this person should be very flexible, because water is pliable and adaptable to its environment—but this water sign is frozen, ice. Therefore the mind is fixed and tenacious in its opinions and almost impossible to change once the individual has accepted an idea as truth. To be wrong is something this person would almost never admit. True humility is difficult. There seems to be a deep abiding pride in whatever ideas they hold on to, as if those ideas were sacred and etched in stone. This is a shrewd, deep and penetrating mind that knows how to solve problems. The person with this Mercury can be a good detective, resolve difficult situations, and find the answers to subtle mysteries. Few things in human nature escape their attention, and they often see from a much deeper level than others. They may be silent in the expression of their opinions—appearing to know nothing—but one day they may cut through our defenses and pinpoint a trait in us that we never knew we possessed. If you never blame them or accuse them of anything, you will have their abiding loyalty. In general, they communicate well with Pisces, Taurus, Capricorn, Cancer and Virgo signs.

Mercury with the Blue Sign Attitude (Sagittarius)

Summary Statement

"I think deeply and seek to understand the meaning of life. I will often skip the details to get the bigger picture. They say that my speech is sometimes too blunt."

Here the mind is full of the fire of adventure, always reaching out across the horizon to another place. This mind may utter prophetic truths or talk endlessly about the daily adventures of life. It is an expansive mind that is interested in principles and has no patience for details—it is only interested in the larger picture, the ultimate meaning. The mind may be focused on law because of some deep need to find justice for others or to enjoy the game. This is a forthright mind not in search of subtlety. It holds on strongly to truth. This person is usually a fair and honest thinker and could rarely be deceptive. However there is sometimes an unkind streak in the words they utter; not by intent, but through brutal honesty about the way they see things. You may not like what they say, but you are never in doubt as to where they stand. At times they seem totally fearless, and they will stand up to anyone. They could be engaged in publishing, writing, teaching, law or philosophy. They have favorable communications with Aries, Leo, Gemini, Aquarius and Libra signs.

Mercury with the Gray Sign Attitude (Capricorn)

Summary Statement

"I think in practical terms and about what can be explained. I am mostly interested in the task at hand and the bottom line. They say I have a conservative mind."

The realm of Capricorn is sensible, practical and useful. A Mercury here is primarily interested in the facts: what is provable by science and practical experience. The mind functions in the realm of practical materialism. This is a very serious mind with a basic understanding of its own gravity. This person seeks to find humor in things. They know they need to "lighten up," but they are conditioned to think seriously. Humor is their best medicine. They usually are good thinkers in business matters because they are very realistic and interested mostly in the bottom line: What are the true results? If it doesn't work, throw it away, or use it for something else. They need to cultivate some mysticism because they tend to get too locked in to the factual or material considerations of daily existence. They usually adhere to tradition and what went before them and are strong believers in the motto "If it ain't broke, don't fix it." They usually communicate well with Taurus, Virgo, Cancer, Scorpio and Pisces signs.

Mercury with the Blue-Green Sign Attitude (Aquarius)

Summary Statement

"I think about the unusual and unpredictable because I have a desire to explore the edge of experience. I like to solve unique problems and go my own way. Some people think I am mentally arrogant."

Here is a very independent mind, usually full of original insights. They always seek the different, the unusual and the creative. This is a very bright mind full of awareness and unique ideas. They look beyond the obvious and can present a perspective no one else ever conceived. They are often found to be very musical and express a world of harmonies no one has ever heard before. A search through the lives of the greatest creators would no doubt show us that many of them had Mercury in Aquarius. Although usually very smart, Aquarian Mercury people tend to express their awareness arrogantly. At times, their speech can be so blunt, impersonal and unfeeling that they cause others to avoid them. Because of this, they often fail to gain cooperation from their friends. This can be quite disappointing to them because their friends are very important to them. However, they do not hang around licking any wounds. They are usually off to the next adventure—they have a great capacity for mental detachment. Aries, Gemini, Leo, Libra and Sagittarius signs can usually communicate well with them.

Mercury with the Purple Sign Attitude (Pisces)

Summary Statement

"I do not think logically. I think with my feelings and am very psychic. My mind often wanders off into fantasy and imagination. Sometimes I can read other people's thoughts. They say I seem to be spaced out."

Here the mind is absorbed in an ocean of sensing. This is not a linear or logical thinking mind. It is a very psychic and highly intuitive mind. The person with this Mercury needs to reach their conclusions through reliable hunches. Their mind can travel to the depths of art, beauty, fantasy, imagination or clairvoyance. They sense and feel the subtle influences around them. They are very attuned to these psychic subtleties, often reading people's thoughts and feelings without knowing how they do this. It is important to understand that they do not do this through reasoning, but through intuition or actually hearing or seeing these impressions from within. They will sometimes say, "He is going to call me," and the phone will ring with that person on the other end of the line. The person with this Mercury needs to protect himself from negative influences or from people who think negatively, because they will absorb those thoughts and think that they are their own. They should surround themselves with positive and beautiful surroundings so that they are free to sense their own inner world without outside influences. They need to practice separating their thoughts from the thoughts of other people. They seem to communicate best with Cancer, Scorpio, Taurus, Capricorn and Virgo signs.

THE DIFFERENCES BETWEEN VENUS AND MARS

Just as the Sun and Moon relate to the father and mother, strength and nurturing—the heart of the woman and the heart of the man — Venus and Mars relate to our feminine and masculine sexuality. While both men and women have Venus and Mars energies in their nature, these energies are expressed differently in a masculine and feminine body.

Being physically a female, a woman identifies with her Moon and Venus nature, but she seeks that other part of herself—the Sun and Mars—in the outside world, which is reflected in the form of a man. Finally she realizes that the outer man she is attracted to is herself—her very own heart and passion. When she discovers how to become totally intimate with this outside male, she will discover that she has become totally intimate with herself. She will come to know and love who she is as a woman, no longer at war with the masculine god of her own heart. She will feel her own inner strength.

Obviously, the same process holds true for a man, but in reverse. That is, being physically a male, he identifies with his Sun and Mars, but seeks that other part of himself—the Moon and Venus—in the form of a woman. When he has awakened the lunar goddess within himself by giving his heart totally to a woman in the outside world, he comes home to his own heart. He feels nurtured and sustained within and knows who he is emotionally.

VENUS (Values/Feminine)

Desire to Relate

It is important to realize that Venus is a planet of value. She shows what we like—our friends, our tastes, our preferred relationships, our refinement and those people we want around us. She is very important in showing us whether we value ourselves or not.

If Venus is afflicted from birth (frustrated by Saturn, Neptune, or Pluto), we will have difficulty taking care of our needs and will tend to give in to the desires of others. We need to honor our own self-worth and understand what we feel or need. The relationship of Venus to the other planets tells us if we do honor ourselves. This is very important because we simply cannot stand up for something that we do not value.

Whether it is a woman's Venus or a man's Venus, she is a planet that shows our desire and need to receive love. Venus is the desire to be appreciated and to receive strokes from our friends, family, lover, beauty and the arts. It also relates to sensuality and sexuality because it seeks intimacy with the lover. This seeking may be motivated by sheer lust or divine ecstasy. The kind of pleasure we receive through Venus depends on our capacity to love and to be truly intimate without fear. Venus is one of the keys to a man's heart because it shows the kind of woman he sees as his ideal. The sign his Venus is in at birth gives us this all-important key.

The sign your Venus is in at birth describes your attitude towards those things you love and appreciate. It shows the type of people you prefer to have in your life, the kind of pleasures you seek, and the type of person you prefer for sharing sex and intimacy. Venus is the key to understanding the relationships you desire in every human experience. Its primary urges are pleasure, love and ecstasy.

Venus with the Red Sign Attitude (Aries)

Summary Statement

"I love starting new things, challenges, fiery friends and lovers. They say I like to take too many risks."

When Venus is found here, her gentle and kind nature turns more into a warring spirit. Venus is not at home here. She will test her friends and lovers with a competitive attitude. If your Venus is here, then you love a challenge and the test of wills. You simply enjoy the forceful energy and sparks that arise from engaging a challenger in a relationship. This energy brings out the competitive spirit in you. You may enjoy collecting guns or war movies. You are attracted to people who are strong and energetic or friends and women of like nature. You tend to like competitive sports that whet your appetite for winning. This position of Venus could be called the "feminine warrior." Love seems to turn into a game of conquest, and sexuality seems to be boundless. The sexual embrace tends to be expressed without reserve or reluctance. In short, this position of Venus makes you an aggressive lover. Check to see if your Venus is "afflicted" by other planets. If so, you would have a difficult time fulfilling your desires because of a poor self-image or fear of intimacy. If your Venus is not afflicted, you will probably have good karma in love, art, money, food and relationships. A man with this position will be attracted to a woman with planets in Aries.

Venus with the Green Sign Attitude (Taurus)

Summary Statement

"I love plenty of money, quality food, a sensual and loyal lover. It has been said that I'm greedy for wealth."

Venus here is very earthy, loyal and predictable. There is love of sensual enjoyments. These relate to food, money and sex. You love good food, are a good cook, and you work hard but are sometimes slow in your responses. You are very sensual and love to touch. You may have a couch-potato side and prefer taking your time to carry out your projects. You are endearing and are very true in your affections, even though you may secretly lust after others in your fantasies. But there is no doubt that you will remain loyal in your affections. You appreciate people who are well grounded in making things happen. You love the simple pleasures of life and enjoy seeing other people enjoy each other. Your friends may find you out in restaurants eating the finest foods. You do love to entertain people and make them feel at home. Singing or speaking may be of interest to you, as you are likely to have a rich voice. Art may be a way for you to express your sensuality. You could have been the person who created the poster entitled, "Poverty Sucks." You are friendly towards people who have their Sun or other planets in Taurus. A man with this position will be attracted to a woman with planets in Taurus.

Venus with the Yellow Sign Attitude (Yellow)

Summary Statement

"I love to have two lovers, smart friends, beautiful words and great ideas. I can complicate my relationships."

You love knowledge, ideas, techniques, methods, books, colored pens and many friends. Because of this, you could be a poet, reporter or writer. Music also appeals to your artistic nature. You are attracted to people who are smart, witty and clever. A great idea can sometimes affect you deeply. You have a love for doing two things at once. Beware of a tendency to flirt and keep more than one lover on the string. You sometimes confuse others by not making a commitment to them. You will express words of love but find it hard to follow through because of a need to keep the door open for someone else. Therefore you may be accused of being fickle. This may be because you find lovable qualities in a lot of people, but can't find all you want in one person. This is why you have to avoid in making promises of love while in your heart you know you cannot keep them. Try to find out why you are attracted to more than one person at a time. You may discover that you have a fear of limiting your options—something your Gemini spirit may find difficult to overcome. You like people who are clever and intellectual because they reflect the things you love. A lot of these people have their Sun in Gemini. A man with this position will be attracted to a woman with planets in Gemini.

Venus with the Brown Sign Attitude (Cancer)

Summary Statement

"I love feeding others, being their mother, nurturing their needs, and having a comfortable home. I have been accused of taking matters too personally."

This position of Venus imparts the love of home and family. The glowing fireplace with family members gathered around with an abundant supply of food is a scene you are attracted to. The sign of Cancer rules the stomach. Therefore you could be very attracted to the culinary arts. Great chefs will often have their Venus in Cancer. There seems to be great pleasure gained from feeding everyone well. Home and security are extremely important to you. You are also quite sensitive to the atmosphere around you and have very deep emotions. You tend to have some strong maternal tendencies and will often find yourself in that role. A man with his Venus here expects the woman to do his laundry, bake his cookies, bring him drinks and be his mother. He will also be strongly attached to the home and family—usually a good family man. He loves his children and wants to sustain the family tradition and values. The danger may be that he expects his wife to replace his mother emotionally; this could put a real burden for her, because he may not yet be a man. He could see his wife as the one who is supposed to nurture him and take care of his needs. A woman with such a man should beware of the temptation to keep this man a boy. You would probably be good at fixing up old houses and selling them for a profit. A man with this position will be attracted to a woman with planets in Cancer.

Venus with the Gold Sign Attitude (Leo)

Summary Statement

"I love romance, expressing my heart, chasing love, and creating an emotional impact on others. I have been accused of being too romantic"

Here, Venus softens the heart. The fiery field of Leo is the natural expression of the heart. Leo manifests the attitudes of romance, children and creativity. With your Venus here, you tend to be in love with love. You could also be in love with the arts, for you are drawn to anything that will enable you to express love on a deeper level. You are drawn to music and drama. A man with his Venus here will be attracted to a woman who is fiery, spontaneous, energetic and very outgoing. He likes drama and is drawn to a woman who is warm and expressive. He can be very romantic and attentive to the things that make a woman happy. His ideal is a Leo woman but another fiery sign will do—Aries or Sagittarius. He also loves sports and the challenge of conquest. He is something of a lion in search of a throne. He is proud, yet easily hurt if rejected. He looks at money as a tool for enjoying life and usually has a very generous heart. There is a love for the dramatic in both sexes. You like to create an emotional impact on those around you. You like to move people to feel the power of love. You love to be the center of a situation where you can make a great emotional impact. You don't like it when others steal your show—the stage belongs to you. A man with this position will be attracted to a woman with planets in Leo.

Venus with the Orange Sign Attitude (Virgo)

Summary Statement

"I love to create order and to stay in touch with the beautiful things of the earth. I respond to those who need my help. I have been accused of being too fussy."

The attitudes of Virgo are to be efficient, to organize information and to keep life together. Virgos place a great deal of value on service and a job well done. If your Venus is found here, you certainly value these traits. The one problem with this is that Virgo is basically very mental in its function. The energy is turned more toward the mind and its capacity to work well, rather than toward feelings or the heart. You love a great plan, a fine work of art, or a beautiful design. But you are too hard on yourself and may overwork yourself in search of perfection. This love for the perfect form causes you to fall short of your expectations. It would help if you would forgive yourself and others more. The pure expression of love may seem a little too mushy for you, feeling that duty and service are much more valuable than a temporary romance. You can be very critical of your lover and require high standards of conduct. But are these attitudes about love? Much can be achieved through art and beauty and there is a keen sense of what works and what does not work. This is why you are very valuable in showing others what real art is about. You could also be a fine chef holding up the highest example to satisfy the palates of adventurous gourmets. You have a strong dislike for anything crude, vulgar, or that shows a lack of taste. But don't set your sights too high. Otherwise, you could end up with a "cold and lonely lovely work of art"—something to look at but never to touch. A man with this position will be attracted to a woman with planets in Virgo.

Venus with the White Sign Attitude (Libra)

Summary Statement

"I love color, music, art, beauty, harmony, and being accepted by my friends. I have been accused of being a social climber."

Venus is a happy planet in Libra because she loves relationship and here she is in the sign of relationship. Libra is the realm of cooperation and blending opposites into harmony. Venus is very harmonious here. She responds to beautiful music, sublime color combinations, and peaceful surroundings. If your Venus is in Libra, you will be drawn to beauty in many forms—beautiful friends, beautiful sounds and a beautiful love. You love options and alternatives and like to keep many relationships going, acting as if you were some kind of social juggler. Sometimes it is difficult for you to take a stand for something because, like Geminis and Aquarians, you want your options open. You may seek a social advantage through your charm and play the butterfly game—going from relationship to relationship in search of an unreachable ideal. This is positive if you are pursuing love from the heart, but detrimental if you are merely seeking a strategic love advantage and not allowing yourself to be vulnerable. Beauty is very important to you. Sometimes you may place too much value on it, letting yourself be deceived by the allure of something that is only "skin deep" and of little substance. You can be charming—but be aware of vacillation in your feelings and lack of commitment. You could do well in the arts; however, indecisiveness could overwhelm you and make you very ineffective. Carry through with the fulfillment of your ideals and you could realize your goals. A man with this position will be attracted to a woman with planets in Libra.

Venus with the Black Sign Attitude (Scorpio)

Summary Statement

"I love the mystery of sex, the joy of intensity, loyalty in love, and being with one person. I have been accused of being too secretive."

If your Venus is here, you are intrigued by sex and mystery. You love to explore the inner workings of a relationship on every level but you find it hard to let other people know how you feel about the things you love. You actually have a certain shyness about sex because you don't want others to know how interested in it you really are. Venus here indicates that you control your feelings until you are safe or can stay in a controlling position. You want to avoid being vulnerable at any cost—but this can be a mistake because you have a great capacity to engage a relationship on the deepest level. Your greatest lesson is to discover true intimacy by turning your heart over to another. Because you are a cautious lover and usually have not allowed another to know you, you can appear to be something you are not. If you can abandon your control and engage your lover on a more vulnerable level, you will have a channel to express your depths. A man with his Venus here is fiercely loyal, but usually reserved emotionally. He is very sexual and is attracted to intense and mysterious looking women. A woman may find it hard to get him to "open up." At times, it will seem impossible. Venus-in-Scorpio types are very reluctant to say how they feel, and some of them may not know how they feel, They may fear the consequences of opening up. Out of their fear of the consequences of opening up, they might be silent pursuers. They can be great sex partners, but they may have a hard time being vulnerable and sharing an open and sincere intimacy; if the heart is not open, there is usually more lust than love. A man with this position will be attracted to a woman with planets in Scorpio.

Venus with the Blue Sign Attitude (Sagittarius)

Summary Statement

"I love the outdoors, wide open spaces, knowledge, foreign countries, traveling, horses and honesty. They say I have too much wanderlust."

This fiery attitude imparts the love for adventure, distant contacts, spiritual truths, publishing, law, writing and foreign countries. If your Venus is here, you are attracted to far away places and foreign cultures. You like a person who is straightforward, honest, and who tells it like it is. You have a love for truth and an aversion for deception and trickery. It is hard for you to keep a secret and you may blurt out confidential information on impulse. You don't like to gather any moss. You love the outdoors and the challenge of new experiences. The adventures of travel and the contacts you make with people from a foreign country who represent a different culture can be of special interest to you. You are sometimes found in higher places of learning trying to unravel your own truth. You are freedom loving and want to take on new adventures and explore new challenges. You want an adventurous partner who is ready to explore the next experience over the horizon. You are always on the move to express your restless spirit. Since you are born with a need to seek understanding, you feel that the more contacts you can make the more awareness of life you will gain. You do not hold on to the past and sentimentality is not your style. A man with this position will be attracted to a woman with planets in Sagittarius.

Venus with the Gray Sign Attitude (Capricorn)

Summary Statement

"I love the tried, the true and the predictable. I am attracted to the past, older friends, and what went before me. I have been accused of being too cold."

This sign of Capricorn imparts a very practical and pragmatic attitude. It tends to limit itself to the physical world and is suspicious of the subtle. It is very interested in matters at hand. If your Venus is here, you love tradition, organization, prestige and status. You are ambitious to find a place in the world, a place of leadership and responsibility. You look toward what worked before and want to continue doing the same thing. Some of your friends might say you are "a stick in the mud," implying that you rarely venture beyond the predictable. You love order, efficiency, and like to be in charge of large enterprises. You like people who have achieved a position in society, and you are attracted to conventional occupations: real estate, law (for status, power and control), medicine, or science. You will probably marry an older person. You tend to honor the family and see yourself as being responsible to the clan. Sometimes you may be too sensible, organized, practical and responsible—not in touch with your deeper emotions. It appears that duty is more important to you than emotions. You want a sensible mate who will help you raise your family well. You will honor a conventional partner who is predictable and reliable and who wants to build a strong family structure. A man with this position will be attracted to a woman with planets in Capricorn.

Venus with the Blue-Green Sign Attitude (Aquarius)

Summary Statement

"I love my friends, the unusual, the hard to get and sexual freedom. I have been accused of having weird tastes."

If you have Venus here, you certainly love your freedom to explore many options. Although you are not as indecisive as Gemini or Libra, you are just as noncommittal. It is difficult for you to stay with one person. You are simply not loyal in your affections to one person because your options need to be open. You may not be promiscuous but people will think you are. You don't see anything wrong with having many different women or men friends—even as lovers sometimes if you so choose. You are not looking for a predictable and committed love life. Other Aquarians understand you perfectly. Your song is "freedom without attachment." The problem with this is that there is not much depth of caring—it is mostly experimentation and lust. You love new technology, new friends, new ideas and kinky sex. You are usually very creative and have the talent to discover new artistic forms that no one ever dreamed of. There is potential artistic greatness because of your capacity to express unique feelings. Maybe you need to get used to the fact that you will always be surprising because you never know what you will be doing tomorrow—and you like it that way. Most people prefer more commitment than you are willing to give. A man with this position will be attracted to a woman with planets in Aquarius.

Venus with the Purple Sign Attitude (Pisces)

Summary Statement

"I love the other world, the unknown, sensitive people and beautiful things. I help those people who need my help. I have been accused of giving too much of myself away."

You are a very sensitive, romantic, idealistic, imaginative, and probably a very artistic person. You are caring and helpful to those in need. You seek a mate who is very emotional, expressive, deep, mysterious and other-worldly. You are attracted to spiritual, artistic or psychic types and may have a strong desire to escape into a fantasy world or pursue drugs or alcohol. The escape tendency is very strong but it can be expressed in a positive way if you are creative and responsible. You may be in pursuit of an unobtainable dream or believe a relationship to be something it is not. Beware of falling in love with people who are "wounded birds." After you help heal them, they will usually fly away and leave you sitting alone. It has been said that you are the most caring of all people. You love to help, but beware of becoming a sacrifice to those people who do not deserve it. Use your sensitivity to create a beautiful world around you without losing yourself in another person's dreams. Try nurturing yourself first and then you will be able to discriminate between those people who will appreciate your help and those who hang around to make you feel guilty and sap your energy. You deserve a lot more than that. A man with this position will be attracted to a woman with planets in Pisces.

MARS (Passion/Masculine)

The Desire to Take Action

Mars shows a man's aggressive energy, his obvious passion—what he pursues. It reflects his male sexuality. Mars is an aggressive energy in both sexes; in a woman, it shows the kind of man she desires sexually. It is the desire to take action, a forward-moving energy but expressed differently. When we consider Mars, we always have to take Venus into account, because she is the other side of sexuality. In a man, Mars shows his sexual behavior towards Venus, the woman he is attracted to and idealizes. He desires to sexually penetrate the woman who relates to his Venus. If his Venus is in Scorpio and you are a Scorpio type of woman, you are the woman he desires. If your Mars, Sun or Moon are in Scorpio, he could be strongly attracted to you sexually. We always have to keep in mind that Mars and Venus are very sexual planets. When the heart is open in love, these sexual energies can bring transcendental experiences of true intimacy.

The sign your Mars is in at birth shows your aggressive desires and the masculine side of your sexuality. In a woman, it shows the kind of man she desires sexually. In a man, it shows his sexual desire when aroused by Venus.

Venus stimulates a man's Mars to sexual activity, shows him the kind of woman he desires sexually, the pleasures he enjoys, and what kind of woman he idealizes. Venus shows a woman her feminine nature and the pleasures she enjoys.

Mars is basically an outward-acting planet and Venus is basically an inward-acting planet. Venus is directed toward receiving love through the senses. Together, Mars and Venus rule and stimulate the sexual centers and magnetize men and women toward each other. When these planetary energies are linked to the open heart in both sexes (Sun and Moon), they can express the deepest possible intimacy between a man and a woman.

Mars with the Red Sign Attitude (Aries)

Summary Statement

"I desire to be first in all my actions. I love a challenge and am energized by competition. They say I am too impulsive for my own good."

If you have this position of Mars, you have an aggressive side. You are good at starting things but not outstanding in finishing them. As a woman with this position, you are attracted to strong and fiery men sexually and would enjoy playful encounters in the bedroom. If the man you are with is not as strong as you, you may not have much respect for him. You need someone who can match your energy. You are an adventurer and you look to the man who has a fiery and active nature who will challenge you. The man you are interested in is a "doer," an initiator, one who is willing to take chances and take action in the moment. Since you are somewhat impulsive yourself, you are attracted to a man of a similar temperament. If your Mars is favorably connected to his Sun or Venus, this could be a very strong attraction.

In fact, if your Mars is conjunct his Venus, the attraction can be so strong that it could be embarrassing. You are attracted to Aries, Leo or Sagittarius men. These kind of men are fiery in nature, which goes well with your own fiery side. Since air feeds fire, you are also attracted to the air signs of Gemini, Libra and Aquarius. Men with this position have an aggressive side. They may be foolhardy at times because they find it hard to walk away from a challenge. A woman with this position will be attracted to a man with planets in Aries.

Mars with the Green Sign Attitude (Taurus)

Summary Statement

"Even though I am slow and steadfast in my action, I am also tenacious, persistent and loyal. I am in pursuit of material comfort. I have a passion for wealth."

Mars in this sign increases the pursuit for material gain. The passion is directed toward money, food, security and acquisitions. Since Taurus expresses all the good things of the earth, money food and sex, Mars here simply energizes all these needs.

A woman with this position will have a strong sexual attraction toward a Taurus man. If his Venus and your Mars are in this sign, the passion can be very intense. You love the Taurus man's sensuality. He's usually into touching and very sexual. He has a very strong mating instinct, and you could be drawn to the intensity of his feelings. Although he is reluctant to verbalize his feelings due to an inherent stubbornness, you understand this because you are very much the same way. He expects his actions to reveal his love for you and he will show it in many ways. That's probably okay with you because you have the same tendency. If you find a Taurus in your life or a man with a lot of Taurus energies (planets in the Taurus sign), a relationship will tend to last. Even if you eventually have trouble, it will be hard to break the bond between you. Neither one of you wants to say good-bye, so you may just have to let your relationship grind down over time if it is not working. Sooner or later, one of you will walk away—it is usually the woman. A man with this position is very tenacious, stubborn and slow to change, but very ambitious for gaining financial security. He is usually a good builder and will work hard and long on a specific goal. Never push him, for he will not budge. A woman with this position will be attracted to a man with planets in Taurus.

Mars with the Yellow Sign Attitude (Gemini)

Summary Statement

"I am restless. I have a million things going on and hate to finish them. I love starting new projects and exploring a dozen things at a time. They say my energies are too scattered."

Here Mars lends its energy to the mind. It gives an intense desire for knowledge, new ideas, techniques, methods and communication. This is an airy, mental energy that does not seem connected to the body.

A woman with her Mars here is attracted to a Gemini man, who is usually lost in thought and has his feelings in the heavens. This position of Mars also imparts the need to have an ongoing interest in two men at once. At first this may be embarrassing to admit because having two men at once certainly can complicate your life. The Gemini's tendency leads you to believe that if you make a choice for one you will miss out on the other. By always trying to keep your options open for another man, you could end up with nothing. But you find it hard to surrender your heart to one man.

As a man, you are bright, sunny, full of new ideas and light energy. You are very intellectual, witty, clever and changeable. Since your Gemini Mars is not connected much to real feeling, your relationships may not last. You will feel that something is missing—that something is usually a lack of feeling. A man with this position usually has several projects going at the same time. He has too many irons in the fire. His challenge is to finish them.

When a woman has Mars in Gemini and someone asks her, "Do you love this man?" Her usual reply is "I think I do." Then she should ask herself this: "What does thinking have to do with love?" A man with this position, usually has several projects going at the same time. A woman with this position will be attracted to a man with planets in Gemini.

Mars with the Brown Sign Attitude (Cancer)

Summary Statement

"I am in pursuit of security, home, family and nurturing. I like to make a nest and store my possessions there. Sometimes my emotions get away from me."

This energy can ignite you to go after security—to maintain the home, country and tradition. You are in pursuit of security for the home and family. You like the hearth. As a man with this position, you would be very emotional. You like to express your feelings and show great sympathy for your children and small creatures that need your help. As a woman, your home environment has to be safe and secure before you feel like being intimate. You have a shy side when it comes to sex, but if you are sure everything is safe around you, you can be the best of lovers. You know feelings and how to express them. Things of the past that were full of family enjoyment touch you deeply, and you identify strongly with a man who feels the same. A Mars-in-Cancer man has a lot of the boy left in him. If home and hearth are your path, a man with Cancer planets would hold strong attraction for you and help you fulfill your family aspirations. A woman with this position will be attracted to a man who has planets in Cancer.

Mars With the Gold Sign Attitude (Leo)

Summary Statement

"I am in pursuit of love, romance and creativity. I seek the center stage and like to be in charge of my affairs. They say I am very dramatic."

A person with their Mars in Leo is in pursuit of love, creativity, and the emotional adventure. Here he or she is the actor who desires center stage. They never want to be last in anything, and love at lot of attention and praise. Because they are proud and full of self, they are easily flattered.

If you are a woman with this Mars, you are attracted to a lionhearted type of man who has a big heart, always full of possibility, who has a strong dislike for negative and dark egos. You love his spirit and the strength he radiates because he reflects your own passion for recognition and achievement. A man with his Sun in Leo stimulates the Mars energy field of love, passion and romance. You are energized by his presence, and his magnetic qualities stimulate your desire for him.

You need to find a way to be creative because you have a deep desire to express yourself and love being spontaneous. You want others to realize how special you are—that you should be treated with honor and respect.

Mars with the Orange Sign Attitude (Virgo)

Summary Statement

"I am passionate for perfection. I pursue order and efficiency, and I like to help others. I dislike anything coarse."

The Virgo sign imparts a very practical life function to Mars. The best in performance is required and expected. Order and perfection are the primary impulses of this energy. When Mars is here, it simply gives a passion for detail, efficiency, and doing one's best. Something organized and neat may give a greater thrill than an orgasm.

If you are a woman with your Mars in Virgo, you are in pursuit of a man who is neat, organized, clean and efficient. Your passion tends to be in your head. Order and efficiency come first, then passion. You probably could not stand to make love in a sloppy bed. You could be a loyal and dutiful wife, but you may have to take occasional foolish risks to counteract a tendency to do everything by the numbers. Being so together all the time can keep you in a rut. The heart must be pushed into the realms of wildness—the realm where your mind has surrendered to the body's desire. Still, you are capable of lasting love and are attracted to a man who has his life together. You will be strongly attracted to a Virgo man but a Taurus could provide the balance in passion that you need. He is practical yet very sensuous. You need that kind of intimacy to keep your body loose and your desires out of your head.

As a man with this Mars, you are in pursuit of excellence. You are interested in smooth-running machinery. Your passion is perfection. You can use up a lot of energy getting something right.

Mars with the White Sign Attitude (Libra)

Summary Statement

"I am in pursuit of togetherness, personal harmony and beauty in all relationships. They say I waffle too much."

Since Libra is an energy field that imparts a desire for beauty, harmony, and idealism in relationship, Mars lends his passion to these tendencies.

If your Mars is here, you are in pursuit of harmony in relationship. But sometimes, because of a desire for an idealized mate, your relationship may not be the one you imagine. Libra can give you the tendency to try and make a relationship fit your idealism—when, in fact, it does not. You could be indecisive when it comes to taking a stand for what you truly need. You can be a master at rationalization. For example, a friend might say that your husband doesn't give you enough attention, and you might reply, "But he does other things that are really great. He's a hard worker and gives me security."

You want a man who seeks harmony in relationship. Therefore, you are strongly attracted to a Libra type. Try to find out where his other planets are, because you don't want to get an abundance of Libra planets. He would be plagued with more indecision than you. With the right balance of idealism and reality you can have a very satisfying intimacy. The fire signs of Aries, Leo and Sagittarius would be very helpful in keeping you from getting stalled with indecision and inspire you to share the many sides of your talent for harmony. A woman with this position will be attracted to a man with planets in Libra.

A man with this position has a passion for relationships. He probably has many friends and has a love of music, harmony and design. He is in search of an artistic form that will fit his ideal. However, he can seem to waver from his goal because of the fear of making wrong choices. He has to learn to deal with his indecision.

Mars with the Black Sign Attitude (Scorpio)

Summary Statement

"I am in pursuit of absolute union with another. I am intensely passionate, possessive, protective, and very sensitive to other people's aggressions. They say I do not forgive easily."

The sign of Scorpio tends to fix the feelings in the unconscious. This field imparts intensity of feeling and desire. There is a strong need for an intense relationship that transcends the ordinary. When Mars is found here it adds emotion and sexual intensity to an energy that already expresses this.

If your Mars is in Scorpio, you are in pursuit of a very intense relationship. You are seeking the depths of intimacy. But sometimes there is a secrecy about your desires because you may be somewhat embarrassed by them. You may not be comfortable with letting other people know how sexual you really are. However, as sexuality is one of your primary interests, you might as well get comfortable with it. There is no greater lover if your desires are linked to a loving heart. The problem may be that lust is greater than love. In this case, sex becomes the goal rather than love. You may have a certain reluctance to turn your heart over to another because you always want to maintain control, to seek a position of safety from too much caring. After all, who wants to give his whole heart to another? No telling what they will do with it—you may actually lose your heart! At some point, you will need to cross the line, be willing to be known, and share your complete depths with another. You have a capacity for great intimacy, once you give your heart to another.

If you are a woman with this Mars position, you are obviously looking for an intense Scorpio type. He may be the quiet and reserved one, but you can feel the intensity of energy between you without a word being spoken. He may not be very adept at saying how he feels. But he may be reflecting your own reluctance. Your challenge together will be in letting each other know how you really feel. After all, if anyone understands the depth of your desires, it is this one. You are strongly attracted to a man with planets in Scorpio.

A man with this Mars also wants to be in control and hates to lose. He is extremely sensitive to insults and has a very powerful will. He has an extremely intense passion and the capacity to endure many hardships.

Mars with the Blue Sign Attitude (Sagittarius)

Summary Statement

"I am in pursuit of meaning and understanding. I will go a long way to find the truth. I have great passion for traveling and discovery. They say that I am sometimes rude."

Like Aries and Leo, this is another fiery sign. This energy imparts wanderlust to the nature. There is a passion for travel, foreign countries, cross-country adventures, camping out, and exploring the unknown.

If your Mars is here, you could have a passion for far away places and always need time to take off on a trip. This position sometimes expresses the desire to pursue spiritual matters. Your father, or someone in your family, may be interested in these things. You see your self as a restless go-getter in search of answers. In some people this energy manifests primarily as a restless quality. You may be someone who gathers no moss. Certainly you rarely look back because you are interested only in the now and the future. When aroused, you have a fighting spirit, but you are not necessarily a warrior. You certainly can be a hard worker. You prefer the outdoors and seek out other people of like mood.

If you are woman with this Mars, you are looking for a man who matches your desires. He is straightforward, honest and adventurous. He will not only go where you want to go, he will add challenge and interest to your life. As a lover, he is not the tender type, but he has a lot of energy that can add to your own. Together you can create a real fire. The Sagittarius man fits your passion the best. But Aries and Leo men are also harmonious with your nature.

Mars with the Gray Sign Attitude (Capricorn)

Summary Statement

"I am in pursuit of leadership, being in charge and reaching the top. I love a challenge. I believe only in the pragmatic. They say I am too ambitious for my own good."

The ancient observers have said that this sign is like a goat. Goats "go at" things and people and this fits the Capricorn instinct. This is an attitude of ambition, achievement and need to reach the top. They love the old, the tried and the true, and are not usually interested in things beyond this world. They function primarily with the material, and are very practical people.

If your Mars is here, you have a strong drive to reach a position of control and leadership. You like to be in front and are willing to take a lot of responsibility if it is to your advantage. You have a passion for organization, efficiency and control. You like to spend your energy moving things or making them happen. You much prefer pulling the strings rather than having others pull yours; and people tend to let you do that because your actions tend to back up your words.

If you are a woman with this position of Mars, you are attracted to a man who is very ambitious, confident and reliable. He is responsible and honors tradition. You like the idea of teamwork and want to share your goals with him. You are inspired by his fatherly, wise nature as well as his head for business and leadership. The passion of Capricorn is not a wild and fiery energy, but it is reliable, enduring and steadfast—never foolish or out of control. Obviously a Capricorn man fits your desires the best, but you would also be attracted to Taurus and Virgo as they also have practical, earthy qualities that support your need for the predictable. You are attracted to a man with planets in Capricorn.

A man with this Mars is in search of a business for himself. He has a passion for climbing to the top and the capacity to endure many obstructions and overcome them.

Mars With the Blue-Green Sign Attitude (Aquarius)

Summary Statement

"I desire independence, sexual freedom and the right to explore. They say I go where 'angels fear to tread.'"

Here, Mars supports the need to be unpredictable. This energy is almost the reverse of Capricorn. This sign imparts the need to explore the unknown, extend the boundaries of the mind and all relationships. It is highly experimental. This is perhaps the most independent of all the signs.

If you are a woman with this Mars, you have a passion for the unusual. You love to have many men friends and keep your options open to all possibilities. You like unusual men who can be eccentric, unpredictable and hard to figure out. You are always challenged and fascinated by the unreachable. It is as if you are only attracted to a man if you can't have him. This is why you may tend to get involved in complicated relationships. You could have affairs with married men who are only available for short periods of time. This way you are guaranteed your freedom. You may be unable to commit your heart totally to any one person because you are already married to the god of freedom. You seem to equate true intimacy with a kind of bondage. You like to explore many kinds of sexual relationships and think nothing of having more than two men in your life at the same time. Loyalty of affection is not something you feel deeply.

You are attracted to the Aquarian man, because he fits your need for the unpredictable. He lives on the edge of experience and you are drawn to these possibilities. There can be a lot of sexual thrills but you need to ask if this has anything to do with love.

A man with this Mars is in pursuit of something new. He has a passion for living on the edge and exploring undiscovered places in technology, science and art. He has a passion for doing things differently.

Mars with the Purple Sign Attitude (Pisces)

Summary Statement

"I am in pursuit of my dreams, ecstasy, and the world of imagination. They say I am an escapist."

Pisces is the sign of the sea of space and the ocean of the earth. It imparts a vast and nebulous feeling to the psyche and a longing to return to the source. It is a mystical and undefined energy that rules the unconscious realms of our mind.

If you are a woman with this Mars, you are in pursuit of a dream man. You are attracted to a sensitive man who is full of feeling and who may need your help. Feelings can run very deep between you and there can be a great capacity for intimacy. You may be drawn to the artistic, the psychic and the creative part of a man. Your passions is deep and full of great feeling, but beware of your tendency to attract men who rely upon you too much for support. There is something of the "savior" in you because you have an unconscious feeling of obligation to save others. Make sure that you don't become a sacrifice in the process. Avoid men who are into drugs or alcohol. These men fear life and cannot give you the support you need. Since commitment and intimacy require a clear and steady heart, this man may fall short. He may be in pursuit of a dream and follow his illusion so strongly that he is out of touch with reality. Avoid weak and emotionally wounded men who look for you to save them. They will sap all of your energy.

You are strongly attracted to the Pisces man, but men with planets in the energy fields of Cancer and Scorpio can also share the emotional depths of your passion. These men will be full of feeling and capable of taking responsibility for an intimate relationship if other things are right in their planetary patterns.

A man with this position is also in pursuit of a dream. This placement of Mars does not give him a strong will, so he will have to take care not to run from life and chase mere illusions. He would do best in the arts or to become involved in humanitarian causes.

Part 2

The Effects of the Impersonal Planets

The planets are part of you. They are not separate from you. They *are* you! If you see another person's planet contacting one of your personal planets, this means that something inside of you is being affected. It is not just an abstract contact of your planet. It is energizing something inside of you, a chakra—a subtle nerve center. Always keep this in mind.

If another person's impersonal planet contacts your personal planets, it stirs a desire or reaction within you in some way. Once you find out which planets are in contact, you can check within yourself to see how it arouses your feelings. Then confirm these feelings with the information in the following pages. For example, if you are a woman and a man's Uranus makes contact with your Venus, first ask yourself what you feel in his company then compare those feelings with what the text says about this combination. Use the tools from Lessons 5 and 6 and the Sign Table to determine the effect another person's planet has upon the personal planets in your birth chart. Use this present section for interpreting the positive and negative effects of birth planets, relationship planets and visiting planets.

JUPITER (Expansion/Optimism)

Desire to Acquire

Although Jupiter shows the desire within us to expand our horizons, to believe and hope for better things, the things he promises are often just full of hot air. Nonetheless, he can bring an opportunity for you to acquire that which you seek. He is a pleasant planet, but prone to excess, exaggeration, and pretense. He brings the feeling that everything is possible, full of hope, and therefore is the planet of great support and optimism. He has dominion over law, publishing, religion, foreign countries, long journeys, higher education, and distant travels. He is expansive by nature. The best way to look at the effects of Jupiter when it makes contact with a personal planet is to expect some kind of increase. Keep in mind that he often promises, but rarely delivers. However, if another person's Jupiter makes a favorable connection to one of your personal planets, he can be very supportive. Don't expect too much from this fellow when he is a visiting planet. When visiting, Jupiter is not very strong—but he can bring opportunity that must be acted on as soon as possible, because the energy is usually short-lived.

Jupiter supports the Sun: If Jupiter is favorable to your Sun at birth, you are a very positive person. You bring hope and an abundance of energy to those around you. Here Jupiter expands and seems to scatter the Sun's energies in all directions and, therefore, has a warming effect on all those he touches.

As a relationship planet: Obviously, if someone brings their Jupiter to your Sun, they bring you hope, support, opportunity and possibility. They will help sustain your ego and offer you positive support. This is a very beneficial connection.

As a visiting planet: A visiting Jupiter that supports your Sun brings a brief opportunity to become successful at what you are trying to achieve. You will feel very positive, as if you could do anything you want. But act swiftly. This energy won't last long.

Jupiter frustrates the Sun: If Jupiter's contact is frustrating at birth, you have to be aware of exaggerating your position in life. Your ego can feel too important and excessive indulgence can drain energy and health.

As a relationship planet: If someone brings you this kind of Jupiter, beware of them promising more than they can deliver or leading you into wasting your own resources on their pipe dreams. They could also lead you into the physical excesses of food and drink.

As a visiting planet: Beware of exaggeration. Things may not be as great as they seem or as what you hear.

Jupiter supports the Moon: When positive connections are formed, Jupiter is a great support to the emotions. This person is a great sustainer of other people—always there to help them—and they feel it. They are also very resourceful in finding creative ways to sustain themselves financially and have an uncanny ability to find opportunities where others fail.

As a relationship planet: If someone brings his or her Jupiter to your Moon in a supporting way, you will always feel nurtured and sustained by them. They will try to give you anything you need. You are blessed by their company.

As a visiting planet: This is time to receive nurturing from others. It is a good phase for family affairs.

Jupiter frustrates the Moon: If there is a frustrating effect on the Moon, the situation is very different. The need to support one's own place in the world takes precedence over the desire to support others and there is a lack of sympathy with others' needs. The person may promise to help, but others will find their offer less than real.

As a relationship planet: The frustrating impact of another person's Jupiter on your Moon is to lead you into excess or promise you more than they can ever deliver. Look for the results before investing too much energy in their suggestions. They could lead you to believe things that are simply not true.

As a visiting planet: This increases emotional enthusiasm but self-indulgence could be the result.

Jupiter supports Mercury: Jupiter adds zest to the mind in this position. The mind has a thirst for knowledge and a keen curiosity. The mind seeks to communicate on a grand scale. Some of our greatest writers had this planetary partnership. There is usually an excellent memory and a great storehouse of knowledge immediately accessible. The accent is on communication. This is an excellent gift for journalists, speakers, philosophers, linguists, planners, writers, and people who do a lot of thinking.

As a relationship planet: If another person's Jupiter relates favorably to your Mercury, they will help you in your communications and add many supportive ideas for any project you might engage. They enhance your thinking and give you confidence in your mental pursuits. You may find yourself talking a lot in their company because they stimulate your mind.

As a visiting planet: This contact brings great mental energy and indicates a favorable circumstance for writing and effective communication.

Jupiter frustrates Mercury: The individual with this position in their own patterns, is prone to exaggeration and overstepping their ability to get things done. They take on more than they can handle because there is a strong outreaching tendency that causes them to bite off projects in big hunks. Then they cannot digest them. There is usually a serious need for organization and planning. Otherwise, little gets done. They love starting things but show little patience for finishing them. Their mind is always racing but they do not know where to go with their ideas.

As a relationship planet: The frustrating effect of another person's Jupiter can lead you into undertaking enterprises that have great promise but little substance in reality. The Jupiter enthusiasm may affect your judgment and cause you to make rash decisions. It is best to check all promises thoroughly before investing time and money. You will soon learn to take what this person promises or says with great restraint. This is simply their effect upon you—it will not necessarily be true in their relationship to another person. They are motivated to add enthusiasm to your thinking but may cause you to make wrong judgments in your decisions.

As a visiting planet: This visit of Jupiter leads to mental overreaching; biting off more mental work than you can handle. Stay organized despite a tendency to scatter your interests.

Jupiter supports Venus: The positive contact of Jupiter to Venus is very beneficial. A person born with this planetary pattern is considered very fortunate. Since Venus rules money, love and relationship, all these areas of life can be full of happy experiences. It is said that this person tends to be at the right place at the right time. Even if they were to back away from success, they would bump into it. They probably have good friends, love people, and are very social.

As a relationship planet: Anyone who brings his or her Jupiter to your Venus in a supporting way can be the channel of wealth for you. They will support your needs and desires completely and even try to get you anything you want.

As a visiting planet: This is a time where you might make a strong contact with someone that will help you succeed in love, money or the arts. It is an opportunity to receive favors and benefits.

Jupiter frustrates Venus: An unfavorable Venus/Jupiter pattern leads the individual to seek a life of excess in money, food and sex. They could lose money through unsafe speculation because they exaggerate their expectations. They find it hard to become truly intimate with others for fear of the demands that might be made upon them. This pattern makes Venus a selfish goddess—she will not go out of her way for others because she is too busy fulfilling her own excessive desires.

As a relationship planet: When someone else's Jupiter forms a frustrating relationship to your Venus, they can lead you into excesses and cause you to waste your resources. These are the fair-weather friends who are never around when you need them. This also tends to blow love expectations out of proportion and a person may seem to be more than they really are. They may make promises they can't keep.

As a visiting planet: During this visit of Jupiter, simply beware of the tendency to overindulge and go beyond your normal boundaries of excess. Your tastes can become exaggerated. Instead of a few pieces of chocolate, you eat the whole box! This can be a time when promises fail, when success and reward become only an apparition.

Jupiter supports Mars: Here Jupiter adds a great increase of energy. Since Mars is already an aggressive planet, a positive impact from Jupiter can give tremendous energy. If Mars is favorably connected to Jupiter from birth, this person may be so full of energy that they rarely rest. This contact also increases the sexual drive and gives a tendency to overdo everything. Their sexual aura can be overwhelming for some people. But if you are looking for sheer energy, you can't beat this pattern. Many great and wonderful enterprises can be completed because of so much available energy. Even though this is an impulsive energy, if it is channeled, it can serve us well.

As a relationship planet: If someone brings a positive contact to your Mars, they will support your ambitions and add their energy to help you achieve whatever goal you want. They will fill you with enthusiasm and creative ideas and show you how it is possible to fulfill your own plans.

As a visiting planet: This is a solid gift of energy for accomplishing your goals. Full speed ahead!

Jupiter frustrates Mars: If a person has this pattern from birth, they are basically rash in their actions, take on more than they can manage, and find it hard to plan and stay organized. Their enthusiasm often gets the best of them and they will have to do things over again because they do not have the patience to work out the details before acting.

As a relationship planet: If another person's Jupiter makes a negative contact (frustrates) with your Mars, then they can persuade you to act rashly or prematurely. Together, you become much more impulsive and find a certain impatience frustrating your lives. This contact will never be boring, but it could be exhausting and lead to many premature decisions.

As a visiting planet: Beware of taking unnecessary chances. It may be that it only looks like you can succeed.

SATURN (Contraction/Restriction)

Desire to Separate

This is a planet you always want to take seriously, because his impact has a sobering effect. Saturn is the desire within us to separate from others, to protect ourselves from being hurt, and to defend ourselves against a hostile world. Saturn works against intimacy; therefore, the feelings he arouses have to be confronted and understood—they are basically fear of intimacy.

Regardless of our great fantasies and dreams, Saturn is about reality. It is the reality of this world—not the next one. It deals only with "the bottom line," the results and the material world. He rules the world of business where only performance counts. Even though he is a cold and serious planet, he can support the five personal planets in a positive way. He rules the energy field of Capricorn, the "dead of winter" sign. His *negative* contact with the personal planets usually brings some kind of denial, fear, or loss. There seems to be some kind of unfinished business involved when Saturn is in the picture. He is always the teacher, but usually the lessons are hard to learn. Although Saturn has character-building power, he doesn't give much support to our ego or our relationships.

Saturn supports the Sun: Saturn always has a stabilizing influence when related positively to a personal planet. When related this way to the Sun from birth, it enables the individual to discipline their energies so they can accomplish the goals of survival (Sun). It helps bring out positive results of the sign in which the Sun is found at birth. For instance, if your Sun is in Capricorn, Saturn's positive relationship would enable you to bring out all the better qualities of the Capricorn nature, e.g., business ability, organizational skills and leadership.

As a relationship planet: Obviously, if someone else's Saturn is related to your Sun in a positive way, they would help you achieve your goals by lending ideas and suggestions that support your ambitions. This is a very fruitful connection that can bring many positive results.

As a visiting planet: When Saturn makes a visit, he usually hangs around for a few weeks and then even returns for another visit. So, his effects last longer than Jupiter's. Here the sustaining energy of Saturn can help you gain solid results with whatever you are working on. Whatever you achieve now will be the result of a positive and sustained effort that has been made possible by the well-defined energy of Saturn.

Saturn frustrates the Sun: Because the Sun expresses the desire to survive (the ego), and negative effects of Saturn can really hinder the ego's freedom of expression, because this usually results in a lack of self-confidence, as well as self-doubt and fear of pushing forward. This situation can be traced to a person's relationship to their father, mother, or to the principal authority in their childhood. They are predisposed to self-doubt and they lack the will to get what they want. This person may have to work very hard to get what they need—when they do, they will have earned it. They do not feel like anything is going to be easy and they expect to work hard for everything they achieve.

As a relationship planet: If someone else's Saturn is frustrating your Sun, you will not want to associate with them. You will feel inhibited, obstructed and unsupported. They will tend to criticize you. These are not favorable patterns for business, marriage, or working together to achieve mutual goals. It is best not to have to work or even associate with this person. If you do, you could be headed for misery. They will always find fault and criticize you.

As a visiting planet: Here Saturn functions as an obstruction. Someone in a position of authority may be working against you. It is wise to practice patience and compromise. The restraint you feel will not last forever but you may have to work under it for a while.

Saturn supports the Moon: As we have seen, the Moon is our sense of being sustained or nurtured by life. Saturn's positive effect on the Moon at birth shows that this person feels emotionally sustained by life. An authority figure in their youth (father, mother, or whoever was in charge of their childhood) had a positive influence on their habits. The discipline they received as a child was tempered with good will and genuine caring for their welfare. Probably a firm, but gentle, hand guided them in such a way that they feel supported emotionally by their own keen sense of self and good judgment. Because this planetary pattern supported them emotionally as they grew up, they have an inherent feeling of self-reliance.

As a relationship planet: Of course, anyone whose Saturn relates to your Moon in this way will also be very helpful and will support your needs for security and well-being. You will be able to rely on them.

As a visiting planet: You may find help in establishing your home and family. It could be a good time to buy a house or help family members, especially your mother.

Saturn frustrates the Moon: A person born with Saturn frustrating their Moon will need to practice "staying in the sunlight" because Saturn here darkens the Moon's spirit. This means that their childhood was austere and without real emotional warmth from the family—especially the mother. It is important to understand that this environment may have conditioned them to feel sorrowful—they did not get the nurturing and support that every child needs. As an adult, they may have occasional bouts with depression and experience heavy moods because their feelings wander back to these unhappy scenes.

As a relationship planet: Obviously, if someone else brings a negative Saturn to your Moon, they will depress you and you will not want to be around them. You may even find yourself saying to them, "You depress me." Look to see if your own Saturn in your chart affects your child, your mate, or some other person who is close to you in this way. It will explain why they react to you the way they do. You can have compassion for them. Usually it is not something that you consciously are doing but the other person may read that repressive and critical feelings are coming from you on a subtle level. It will take some observation to understand the specific reasons for their reactions.

As a visiting planet: Hopefully, this visit of Saturn will not last long. You will be inclined to depression—perhaps having to move, leave home, or become separated from your roots. You may feel undernourished and cut off from that which makes you feel good. But take heart. It will soon pass.

Saturn supports Mercury: Actually, Saturn is not much of a friend to many planets. Even though he may be related to Mercury in a positive way, he still adds a serious quality to the mind. Here the mind is able to carry out the expression of its ideas efficiently and to express them fully through discipline, and it is capable of deep thought—yet, it gives a tendency towards thinking that is too grave, and prone to depression and self doubt. This person can think and write for long hours without a rest because they have a disciplined mind. It is a positive pattern for scientific work involving research and can power the thoughts to be able to create form and meaning out of chaos.

As a relationship planet: If someone brings Saturn to your Mercury in a supporting way, they can add practical advice and depth to your understanding and help clarify your thinking. This connection could add a new dimension to your relationship and make you feel supported by the other person's practical suggestions. This could be a good pattern for business pursuits and could produce solid results.

As a visiting planet: This is a time to achieve your mental goals. Writing projects can go forward effectively now and your thinking is very productive. You could work long hours and show unusual tenacity in carrying a project to completion. If you need this kind of planetary support, now is the time to take advantage of it.

Saturn frustrates Mercury: These positions affect the mind in a negative way. These people do not trust their mind; they hate studying and have inherited painful memories related to school and learning experiences. They may feel blocked in saying what they think, or simply unclear about what they do think. They could have a fear of speaking before large groups of people. Their tongue sometimes gets tied. Stuttering is possible. They are capable of deep thought but doubt their mental abilities. They may stick to the tried and true ways of thinking without venturing into creative realms because they do not want to take risks. This connection could limit their thinking. The limitations may not really be there, but they are set up to believe they are. These basic inhibitions may relate back to the first teacher or a critical parent's remark when they were studying at an early age.

As a relationship planet: If another person's Saturn relates to your Mercury in a frustrating way, they can be your worst critic. They don't think your ideas are worth much and will not support the projects you create. They always seem to find something wrong with what you say, write or express in meetings. Basically, there is just a lack of support for any of your communications. It is rare that their criticism would be constructive for you.

As a visiting planet: Saturn visiting your Mercury may serve as an obstruction to your goals. Communications may be impossible. It may be hard for you to get anyone to listen to your ideas. They do not seem to understand what you are saying, or don't agree with your suggestions. Be patient. Don't force it. You don't have the advantage.

Saturn supports Venus: Venus is a very human planet that shows what we like and appreciate. It rules money and relationships. Therefore when it is related positively to Saturn, Venus feels sustained and supported by the material world. Saturn imparts feelings of loyalty in affection to friends and lovers and honors business transactions. If these planetary patterns are present at the time of birth, this person has the endearing qualities of steadfastness and honesty in their relationships. They are usually good at handling money and have a cautious attitude about spending on frivolous things. In matters of love, they are the "true blue" type and take relationships quite seriously.

As a relationship planet: If another person's Saturn relates favorably to your Venus, you will feel that they support your sense of self-worth and will also be there for you when you need their help. This would be a good relationship for working together in business because it generates a sincere cooperation that makes success possible.

As a visiting planet: This visit of Saturn could bring you solid financial results, artistic achievement, or discovery of a lasting friendship. You should be able to produce something of value during this time.

Saturn frustrates Venus: A negative Saturn robs you of a sense of self-worth, worldly benefits, and it may lead you into abusive relationships where you become the victim. If these patterns exist at birth, the lifelong journey will one of trying to prove that you are a valuable human being, that you don't deserve to be abused, and that you need nurturing and support like everyone else does. You may tend to become a sacrifice in life, because you were criticized as a child and felt neither loved nor supported. You gravitate towards those people who do not love you and engage in relationships where you have to do all the giving and make all the concessions just to get a little attention from your mate. They usually are not worth your generosity. But, not used to getting what you want, you tend to endure these insults. This conditioning can be overcome through creative hypnotherapy and by pursuing that which you love. You must not be so willing to be the sacrifice. You must go after what is good for you and reject those who do not support you. This will hurt, but you will soon realize real self-love if you do this. You will refuse to be someone else's lover if you don't truly love them. Sooner or later you will discover that you are a very valuable person and deserve to have the best like anyone else.

As a relationship planet: If someone brings a frustrating Saturn to your Venus, turn around and walk off in the opposite direction. They will not give you what you want. If you have to establish a relationship with them, you will find that you are the one who is expected to be the giver. You cannot possibly come out ahead. The problem is that you may feel guilty or obligated to them. But don't give in to these feelings. This is a trap. Avoid it at all costs. It is important to remember that this person is not necessarily bad. They are simply bad for you.

As a visiting planet: This visit of Saturn is certainly no fun. You may say good-bye to someone you love, or they may say good-bye to you. People don't seem to show you much love during this time. You may feel cut off or disconnected from others. You may be taking a second look at your friends and discover that you have to let them go because you no longer have anything in common.

Saturn supports Mars: Think of Mars as an energy that makes things happen. It is naturally aggressive because it supports the survival instinct in all of us. We all have to go after things to survive. But this energy can be expressed aggressively, creatively, wildly or with hostility. It depends on how Mars is affected by the other planets. A positive influence from Saturn enables Mars to work efficiently without any waste of energy. If this is the way your Mars is related to Saturn, then you have the ability to get things done without wasting your time on false starts or impulsive behavior. There is a certain positive restraint in everything you do. You know how to complete your projects in the shortest available time. You have the ability to focus your energy and concentrate on the task at hand without getting distracted.

As a relationship planet: If another person brings you a supporting Saturn, they will help you complete projects and show you a better way to do things. This is a positive support for joint enterprises and for achieving goals together.

As a visiting planet: Your energy is strong during this time and you are able to focus and get things done. Saturn here gives you focused energy. Use this energy to finish incomplete projects.

Saturn frustrates Mars: Here the energies of Mars are repressed by the conjunction or square. A person has to be careful with this energy because there is potential violence due to an inner rage. There is usually some kind of anger associated with a repressed Mars. Saturn is the repressor. This person needs to find positive release for his energy and be careful in his association with people. Somewhere in his childhood someone "sat on him" and he is resentful for that. Therefore, anyone in his adult world who tries to "sit on him" should be very careful. There could be a confrontation.

For a woman, this position indicates some kind of abuse from the father. Therefore, there could be a lot of anger toward men and a deep fear of physical and emotional vulnerability.

As a relationship planet: If someone brings you this negative Saturn, you will feel very repressed by them. They represent a real obstruction to your intentions. It is best to find a way out of this relationship, as it will eventually create problems. If that is not possible, then you will have to bite the bullet or seek a compromise. Also, should you have your Saturn related negatively to another person, you might be repressing or controlling them without realizing it. It is wise to check out your planetary patterns with them if you suspect something is wrong.

As a visiting planet: Something or someone is blocking your efforts. You may be having trouble with a man or a boss, yet feel unable to do anything about it. Try to cooperate and work around the problems. They will soon pass. Try not to force the issue. It doesn't appear that you would win if you do.

URANUS (Radical Change/Independence)

Desire for Freedom

This is a very radical and volatile planet that will not tolerate any form of restriction. Uranus represents the desire within us to be different, to be independent and not follow the herd. It seeks to find its own unique way in the world. It is that part within us that hates to take orders, bend to authority, or follow other people's advice.

Uranus has a sudden, unpredictable quality. It often brings the unexpected. "I just turned the corner and there he was" or "It hit me from out of no where" are statements people tend to make when Uranus is involved. Uranus is also a very creative planet because contacts with it tend to push us in new directions. It can add brilliance, uniqueness of action and unusual artistic expressions. Consider four Aquarians ruled by the planet Uranus, and you will get the idea: Mozart, Schubert, Edison, and Jerome Kern. All of these very unique individuals expressed great originality in their work.

Uranus can also add a cruel side to the nature. It seems indifferent to personal feelings and holds a certain detachment from others. People with positive connections to Uranus are special individuals. If the connections are negative, they can be downright obnoxious.

Uranus supports the Sun: This energy gives the Sun a strong impulse to explore the unusual. The ego is in search of new ways to express itself. This energy is very creative, full of life and originality. If you have this placement at birth, you are attracted to people who are offbeat and unusual. If you are a woman with this position, you are strongly attracted to a man who is quite different from the normal herd. When you "fall in love" it is usually at first sight, but you can be bored just as quickly. You may have difficulty staying with one man due to an overt desire for new adventures.

What you really have to offer to the world is a unique perspective of life and an individuality that inspires others to be adventurous.

This is because you are something of a character yourself—you are considered to be "off-beat" by others.

As a relationship planet: If another person brings this Uranus to your Sun, they could inspire you to try new experiences and lead you into radical encounters with life.

As a visiting planet: It is time to try something new, to be your own person. Take the chances you have been thinking about—you may land in a better place. Now is the time to move on your imagination, because you will enjoy the journey and be pleasantly surprised.

Uranus frustrates the Sun: If Uranus makes this contact with the Sun, this person will have the desire to break away from established conditions and establish their own rules. They are strongly independent and unlikely to cooperate with others. Their ego may be so strong that they have very little tolerance for rules, regulations, authority and routine. Cooperation and compromise are important virtues for them to learn, but they will have to do that on their own terms.

As a relationship planet: If someone brings a frustrating Uranus to your Sun, they will bring a wild and unpredictable energy into your life. They will "push your buttons," lead you to take foolish chances, and challenge your will. The ego is very strong and uncooperative. This person can be very unreliable: here today and gone tomorrow. Don't invest a lot of energy and expectation in them. If you do, you will set yourself up for disappointment.

As a visiting planet: Sudden and unexpected experiences can create a lot of tension for you. Your goals are frustrated. You may want to make a change but don't feel like you can. You are forced to compromise to make it work out.

Uranus supports the Moon: People born with this position have habits that are most unusual. They do not hold on to experiences very long and therefore are not sentimental and rarely look back to lick their wounds. They have an impatience for solving problems and are quick to get to the heart of a solution. They can be very impulsive. However, they are very interesting people full of new and unusual ideas, and most of us like to be around them. Life is never boring when they are in the vicinity.

As a relationship planet: If someone brings a positive Uranus to your Moon, they can be responsible for getting you out of a rut. They will upset your normal surroundings and expectations, and will urge you to change your way of doing things. This can be a very positive influence because they can show you many possibilities for achieving your own life goals.

As a visiting planet: You will find some very unusual experiences coming your way, which can help break you out of a rut. Uranus visiting a man's Moon can suddenly bring a new woman into his life.

Uranus frustrates the Moon: This person could have a hair-trigger temper and surprise us with their reactions. They may explode when they are pressured to do something they don't want to do. They do not take kindly to any form of domination from others, and you will certainly hear from them if you attempt to tell them what to do. They are fiercely independent and sometimes quite volatile. As the Moon is involved here, this anger could relate to reactions to the mother or to women. Violence could result; however, this violence could be inflicted on self as well as on others.

As a relationship planet: If someone brings you a negative Uranus, then they can upset you more than any other person. They can stir reactions within you that you never thought you had. They will "get your goat." You might feel very nervous and constantly agitated in their presence.

As a visiting planet: This visitation of Uranus can bring very tense situations where you will feel like exploding. There can be some real upsets when the family and home environment are involved. Try to find a way to stay calm.

Uranus supports Mercury: A person born with this pattern is very bright. They are advanced in their understanding and have a very sharp mind, usually full of original ideas. This is a mind that knows that it knows and is capable of achieving a high position in life if so desired.

As a relationship planet: If another person brings Uranus to your Mercury in a positive way, they add clarity and brilliance to your own thinking and greatly inspired you by their presence. You see them as a source of knowledge and you like the mental stimulation they bring to you. They could be your teacher. You could work extremely well together and bring forth some very special ideas that would benefit you both—they would enjoy your interest in them and you would be inspired by their unusual insights.

As a visiting planet: It is now time to make huge mental advances for finishing writing projects, speaking to others and sharing inspired communication. It's a time when you can be very original with new ideas. Explore Internet possibilities.

Uranus frustrates Mercury: This could be a pattern of agitated impatience. The mind is bright, but gives this person a streak of intolerance for slower thinkers, a certain amount of arrogance and pride of knowledge. This could be the person who "knows it all." They do get flashes of insight that startle people, but their obnoxious way of showing their intelligence may be a "turn off". They are impatient and intolerant of other people's ideas and are very insensitive to another person's viewpoint.

As a relationship planet: Anyone whose Uranus affects your Mercury in an adverse way will challenge your thinking. They will not simply criticize your mind but will steamroll over it. They may oppose your ideas, interrupt you when you are speaking, or simply refuse to associate with you. They will find what they call "holes in your thinking." It may be humorous to them, but very obnoxious to you.

As a visiting planet: This visit of Uranus may show that you have to change your way of looking at things. The concepts and opinions you have been holding onto may no longer be valid. The pressure is on to re-examine the ideas that could be holding you back. Other people's ideas may be a challenge for you. Seek to compromise your position if it is for the better in the long run.

Uranus supports Venus: Since Venus is the desire to seek beauty, love and relationship, the planet Uranus here adds to the uniqueness of this search. Anyone born with this position seeks fulfillment in special ways. They can express themselves with a surprising originality in music, art, design or style. They are always open to new relationships and love to be with creative people who can stimulate their insatiable desire for new and exciting encounters. Because they like to associate with the unusual, they learn a lot of things other people don't even know about. They could be lucky with money and posses a sixth sense of how to invest it. There can be sudden financial gain. Their life is never boring because they cannot stand routine. They live on the edge of relationships because they believe in the freedom of love and the adventure of new encounters, which can make it difficult for them to remain loyal in relationship with others.

As a relationship planet: If someone brings their Uranus to your Venus in a supportive way, they will urge you to explore places you have never seen. If you are an artist, they can inspire you to create something unique and lasting. They will help you see through different eyes. They can stimulate you to a sudden love experience and cause you to fall quickly in love. But the attraction may not last because the need for constant stimulation may create a strain on the relationship. Sooner or later, one of you may not be able to keep up the pace.

As a visiting planet: This could bring sudden love and a sudden good-bye. Also, you could have sudden gains. You could be lucky during this period. Sexuality is also strong.

Uranus frustrates Venus: A person born with this kind of pattern can be very inconstant and unreliable in their feelings. They seem to feel that if they commit to one person they will lose the opportunity to be with another. But behind this strategy lies the real truth: They don't want to be vulnerable. They will fear that if someone has their heart it would destroy their freedom. So they tend to dance around the idea of intimacy, but rarely truly engage it. Their need to seek out another relationship even while they are already with someone is simply an avoidance of true intimacy. In true intimacy, we give our heart away. This person is afraid to do that.

As a relationship planet: If someone else's Uranus relates to your Venus in a frustrating way, they may seduce you into an affair because they stimulate your sexual energies. But beware—the relationship may not last long. This kind of contact tends to be short-lived. This person can also lead you into financial excess and cause you to waste your resources through wild enterprises. Think carefully before getting involved with them.

As a visiting planet: You will want to take chances in love and finances during this period, but don't do either. It may not turn out the way you expect.

Uranus supports Mars: If Uranus is related in a positive way to a person's Mars, it creates an unusual character full of the spirit of adventure. People with this position like to explore unknown territory, do things no one else has ever done before, or take up a challenge just to prove their uniqueness—even when they know it is risky. Not afraid to take a chance, they are competitive and seek to win at large enterprises. They are not afraid to take a chance. They may be outstanding in sports that require great skill and physical strength. (Chuck Norris, the famous martial artist, has this position.)

As a relationship planet: If someone brings a positive Uranus to your Mars, they can inspire you to act with courage and give you the confidence you may need to take action. They offer you a new way of doing things and can help get you out of a rut. You will find them very interesting and fascinating. Since Mars is also a sexual planet, this can mean love or sex at first sight. This contact can be very stimulating and you will need to be aware of the tendency to excess. You could become exhausted through mere association with this person. This is especially true for a woman whose Mars is stimulated by a man's Uranus.

As a visiting planet: Uranus functions as an increased feeling of possibility that any goal can be achieved. This visit of Uranus brings creative energy to accomplish your goals. You could be very effective.

Uranus frustrates Mars: The negative effect of Uranus promotes a wild and sometimes foolish lifestyle. This person will need to practice caution in all of their undertakings because they are always pushing their boundaries beyond what most of us would call good sense. Like the positive Uranus, they also take unnecessary risks just to prove a point, but they usually lose in the doing and may suffer a serious accident or cause something regrettable to happen. They should be careful with any kind of machinery as they tend to overlook safety precautions. When they push their boundaries and try to do things no one else has ever done, they may end up flat on their face. This is definitely the kind of planetary pattern that evokes the saying, "Don't push your luck."

As a relationship planet: If someone else has his Uranus in a negative relationship to your Mars, he will prompt you to act against good judgment and lead you into experiences that could be risky for you. Always think twice before doing anything this person suggests. If there is a sexual connection between you, don't expect the relationship to last or turn out the way you want—there is always something unpredictable in this kind of chemistry. Take caution.

As a visiting planet: A visiting Uranus brings stressful energies. Take care driving and practice being calm. Sudden frustration or anger could lead you to take an unwise course of action. Back off and don't force the situation.

NEPTUNE (Imagination/Escape)

Desire for Ecstasy

Neptune is a most mysterious planet because its energy works on a subtle level. It gives us the urge for ecstasy, to seek peak experiences, and to transcend the trials and troubles of the world through romantic love, art, beauty, film, music, writing, poetry or spiritual self-transcendence. These are its positive expressions. A strong Neptune can give us the need to get away from the world—to escape through positive or negative channels according to how it affects our other planetary patterns. On the negative side, this desire for ecstasy can move people into drugs, alcohol, fantasy, deception, weakness, dependency, swindling, lying, cheating and stealing.

This is an important planet for determining ancient connections that you may have with some of the people you are in contact with here. You will discover whether such connections exist in your relationships by exploring the kind of contact other people's Neptune makes with your own planetary patterns. If you find these connections, you will understand why the feelings you hold for such people are so extraordinary.

Neptune supports the Sun: Neptune manifests in the realm of the unseen; therefore its effects are subtle. Since it expresses within us the desire for ecstasy, its contact with our personal planets arouses this impulse. If Neptune supports a person's Sun at birth in a positive way, it can impart the highest aspirations. This person is very interested in the subtle things of life and considers love to be beyond this world. Very sensitive to other people's needs, they cannot endure the suffering of another person without wanting to do something to help them. This person has to be careful about creating illusions about their friends and lovers—they are sometimes too open and trusting because they see good qualities in just about everyone. They can be very musical, artistic, and creative with keen imagination. If this person is well grounded, they can handle flights of imagination and the need to help others, but they still must be careful to protect themselves against negative influences. Even a supportive Neptune can instill fear of dealing with the world.

As a relationship planet: If someone else brings their Neptune to you in a positive way, you could feel that you have known them for a thousand years. Past life or ancient connections are often felt. They could inspire you with their kindness and genuine support from the heart. This person can be a true friend or lover where the love between you runs deeper than the experiences of this lifetime.

As a visiting planet: This visit of Neptune can bring creative inspiration into your life. Your sense of the subtle is stronger. Your feelings are tuned more toward helping others or your creative capacity is enhanced. It is time to express your feelings and get in touch with the deeper meaning of life.

Neptune frustrates the Sun: A negative Neptune can lead us into difficult circumstances. A person with this pattern will have to exercise great will and develop a deep understanding of themselves to avoid self-destructive habits and actions. They have a longing to escape from the world because there is a lack of emotional support from within. They tend to associate with people who need their help, but they should beware of negative and deceptive friendships. Because they tend to rely too much upon others to give them some sense of direction, they can be taken advantage of by showing their weakness. Women with this pattern often attract men who are weak and wimpy because they have the need to help wounded men.

As a relationship planet: If someone brings a negative Neptune to your Sun, they will sap your energy, appear other than they really are, and deceive you in some way. They may cause you to deceive yourself because you will tend to see them other than they are. This kind of relationship is hard to figure out—there is always something illusive about it. But behind this illusive quality can be lurking a true deception. Even though you will really want to, don't believe anything this person tells you. Always check them out first.

As a visiting planet: You may not know what to do with your life at this point because your goals appear confused. It is not a time to move forward on any plan because you could have some feelings about it that are not realistic. Wait until this period passes and you will be able to make better decisions.

Neptune supports the Moon. This connection is very nurturing. A person with this combination can be an extremely helpful person with a loving, motherly spirit. They are unusually sensitive to the emotional needs of others and show the deepest kind of caring—always being there when people need their kind and comforting words. Deeply sensitive to their environment, they like to create peaceful surroundings. They have the power to attract very harmonious and benign forces into their life and often have a mysterious spiritual quality that draws others to them. They are naturally attuned to the subtle and may do a lot of meditating. Theirs is truly a caring heart.

As a relationship planet: If someone else brings you a positive Neptune, you will feel their support right away. What they do for you tells you that they really do care. Sometimes you will even feel healed in their presence. There can be a deep bond between you and your connection may go beyond this lifetime. You will feel that this person really understands you.

As a visiting planet: This brings an increase in imagination, sensitivity, sympathy and caring for others. Neptune is supporting your creativity. It is time to heal old wounds with the mother.

Neptune frustrates the Moon. A person with this connection wears glasses of illusion. They tend to see the world the way they want to and are consoled by what might be or what they pretend the situation to be. The difficulty is when reality knocks on their door. They have a great need for support and comfort because they were not sustained or nurtured as a child. They may look for this support from the wrong kind of people. The price they personally pay in money, energy and attention for that comfort may be too high. They often sacrifice themselves in situations with people who are not good for them and sometimes get swindled by those they trust. They tend to choose negative people who are weak and who feed off of others. They tend to trust the wrong person.

As a relationship planet: If someone else brings you this kind of Neptune, you may have to take care of their needs—but your needs will not be met. You could feel obligated to this person for no apparent reason and they can make you feel guilty if you start to abandon them. They will usually bring out your need to help. Be cautious: they may be using you. As always with negative Neptunian influences, you have to work at keeping the situation out in the open and confront what is really going on. Any attempts to pretend or to avoid the reality should be confronted immediately so misunderstandings do not develop. If you have suspicions about this person, you are probably right.

As a visiting planet: You may become consumed emotionally, feeling that you are caught between satisfying your needs and those of someone else. A woman or family member may need your help at a time when you don't feel you have the energy to give. Try to work out your priorities—first things first.

Neptune supports Mercury: This connection adds great inspiration to a mind that taps the superconscious realm of the mind—the world of imagination and creativity. Neptune reveals our desire for ecstasy; therefore, this is an ecstatic mind. The thoughts are infused with subtle impressions of imagination, sound, words or dreams. This is a wonderful pattern for a musician, artist or writer. If this is your Mercury, you have been given a great gift.

As a relationship planet: If anyone brings Neptune to your Mercury in a supporting way, they can inspire your mind. Their mere presence has a calming effect on your thinking and you may perceive in them some kind of spiritual quality. This is an excellent connection for delving together into the subtleties of life. They will add intuitive inspiration to your thinking and help you find insights into difficult problems.

As a visiting planet: This visit of Neptune brings sheer inspiration and the capacity to understand the subtleties of life. This is an extremely helpful planet for doing very creative and artistic work of any kind. You could discover some very helpful insights that have a direct emotional impact upon others.

Neptune frustrates Mercury: A person with this pattern has to be careful to tell the truth and not distort reality to suit their expectations. In some sense, they refuse to see the truth. They seem to have a deep fear of reality because it has been so painful in the past. These people could lie to themselves or refuse to accept the facts. They can be woolly-minded and seem confused at times. Logical thinking is difficult for them because unconscious fears distort their reasoning or perceptions.

As a relationship planet: If someone has their Neptune adverse to your Mercury, you need to be careful in your communications. Often there is a web of misunderstanding because the conversations are unclear, or unconscious assumptions take over to distort the messages. You may disagree over artistic and creative matters. Be careful to read between the lines if this person wants you to sign an agreement or contract. They may be hiding something. Keep your communications and agreements out front so no misunderstanding will develop. Remain on the cautious side.

As a visiting planet: Time to double-check all your communications because it is a time when you may become very confused and unable to get your ideas across. You may feel like your mind is jelly and that you can't function mentally like you used to. Don't worry—you will soon come out of the fog. Be careful with any legal agreements that require your signature. Something important could be overlooked.

Neptune supports Venus. These positive patterns of Neptune exalt the energies of Venus. This person has unusual artistic abilities and can communicate something of the sublime through their creative imagination. Their imaginative wings can take them to places where they find remarkable inspirations. Whatever form of art they choose, they have the capacity to make it the best. Musical tones or colors in paintings, can move the listener or viewer to profound feelings. This position of Neptune also gives great love of friends and people in general, and this person is very supportive of others due to a deep sensitivity to other people's needs. They are full of romantic ideas and fantasy—always seeking the absolutely perfect love.

As a relationship planet: If someone brings his Neptune to you in a positive way, you will consider them your dearest friend, as if you had always known them. Your love and friendship can extend far beyond any difference you may have between you. This is a relationship you feel will last forever regardless of what might really happen in life between you. Your love is deeper than what most people experience and has an enduring quality. This is something you will feel to be true in your heart.

As a visiting planet: This is a visitation of inspiration, a time to create something beautiful. Love that comes to you during this time can be of the highest kind. If you are in the arts, it is a great time to make things happen—a very creative period.

Neptune frustrates Venus. If someone has this negative pattern, they will tend to get involved in relationships that are full of complication and intrigue. One reason for this is that they tend to see in their friend or lover only what they want to see rather than who they really are. Therefore, there is most always a real disappointment with friends and lovers when the reality of the relationship comes home. They may often find themselves being deceived by others either financially or emotionally because they trust them without question. Any devious person lurking in their life will reach out and take advantage of their trusting nature. Because of this, they feel abused and ripped off. The person with this pattern has a profound need to be loved and will often make great sacrifices just to get a little affection—but what a price to pay.

As a relationship planet: If someone brings your Venus a negative Neptune, you should be very cautious. They could be setting you up for a fall. This individual may promise you the sky, but obviously can't deliver. You have to look at the potential karma of your relationship because another person's negative Neptune can distort your impression of them. They will stir your feelings of love and appear to be your friend, but if you invest your heart and time in them, expect to find something about them that you didn't know before. There can be a real sense of betrayal when the truth is finally known. This connection can generate craving for sexual ecstasy. It, however, can be treacherous because alcohol, drugs or perversion can be involved. There could even be entrapment. The person with the Venus can feel "sucked in" by the Neptune person. All illusions about the relationship should be confronted, because lovers with this pattern will tend to deceive each other.

As a visiting planet: This visit of Neptune is definitely a time of confusion in relationship. It may be that you are totally swept away by someone but are not sure whether it is illusion. The reality of a person may be saying one thing while you are feeling another. Check out everything against the real truth. Also, be especially careful not to listen to grand schemes for making money. It is likely that you will lose out if you buy into promises that may only be full of air. Friends may not turn out to be your friends after all.

Neptune supports Mars. If Neptune is related to Mars in a favorable way at birth, this person has a wonderful healing energy. Their effect on others can be very soothing. People feel sustained and nurtured in their presence even without them doing anything. The person with this Mars is driven towards an ideal and wants to realize a creative goal. They would be outstanding as a physical therapist or counselor. People feel their warmth and are drawn to their company. They will be favorably associated with other people who are very helpful and nurturing. They may relate to each other on a very deep level. Neptune's energy heightens the sexual desire, refining it and giving this person the capacity to relate to a lover in a very intimate way. They may be too idealistically attracted to those who need their help. Even with this positive energy, a person must be careful not to get drawn into a relationship that will be hard to dissolve because Neptune here can generate a kind of magnetic attraction that can be sexually very satisfying but also debilitating due to excess of appetite or craving.

As a relationship planet: If a person brings a positive Neptune to your Mars, they will be your dearest friend and possibly your greatest lover. They will always be there for you—ready to help when you need it. There is an opportunity to establish a very loving and deep connection between you that goes beyond the spoken words of "I love you"—your intimacy can be transcendental, transporting you to a higher level of ecstasy. You may feel like you have known each other before, sharing a familiarity that you cannot explain. These are often past life connections that are shown by Neptune's positive support of Mars.

As a visiting planet: This visit of Neptune brings creative magnetism. Your personal magnetism and sexual energy are increased and people will feel the warmth coming from you. They will read that warmth as love, or that you really care. This is a time to heal yourself and respond to subtle energies that can bring you a more peaceful life.

Neptune frustrates Mars: Since Mars is masculine in nature, a woman born with a negative relationship between her Mars and Neptune, will tend to see men through foggy lenses. She may imagine them to be someone they are not. She tends to attract men who take advantage of her because of the martyr tendencies that make her a willing victim. There is often a history of sexual abuse and deep-seated pains relating to childhood experiences with men. Neptune functions here as the robber or deceiver. This woman may often play the role of being used by men—to later find that this has always been her unconscious expectation. If she has been mistreated or rejected by men in her childhood, she may unconsciously expect to be the one who makes the sacrifices in her relationships with men. At some point, she must take a stand for her own goodness by walking away from those men who do not love her. Sometime, she will get tired of being the one to fix up the relationship by always giving in to what the man wants. When she refuses to be with the men who neither love her nor give her their heart, she will begin to awaken to her own power as a woman. Great growth can come from this courageous gesture—it is a fire that will transform her.

A man with this pattern was probably born with a weak will and needs to find strength within himself. His father may have given him little support and was probably an alcoholic. He will sometimes feel helpless to act upon his desires. He needs to awaken his will through disciplined exercises and take conscious responsibility for his own life.

As a relationship planet: If a man brings a woman's Mars a negative Neptune, she should realize that he may try to seduce her through beguiling romanticism. He can cause her to see him idealistically rather than realistically. Whatever he promises or proposes should be looked at carefully. Chances are he is not sincere and is only satisfying his own appetites. If she detects any deception or contradiction at all, she is probably right. She should walk away and not look back.

If someone brings a man a negative Neptune, he should be careful and check them out. They may be looking for a favor and may not be totally honest.

As a visiting planet: This is primarily an energy of confusion, deception and uncertainty. It is not wise to trust your own actions or the actions of others, because you may be functioning from a weak position. You may not have all the facts and may give too much to others. Take care of your health. Your physical energy seems to be low. You may be tired a lot, not your usual energetic self. It is time to simplify your life and let go of a lot of activities. You need rest.

PLUTO (Transformation/Extreme Pressure)

The Heart's Desire

Not enough can be said about Pluto. It is a planet of such powerful, transforming energy that its fallout effects can last a lifetime. Pluto is the urge within us to move beyond our human existence, transcend our limitations, and express our heart's desire to merge with another—the Source. But this urge is so deep within our psyche that few of us are aware of how to do this. Pluto is the "fire of Shiva," the God that destroys darkness and ignorance. That is, the energies of Pluto try to move us toward an open heart, but this energy is so intense that we often find it difficult to bear the pain of feeling our own resistance to the overwhelming love within us.

My own personal discovery of Pluto led me to the remarkable vision that a man's heart bears a feminine form and a woman's heart bears a masculine form. But beyond these lunar and solar energies is the heart's essence, the soul. Pluto is our soul—our purest and deepest desire. It is the core of our heart, beyond our masculine and feminine forms, and therefore Pluto is the deepest part of us. The heart reflects the soul and the soul is the heart's desire. This is to say that the woman's heart (the Sun) reflects her soul, and the man's heart (the Moon) reflects his soul. (The true meaning of the esoteric relationship between a man and a woman is explained completely in my other book *The Heart of a Man is a Woman*, which was written under the name of Randall Curtis.)

When you have planetary contacts with Pluto, there is nothing ordinary in the energy expressed. When Pluto makes favorable contacts, all the great qualities of the soul and its capacity for the deepest love are expressed. When Pluto makes unfavorable contacts, its energies are thwarted and a tyrannical battleground may become the foreground of your life. It is extremely important to understand how Pluto is operating in your life; it holds the key to your ultimate freedom as a lover and as a creative human being.

Pluto supports the Sun: When we combine these two energies in a positive way, we have one of the most powerful emotional patterns possible. A woman with this pattern in her chart has more capacity to love than anyone. This is not a love nature that makes demands. At the same time, she will not tolerate an insincere relationship made up with devious games. She wants the ultimate love expression with her mate, but she will not lay claims. Her feelings are very clear to her and she is not fooled by her own emotions. She tends to give love generously to others but will not be abused by a manipulating lover. Yet she is not trying to be in control—she simply wants her relationships to be deeply satisfying.

For a man, this position will increase his will. His power to achieve and accomplish is very great. He may have a powerful charismatic quality that reflects the depth of his feelings. He has a quiet will that endures through time.

As a relationship Planet: If a man brings a woman a supporting Pluto, he could be the love of her life. This could truly be a past life connection and she could see her soul in this man. She may feel so connected to him that her love is greater than any other experience she has known. He could be the one she has always wanted.

A woman who brings a favorable Pluto to a man's Sun can support his greatest desires and ambitions. She will always be there for him.

As a visiting planet: Pluto's visit here brings a very sustaining energy that supports the ego, and goals are achieved with much less effort. Doors seem to open and life situations seem more graceful. A woman experiencing Pluto's visitation to her Sun may meet her soul mate, because the Sun is her heart.

Pluto frustrates the Sun: This person has a power struggle with life. They can be very aggressive and show a cruel streak because of intense desires. They feel as though their life is always being threatened.

A woman with this pattern will demand more from life than she can possibly receive. She must find the answer to love from *within* herself rather than requiring it from the man she overcomes with her intensity. Pluto next to her Sun sets up an unusual life situation. Even if her Sun is not negatively related to other planets, she will still look for complete and absolute love from the man in her life—in fact, she demands it from him. But at the root of this need is a great fear. She was probably abandoned by her father or else lost him at an early age. Even if this did not actually occur, she was born feeling that. She was born with a great sense of threat—a fear that something is going to happen if she does not protect herself. Bearing a deep disgust of weak men, she will test her lovers all of her life to see how strong they really are. Perhaps she needs to ask a very important question: "Do I really want to stay in control of the relationship or am I willing to surrender my heart without seeking protection from loss?" What she must eventually realize is that the love she is looking for must come from within herself.

A man with this position can be quite obnoxious because Pluto moves his will into a position of confrontation. If he feels thwarted in the smallest way, he may react with anger and even violence. He has the feeling that nothing is going to stop him from getting what he wants. The frustrating effect of Pluto upon his survival instinct (Sun) makes him feel that he has to have his own way. He is probably reacting against an abusive or demanding father.

As a relationship planet: If someone brings your Sun a negative Pluto, you will feel threatened by them. They will tend to make impossible demands on you that you feel you cannot possibly fulfill or refuse to submit to. They seem to have all the power, and you may feel compelled to give in just to keep the peace. But this is a one-sided concession and no real peace will ever come from it. You can never win in this situation because it will feel like they have a gun to your head. This relationship can be a very negative piece of karma. You may need to get yourself away as soon as possible because it could eventually turn violent. At some point, you may find yourself saying, "I'm not going to take this anymore."

As a visiting planet: You feel "under the gun." The situation seems unbearable. You may be at war with someone. You need to decide which is the best course of action: Give in and compromise or oppose your enemy. Choose carefully.

Pluto supports the Moon: This position intensifies the feelings and relates closely to experiences with the mother, home and family. There is a deep caring love nature that is very supportive and nurturing to others. Sensitivity is heightened as well as a psychic sense of the surroundings. This pattern lends greater awareness of the needs of others. Therefore, this person has a natural inclination to help the homeless, the aging, the hungry and the forsaken.

As a relationship planet: If another person's Pluto is related favorably to your Moon, they certainly would be your greatest support. They will always be there when you need them and will endure your hardships to help you through a crisis. Their connection to you can go beyond words because there is an unspoken love that endures through time. Such love is very strong.

As a visiting planet: You will be totally nurtured by someone or by a life situation. You could be going through a real healing process with members of your family—especially with your mother. It is a time to be completely open and share your deepest feelings with others, because there is a potential for creating very lasting bonds of love.

Pluto frustrates the Moon: This pattern presents an altogether different picture, which includes some form of emotional loss. Even though the mother may not have literally abandoned this person, they feel like she did. The person has a deep emotional fear that they will be forsaken. This is usually not conscious, yet it plays out in daily life. Therefore, with any hint or threat of loss of security, they go into a panic. Driven by fear and anxiety, they are intensely emotional and very demanding in getting their needs fulfilled.

As a relationship planet: If another person relates to your Moon in this way, you will feel very threatened by them. One man whose wife had her Pluto square his Moon said, "It felt like she had a gun to my head." This person makes intolerable demands upon the Moon person. This is definitely a pattern to avoid in a relationship—it is very difficult to live under and it is hard to say "no" to the Pluto person because of the threatening quality of their demand. They feel like performing psychological surgery on the Moon person.

As a visiting planet: You can be very upset emotionally. There seems to be an intense emotional response required of you at this time. You may be feeling fears that you never felt before because of the situation. You may experience the loss of a family member or feel that you don't have a home anymore. There can be a deep sense of loneliness because you are not being nurtured by others or your life situation has become intolerable. But from this struggle, you may find out who you are.

Pluto supports Mercury: This pattern imparts to the individual a very keen mind. The mind works like an X-ray. President Clinton has this pattern and he has mentioned that the mind has to be like a laser. There is great perception and deep understanding of any subject the mind wishes to focus on. The energies of Pluto intensify the mind's capacity to see into things. This is a detective's mind— one that can ferret out the truth from a bundle of lies. The person can have a great capacity for research and penetrating the causes of things. These people can be great writers, speakers or researchers because they have the ability to go directly to the issues that matter. They can be threatening because they tend to have a penetrating gaze that can make others feel naked or uncomfortable in their presence.

As a relationship planet: If someone has Pluto related to your Mercury in a positive way, they can certainly help you reach the depths of your thinking and challenge you to look deeper. You may feel like you have learned a lot in their company because they can actually help you awaken a new level of awareness. At times, you may feel pressured in their company but you will usually find it is a positive and beneficial association. You could work well together.

As a visiting planet: This is really a boon for stretching your mind and actually seeing that you can accomplish a lot mentally if you set your mind to it. Your insights at this time can be most penetrating. They could be very valuable and will probably be very accurate. Trust them and keep a record of your discoveries.

Pluto frustrates Mercury: This person has a very coercive mind. They know what they want when they want it, and tend to project this demand upon others. They are obsessed with their ideas, documents, writings or papers and seem to have a deep fear that something awful may happen to their communications. Fear drives them to make impossible demands upon other people. They have a very keen intellect but it is expressed with such a dominating attitude that other people avoid them. Most people who work with this person will feel threatened by their anger or intensity of demand. They have an amazing capacity for arousing hostility.

As a relationship planet: If someone has his Pluto adversely related to your Mercury, you will have a terrible time trying to please them. They will place such exacting demands upon you that you may begin to act strange and feel unsure of yourself. You will become plagued with trying to second-guess what this person wants. If they are your boss or superior, ask for a transfer, because you will never be able to please them. Whatever you do for them, it will never be good enough. They will make you feel inadequate and stupid, when you obviously are not. If you continue this association, you will only make more mistakes and matters will get worse. Get away as fast as you can. This could fester into a serious communication problem.

As a visiting planet: Someone may be undermining or criticizing your work. This could put you under tremendous mental pressure with a feeling that it is impossible to measure up to the demand. You could be under unreasonable mental pressure. Try to get some help or seek advice for another avenue of action. You may be banging your head against the wall when you don't have to. Consider another way out or a better way to do it.

Pluto supports Venus: This increases the love nature and desire for a quality relationship. There is little tolerance for casual or shallow love affairs. This person is deeply loyal in their affections and they look for real substance in love. The intense energy of Pluto exalts the desire of Venus and shows that they have a deep love nature. Because of this sensitivity and refinement of feeling, there can be remarkable expressions of beauty through art.

As a relationship planet: If someone has their Pluto relating to your Venus in this way, you will feel a close connection to them. They may feel like an old friend, someone who really relaxes you.

If a man's Pluto is next to a woman's Venus, this can add a compulsive quality to the relationship—even seem like an obsession--but it simply shows the intensity that each person is capable of feeling for the other. In some cases, this connection can bring the deepest love and friendship possible between two people. Such connections are often experienced as profound love upon first contact.

As a visiting planet: Now is the time to express the deepest love in your heart. You are more moved to connect with someone or something on a more intimate level. As a result, you could gain a deeper understanding of how you really feel about other people. The person or situation in your life now may help you see this. This is a great time to share more intimately—and then you will find a relationship with greater emotional depth.

Pluto frustrates Venus: This pattern can drive a person to be very demanding in matters of love and they can be very manipulative in getting what they want. They want the heart and soul of their lover and their friends, and require a great deal of attention. They may have suffered loss of the mother or experienced abandonment at an early age. If other planets relate favorably to this pattern, the person's compulsive demands—their attempt to quell their deep fear of loss, may be less deceptively expressed. This person will find it difficult to be truly vulnerable because of an inherent fear of rejection and loss. While they expect a lot from love, they find it difficult to give someone else their heart without a solid guarantee. They will always seek the safer position.

As a relationship planet: Obviously, if someone has their Pluto negatively related to your Venus, they will make compulsive demands upon you. Be careful to see if this is real love or possession. Sometimes lovers with this connection have been together in a past life and have come together again to work out or complete their relationship. Beware of being coerced into a relationship that you instinctively know is not good for you. It will be difficult to break the connection once it has been established because of the intensity of the energy between you.

As a visiting planet: Relationships will be very intense at this time and you may fall under the spell of a love obsession. You may be intensely pursuing love because you are trying to discover what it really means. While you may not end up with any of the people you engage now, you are so intensely involved with them that you will learn a great deal about yourself. This will probably be very beneficial for you in the long run—or maybe not. It all depends on what you learn at this time about the way you love people.

Pluto supports Mars: A person with this pattern has an intense drive and strong sexual energy. They usually have a strong will and an amazing capacity to endure many hardships. They know how to use energy effectively and can be extremely creative. But Pluto here primarily moves the passions.

A woman with this favorable position can threaten men because of the intensity of her desire—but no harm is intended. Her desire is great. If the pattern is a conjunction, she can challenge men to take her if they can handle her. She is fiercely attracted to strong men who can match her intensity. She is a fighter or champion of causes and may have had an intense relationship with her father.

As a relationship planet: For a woman, if a man's Pluto comes into relationship with her Mars, she could be in for an intense sexual journey. This is passion in its highest state. She could become obsessed with her desire for him and may not be conscious that the relationship may be about love lust rather than love. It is very difficult to refuse to engage this affair because it goes deeper than a mere romance. This energy will really spin the chakras!

As a visiting planet: This is the time to get a lot accomplished. Your projects are easier to finish now because you have a lot of energy available. You can be successful in any endeavor requiring huge amounts of endurance and expenditure of energy. Relationships with men in general may be very supportive.

Pluto frustrates Mars: This is a pattern of intense feeling that can be very threatening to others. If the energy is triggered in the wrong way, violence could occur. A woman with this configuration may have been sexually abused as a child. She could be full of great rage and carry a psychological weapon, ready to emotionally castrate any man who is too weak to stand up to her. She can be very challenging and desire confrontation.

Men with these positions can basically be very aggressive and often find themselves in situations that can be quite dangerous. This is a very volatile pattern.

As a relationship planet: If a man has his Pluto related negatively to a woman's Mars, she will have to be careful of the relationship. He will want to take her over, control her life, and be in charge. This connection is so intense that she may have to be very careful not to play out negative and compulsive games with him. She may be fascinated by this man because he is able to reach the depths of her desire, but it is still a fiercely possessive energy. Negative reactions can be very damaging. Also, this could be pure lust.

In general, any person whose Pluto frustrates your Mars will be at war with you. They will stand in your way and can be very difficult to deal with. Avoid confrontation with them because they would likely win the battle.

As a visiting planet: You may feel like you are being coerced into doing something against your will. Consider this carefully. Consider the consequences if it does not turn out the way you expect it to. Try to avoid ultimatums and head-on encounters with others. Make compromise your watchword. It may be better to give in if you do not lose all that much. You could prevent a serious mistake by doing so.

Appendix

MASTER TABLE

DEGREES OF SIGN	SYMBOL FOR SIGN	NAME AND DATES	ELEMENT
0 - 30	♈	ARIES 3/21-4/19	FIRE
30 - 60	♉	TAURUS 4/19-5/20	EARTH
60 - 90	♊	GEMINI 5/20-6/21	AIR
90 - 120	♋	CANCER 6/21-7/23	WATER
120 - 150	♌	LEO 7/23 - 8/23	FIRE
150 - 180	♍	VIRGO 8/23 - 9/23	EARTH
180 - 210	♎	LIBRA 9/23 -10/23	AIR
210 - 240	♏	SCORPIO 10/23 -11/23	WATER
240 - 270	♐	SAGITTARIUS 11/23 - 12/21	FIRE
270 - 300	♑	CAPRICORN 12/21 - 1/19	EARTH
300 - 330	♒	AQUARIUS 1/19 - 2/19	AIR
330 - 360	♓	PISCES 2/19 - 3/21	WATER

APPENDIX

MASTER TABLE

POSITIVE/NEGATIVE ATTITUDES	PLANETARY RULER	AREAS RULED BY THE PLANET
Aggressive, fearless, unyielding initiator	MARS ♂	Fire, iron, surgical instruments, knives, spears, guns, war, masculinity
Slow, tenacious, persistent, materialistic, stubborn, and sensual	VENUS ♀	Banks, idealism, femininity, relationship, marriage, and partnerships
Witty, versatile, light-fingered, impatient, dishonest, and crafty	MERCURY ☿	Communication, transportation, letters, contracts, neighbors, and mental activity
Sensitive, imaginative, moody, protective, security-minded, and crabby	MOON ☽	Stomach, grocers, chefs, bakeries, houses, mother, silver, habits, family, and security
Proud, independent, soft-hearted, dramatic, and egocentric	SUN ☉	Gold, children, theatres, entertainment, heart, ego, speculation, and gambling
Serving, neat, critical, analytical, and efficient	MERCURY ☿	Small animals, employees, health, work, and service
Social, artistic, indecisive, harmonious, and wishy-washy	VENUS ♀	Marriage, partnership, public relations
Intense, jealous, proud, cautious, vengeful, and secretive	PLUTO ♇	Death, regeneration, mysteries, taxes, insurance, sexuality, and the occult
Restless, blunt, bigoted, aspiring, hard worker, truthful	JUPITER ♃	Publishing, law, foreign countries, churches, long trips, ministers, philosophy, higher education
Practical, ambitious, austere, cold, stingy, honest, limited spirituality	SATURN ♄	Bones, real estate, knees, business, government, tradition, responsibility
Ingenious, unpredictable, opinionated, indifferent, detached	URANUS ♅	Television, computers, airplanes, telephones, high-tech, planetary psychology, electricity, higher awareness
Impractical, sympathetic, artistic, creative, dreamy escapist, sacrificial	NEPTUNE ♆	Hospitals, drugs, alcohol, gas, ocean, music, poetry, meditation, monasteries, and prisons

THE ELEMENT CHART

	FIRE Aries Leo Sagittarius	EARTH Taurus Virgo Capricorn	AIR Gemini Libra Aquarius	WATER Cancer Scorpio Pisces
FIRE Aries Leo Sagittarius	S	F	S	F
EARTH Taurus Virgo Capricorn	F	S	F	S
AIR Gemini Libra Aquarius	S	F	S	F
WATER Cancer Scorpio Pisces	F	S	F	S

S = Supported
F = Frustrated

The chart above enables you to know at a glance whether two signs are in harmony (supported) or in discord (frustrated). This allows you to determine that the attitude, or sign, expressed by an impersonal planet is in harmony or conflict with the attitude expressed by a personal planet. After finding out if the planets' signs support or frustrate each other, use the Sign Table to determine whether they are in orb. To use the Element Chart, first determine the sign of an impersonal planet and locate that sign in the left column of the chart above. Then determine the sign the personal planet is in and locate it in the appropriate column to the right. Notice that there is an S or F letter where these two points intersect. When using the Element Chart, make sure you keep the 10-degree orb in mind and that you follow the rules in Lesson 5. Here are two examples:

1. Your friend's Uranus is at 10 degrees of Libra and your Venus is at 6 degrees of Libra. Locate Libra in the first column, which is where Uranus would be, then move your finger across the page to your right until you come to the air column where the sign of Libra is located. Notice that there is a an "S" there. This means that your friend's Uranus supports your Venus.*

2. My Saturn is at 20 degrees of Scorpio and my Moon is at 3 degrees of Leo. Locate Saturn in the water sign of Scorpio in the first column of the Element Chart and move your finger over to the fire column where Leo is located. There you will find the letter "F". This means that these attitudes would be frustrated EXCEPT they are 17 degrees from being a square. Therefore, they are out of orb and are not readable. Always keep the orb in mind when using the Element Chart, because the energies of the power points described in Lesson 5 are not activated outside the 10-degree orb—regardless of whether or not the signs are compatible.

* This pattern is obviously a conjunction (see Lesson 5). This is read as supporting if Venus in your birth chart is *not* afflicted (frustrated) by an impersonal planet in your birth chart. If your Venus is afflicted at birth, then your friend's Uranus would not support your Venus. He would only activate the frustration that is already felt by you. Note that Uranus and Venus are only 4 degrees from an exact conjunction.

THE SIGN TABLE

1 Fire	2 Earth	3 Air	4 Water	5 Fire	6 Earth	7 Air	8 Water	9 Fire	10 Earth	11 Air	12 Water
ARIES ♈	TAURUS ♉	GEMINI ♊	CANCER ♋	LEO ♌	VIRGO ♍	LIBRA ♎	SCORPIO ♏	SAGITTARIUS ♐	CAPRICORN ♑	AQUARIUS ♒	PISCES ♓
1°	1°	1°	1°	1°	1°	1°	1°	1°	1°	1°	1°
2°	2°	2°	2°	2°	2°	2°	2°	2°	2°	2°	2°
3°	3°	3°	3°	3°	3°	3°	3°	3°	3°	3°	3°
4°	4°	4°	4°	4°	4°	4°	4°	4°	4°	4°	4°
5°	5°	5°	5°	5°	5°	5°	5°	5°	5°	5°	5°
6°	6°	6°	6°	6°	6°	6°	6°	6°	6°	6°	6°
7°	7°	7°	7°	7°	7°	7°	7°	7°	7°	7°	7°
8°	8°	8°	8°	8°	8°	8°	8°	8°	8°	8°	8°
9°	9°	9°	9°	9°	9°	9°	9°	9°	9°	9°	9°
10°	10°	10°	10°	10°	10°	10°	10°	10°	10°	10°	10°
11°	11°	11°	11°	11°	11°	11°	11°	11°	11°	11°	11°
12°	12°	12°	12°	12°	12°	12°	12°	12°	12°	12°	12°
13°	13°	13°	13°	13°	13°	13°	13°	13°	13°	13°	13°
14°	14°	14°	14°	14°	14°	14°	14°	14°	14°	14°	14°
15°	15°	15°	15°	15°	15°	15°	15°	15°	15°	15°	15°
16°	16°	16°	16°	16°	16°	16°	16°	16°	16°	16°	16°
17°	17°	17°	17°	17°	17°	17°	17°	17°	17°	17°	17°
18°	18°	18°	18°	18°	18°	18°	18°	18°	18°	18°	18°
19°	19°	19°	19°	19°	19°	19°	19°	19°	19°	19°	19°
20°	20°	20°	20°	20°	20°	20°	20°	20°	20°	20°	20°
21°	21°	21°	21°	21°	21°	21°	21°	21°	21°	21°	21°
22°	22°	22°	22°	22°	22°	22°	22°	22°	22°	22°	22°
23°	23°	23°	23°	23°	23°	23°	23°	23°	23°	23°	23°
24°	24°	24°	24°	24°	24°	24°	24°	24°	24°	24°	24°
25°	25°	25°	25°	25°	25°	25°	25°	25°	25°	25°	25°
26°	26°	26°	26°	26°	26°	26°	26°	26°	26°	26°	26°
27°	27°	27°	27°	27°	27°	27°	27°	27°	27°	27°	27°
28°	28°	28°	28°	28°	28°	28°	28°	28°	28°	28°	28°
29°	29°	29°	29°	29°	29°	29°	29°	29°	29°	29°	29°
30°	30°	30°	30°	30°	30°	30°	30°	30°	30°	30°	30°

Note for the Sign Table:

If two planets are more than 180 degrees from each other, count backwards. For example, if Uranus is at 8 degrees of Taurus and Mars is at 2 degrees of Capricorn, you would cover 270 degrees to get to Capricorn (column 2 to column 10). Since this is more than 180 degrees, count backwards from Taurus to Aries, to Pisces, to Aquarius, and then to Capricorn. By going in this direction, you discover that these two planets are trine each other (120 degrees apart).

THE PERSONAL AND IMPERSONAL PLANETS

Personal Planets

- ☉ Sun
- ☽ Moon
- ☿ Mercury
- ♀ Venus
- ♂ Mars

Impersonal Planets

- ♃ Jupiter
- ♄ Saturn
- ♅ Uranus
- ♆ Neptune
- ♇ Pluto

THE RELATIONSHIP TABLE

Positive Attraction Indicators
(Supports Your Personal Planet)

♅/☉ = Never a dull moment
♅/☽ = Challenges you to adapt
♅/☿ = Creative communication
♅/♀ = Love at first sight
♅/♂ = Sex at first sight

Can you take the stimulation?

♆/☉ = Deep soul connections
♆/☽ = Feeling of being nurtured
♆/☿ = Psychic communication
♆/♀ = Love is very deep
♆/♂ = Seductive sexuality

Love and personal attachment seem to be present upon first contact.

♇/☉ = Potential soulmates
♇/☽ = Intensely caring
♇/☿ = Intense communication
♇/♀ = Intensely loving
♇/♂ = Intensely sexual

Moderate these obsessive energies with compromise.

Negative Attraction Indicators
(Frustrates Your Personal Planet)

♅/☉ = Obnoxious behavior
♅/☽ = Emotionally upsetting
♅/☿ = Disagreements
♅/♀ = Attraction without satisfaction
♅/♂ = Angry reactions

♆/☉ = Will not support you
♆/☽ = Only appears to care
♆/☿ = Confused communications
♆/♀ = Deceptive lover
♆/♂ = Lust without love

♇/☉ = Tries to control you
♇/☽ = Emotionally demanding/coercive
♇/☿ = Critical of your thinking
♇/♀ = Possessive love
♇/♂ = Sexual dominance/tyranny

Potential danger

Note:
Even though the attractions may be strong, avoid all the "negative attraction indicators." Also avoid all relationships where another person's Saturn is conjunct or square your personal planet.

ANALYSIS FORMS

Re-create these forms for your use as they are too small for copying.

Sign Positions for Personal Planets

1. **Descriptions of the Sun**

    The Sun (_____) is in the _____.
    Therefore the _____ is influenced by the _____ Attitude.

    Example of how to fill in the above sentence: The Sun (<u>ego, survival instinct</u>) is in the <u>red sign</u>. Therefore the <u>ego or survival instinct</u> is influenced by the <u>red sign</u> attitude. My Summary Analysis of the ego and survival instinct (the Sun) after studying the text descriptions I have compiled is. . .

2. **Descriptions of the Moon**

    The Moon (_____) is in the _____.
    Therefore the _____ is influenced by the _____ Attitude.

    Example of how to fill in the above sentence: The Moon (<u>feelings, habits, and desire for security</u>) is in the <u>blue sign</u>. Therefore the <u>habits, feelings, and desire for security</u> are influenced by the <u>blue sign</u> attitude. My Summary Analysis of the feelings, habits, and desire for security (the Moon) after studying the text descriptions I have compiled is. . .

3. **Descriptions of Mercury**

    Mercury (_____) is in the _____.
    Therefore the _____ is influenced by the _____ Attitude.

APPENDIX

Example of how to fill in the above sentence: The Mercury (<u>thinking, communication, and desire to think</u>) is in a <u>yellow sign</u>. Therefore the <u>thinking</u> is influenced by the <u>yellow sign.</u> My Summary Analysis of the thinking, communications, and desire of the mind (Mercury) after studying the text descriptions I have compiled is. . .

4. Descriptions of Venus

Venus (_____) is in the _____.
Therefore the _____ is influenced by the
_____ Attitude.

Example of how to fill in the above sentence: Venus (<u>values, feminine nature and desire to relate</u>) is in the <u>purple sign</u>. Therefore the <u>values, feminine side, and desire to relate</u> are influenced by the purple sign attitude. My Summary Analysis of values, femininity, and the desire to relate after studying the text descriptions I have compiled is. . .

5. Descriptions of Mars

Mars (_____) is in the _____.
Therefore the _____ is influenced by the
_____ Attitude.

Example of how to fill in the above sentence: My Mars (<u>passion, masculine nature, and desire to act</u>) is in a <u>green sign</u>. Therefore these are influenced by the <u>green sign</u> attitude. My Summary Analysis of the passion, masculine nature and desire to act (Mars) after studying the text descriptions I have compiled is . . .

Note: After re-creating your own forms and completing them, attach them to the descriptions of the personal planets you are analyzing.

IMPORTANT STEPS FOR OBTAINING CHART INFORMATION

You will need to obtain the correct planetary information on yourself or on another person(s) before you can analyze the birth chart, which also contains the condensed chart(s). If you are the purchaser of this book, you are entitled to receive a birth chart with your condensed chart at a discount, which you can also use to compare with another person's chart. Send $5.00, a self-addressed stamped envelope, proof of purchase with the date, time, and place of your birth to Amrita Publications, P.O. Box 367, Kentfield, CA 94914. If you have not purchased this book, you can still use the following order form to get your birth chart with the condensed chart for $10. To order more than one chart, simply include the other person's birth data.

ORDER FORMS

OPTIONS

Please find enclosed:

❏ $10 for a laminated **Planetary Profile Card** made from my condensed chart.

❏ $10 for a laminated **Planetary Profile Card** made from another person's condensed chart.

❏ $ _____ for _____ laminated **Planetary Profile Cards** made from the additional condensed charts of _____ individuals. Their chart information is also enclosed ($10 per person).

❏ $10 for a laminated **Attraction Indicator Card**.

❏ $ _____ for _____ laminated **Attraction Indicator Cards** ($10 for each).

❏ Please send me a computer readout of my currently **Visiting Planets** with instructions. I enclose my check for $15.

APPENDIX

CHART ORDER FORM

(Please make a copy of these forms for your use.)

Your Birth Data

Name _____

Address _____

City _____ State _____ Zip _____

Date of Birth _____ Time _____

Place _____

E-mail Address (optional) _____

I also wish to compare my planets with the planets of someone else. Please send me their birth chart, which contains the condensed chart. I enclose my check for $_____. ($10 for each chart.}

Please make check payable to: **Amrita Publications**
    P.O. Box 367
    Kentfield, CA 94914

Second Person's Birth Data

Name _____

Address _____

City _____ State _____ Zip _____

Date of Birth _____ Time _____

Place _____

E-mail Address (optional) _____

SPECIAL REPORTS ORDER FORM

❑ Please send me the special report on:
(See Internet at www.skysage.com to find more reports or E-mail amrita@skysage.com.)

❑ **How to Choose the Right Mate**

❑ **How to Avoid Fatal Attractions**

❑ **How to Understand Your Children the First Day They Are Born**

❑ **Why Some People Love You While Others Avoid You**

I enclose _____ ($12 each report).

SPECIAL INSTRUCTIONS

Extra copies of this book can be ordered by calling 1-888-265-2732.

All other items can be purchased by sending your order to Amrita Publications, P.O. Box 367, Kentfield, CA 94914. Make sure we receive the date, time, and place of birth of any person or person's being charted or who are ordering a chart.

OTHER OPTIONS

Another option for obtaining planetary information is to purchase a simple astrological program for your computer. If you anticipate looking at a lot of people's planets, this may be the least expensive route for you to go. There are some very simple programs available for as little as $50. Here are some untested sources that you might try:

American Federation of Astrologers 602/838-1751. Ask for inexpensive software for generating a natal chart.

Astro Communication Services 619/492-9919. Ask for the "Electronic Astrologer" program. Current price is $59.95.

Steve Hines at **Microcycles** 1-800-829-2537,
P.O. Box 78219, Los Angeles, CA 90016-2537

Look for advertisements in astrological publications, such as *The Mountain Astrologer* and *Horoscope Magazine*.

You may also be able to access charts through the Internet. Please check out your online possibilities. We can be reached at www.skysage.com.

If you do not have a computer and do not want to order from us, you can purchase *The American Ephemeris for the 20th Century* from your local bookstore (about $25.00) and visually select the planets for any particular birth date. While this is not a completely accurate way, it is a fast approach for getting an instant look at any person you are interested in.

Here is what to do if you generate your own readouts from your astrological program or simply look up your planets from *The American Ephemeris:*

1. Use the Master Table from your appendix to help you translate the symbols of the signs in which the planets are located.

2. Use the Sign Table from your appendix and instructions in Lesson 5 to determine which personal planets are supported and which personal planets are frustrated by the impersonal planets.

3. Use the forms provided in the appendix to compile your individual planetary profiles based on the information in this book.

Note:
To determine the positions of visiting planets mentioned in this book you may need more expensive software. You can either order these computer readouts from us without having to purchase software, or contact Steve Hines at Microcycles, 1-800-829-2537, P.O. Box 78219, Los Angeles, CA 90016-2537 and ask for a brochure on software programs available.